THEATER
IN THE
AMERICAS

A Series from
Southern
Illinois
University
Press
ROBERT A.
SCHANKE
Series Editor

Other Books in the Theater in the Americas Series

The Theatre of Sabina Berman: The Agony of Ecstasy *and Other Plays*
Translated by Adam Versényi
With an Essay by Jacqueline E. Bixler

Women in Turmoil: Six Plays by Mercedes de Acosta
Edited and with an Introduction by Robert A. Schanke

"That Furious Lesbian": The Story of Mercedes de Acosta
Robert A. Schanke

Teaching Performance Studies
Edited by Nathan Stucky and Cynthia Wimmer
With a Foreword by Richard Schechner

Staging America

STAGING AMERICA

Cornerstone and Community-Based Theater

Sonja Kuftinec

Southern Illinois University Press
Carbondale and Edwardsville

Library of Congress Cataloging-in-Publication Data

Kuftinec, Sonja, 1966–
    Staging America : Cornerstone and community-based theater / Sonja Kuftinec.
        p. cm. — (Theater in the Americas)
    1. Community theater—United States. I. Title. II. Series.
PN2267 .K84 2003
792'.022—dc21
ISBN 0-8093-2496-2 (alk. paper)   2002008705

Printed on recycled paper. ♻

The paper used in this publication meets the minimum requirements of American National
Standard for Information Sciences—Permanence of Paper for Printed Library Materials,
ANSI Z39.48-1992. ∞

To Mara Sabinson,
an inspiring teacher who staged a revolt on the banal
and connected art to life

Art is supposed to be a part of the whole life of a community. . . . It's supposed to be right in the community, where they can have it when they want it. . . . It's supposed to be as essential as a grocery store.
—LeRoi Jones/Amiri Baraka
"They Think You're an Airplane and You're Really a Bird"

CONTENTS

ILLUSTRATIONS

PREFACE

Approximately halfway through drafting *Staging America,* two hijacked planes crashed into the World Trade Center towers. Like almost everyone I knew, I began to reassess my work in relation to this event. I felt compelled to contemplate this project, which examines the negotiation between theater and identity, within a violently altered context, to ask again what I was doing, why, and for whom. At the same time, my thoughts about community and contradiction informed how I perceived and understood the events that continued to unfold. The country seemed united in its horror and grief. Americans came together across racial, social, and geographic boundaries, joined by shared images communicated through the mass media that Benedict Anderson cites as essential to the construction of an imagined national community.[1] Within these media, printed or downloadable American flags reinforced a sense of mass symbolic association. On a more personal level, I witnessed stories of individuals compelled to connect through voluntary efforts. I heard of a college student who drove all night from Boston to New York just to "give water to firefighters, lift rocks, anything." Testimonials on television, radio, and the Internet heightened these perceptions of communal sensibility.

But as reliable theorists of community point out, affinity depends upon a sense of not only "us-ness" but also "them-ness." More complex and difficult stories emerged from the youth I work with at Seeds of Peace, an organization that advocates coexistence among Middle East teens. A Muslim student at Phillips Exeter Academy wrote of her public prayer for peace in Arabic, which was followed by another student's muttered remark, "Great, first they bomb us, then we have to listen to them pray." Another student reported being slammed into her locker for supporting Arab Americans in her Midwest school. In the days following, some Arab-looking men were removed from passenger planes due to the discomfort felt by fellow passengers and flight crew. In light of these contradictory events, the importance of examining the complex relationship between inclusion and exclusion that helps to shape community and to stage America seems undiminished, as does the importance of theater in shaping and focusing these relationships.

About a week after the bombing, I walked through Union Square, a public space that had become devoted to memorials of the missing. The memorial offered a site for witnessing as well as participation, in what the *New York Times* referred to as a kind of public street performance.[2] Theater links narrative reflection with physical embodiment and relationships. It is a space where people can literally come together, sharing images and experiences, without recognizing the probable disparateness of their individual interpretations of those images. Community-based theater, with its emphasis on participatory artistry and a more direct reflection of its audience base, inflects community in an even more intimate and complex manner. I am now more than ever convinced of the vitality of community-based theater not only as a social, aesthetic, and civic initiative but also as a site for philosophical and ethical inquiry into the forging of identity.

But writing rigorously about a practice rooted in notions of inclusion and accessibility has its challenges. Commenting on an early draft, Cornerstone Artistic Director Bill Rauch cautioned, "I was really struck by how densely intellectual the writing is. I had trouble keeping up sometimes, and I know this stuff better than many."[3] Another staff member confessed that she had difficulty making her way through the book's introduction. In continuing to work on the text, I had to grapple with striking balances between the concrete, descriptive and more abstract, theoretical writing. The results are perhaps fittingly mixed. Scholars and practitioners of community-based theater work with concepts that deserve and demand a more sophisticated kind of thinking than that required by everyday life. Sometimes a dense vocabulary can unpack the delightful difficulties of representation. The point is that these concepts are not always easy, nor should they be, as theater is by nature difficult and inefficient. The signs of theater do not offer one-to-one correspondences or simple platitudes, but rather multisensory phenomenal occurrences that communicate through presence, memory, and affect as well as narrative. It is not always easy. And this is what maintains both theater and community.

ACKNOWLEDGMENTS

C ommunity-based theater is an inclusive enterprise, and its scholarship no less so. Over the eight years since this project began at Stanford University, I have received invaluable support and feedback from colleagues, friends, and critics. In early stages, fellow graduate students Caroline Bicks, Kirstie Gulick Rosenfield, and Ehren Fordyce offered comments, camaraderie, and coffee. Ron Davies proffered his vast technological, editorial, and administrative skills. Conversations with Bruce McConachie, Doug Paterson, Tobin Nelhaus, David Feiner, and Mark Weinberg stimulated both thought and praxis. Jan Cohen-Cruz imparted warm, insightful feedback at many stages of the book's development, as did my colleagues at the University of Minnesota, Michal Kobialka, Tamara Underiner, Matthew Wagner, and Aleksandra Wolska. The University of Minnesota College of Liberal Arts also supported me with a leave term, and the Office of the Vice President for Research and Dean of the Graduate School supported the project with a Grant in Aid, which included the extraordinary assistance of graduate student John Fletcher. John served as a textual dramaturg, procuring obscure source materials and offering witty, engaged editorial feedback and unflagging support. Several times he suggested articles or ideas that significantly strengthened the book's focus while elegantly refining its arguments. John's summer internship with Cornerstone in Fresno, California, lent him an informed critical awareness, and I thank California State Universities for helping to support this work. Andy Arsham provided the expertise of a humanist scientist, dissecting improbable clauses, and offered endless encouragement. An inclusive research process relied on input from Cornerstone Theater, whose many members proved essential in their openness, support, and critique of the project, beginning with my friend Patty Payette, who introduced me to the company. During a residency in 1994, I was invited to listen and at times to participate in ensemble meetings, planning days, and several projects in Watts. Input from participants in Watts, Anacostia, and New Haven and at Arena Stage kept me humble about the limits of my knowledge and alive to the impact of theater on individuals.

As I detail in my introductory chapter, my undergraduate and graduate experiences were essential in formulating and shaping my thoughts about community-based theater. I wish that my college advisor, Jim Steffenson, and graduate professor, Charles Lyons, were alive to see the results of their mentorship. Special thanks are due to my dissertation advisor, Harry Elam, who encouraged me to "think until it hurts." It has. But there has been pleasure as well as pain.

Parts of chapter 3 previously appeared in "A Cornerstone for Rethinking Community Theater," *Theatre Topics* 6.1 (1996): 91–104. Sections of chapter 5 appeared in "Cornerstone's Community Chalk Circle," *The Brecht Yearbook* 22 (1997): 239–51, and in "Beyond Brecht: An Interview with Bill Rauch," *Theater InSight* 16 (1996): 35–41. Chapter 6 includes excerpts from "Staging the City with the Good People of New Haven," *Theater Journal* 53.2 (2001): 197–222. Chapter 7 includes excerpts from a review of *Broken Hearts: A BH Mystery, Theater Journal* 52.3 (2000): 397–99. I would like to thank the various journals for publishing these articles and for allowing me to make use of them again in this book.

All photos are from the Cornerstone Theater Company's archives. I gratefully acknowledge the Cornerstone Theater Company for permission to reproduce these photos and to quote from documents in the company's archives. For permission to quote from interviews, e-mails, and similar material, I also gratefully acknowledge Christopher Acebo, Linda Burnham, Alison Carey, Deb Clapp, Dana Fripp, Peter Howard, Doug Hughes, Geoff Korff, Shishir Kurup, Allison Lee, Bob Leonard, Laurence Maslon, Armando Molina, Christopher Liam Moore, Damion Teeko Parran, Patty Payette, Bill Rauch, Jean Routt, Leslie Tamaribuchi, Pamela Tatge, Mark Valdez, José Luis Valenzuela, Doug Wager, Shana Waterman, and Antoinette White-Richardson.

Staging America

1

INTRODUCTION: SURVEYING THE TERRAIN

I begin a work based on many years of participation and reflection in the theater with the confession of a guilty secret: I often don't like going. I approach most productions with a dull sense of dread and a faint whiff of hope. The dread arises from years of attending overproduced deadly professional and academic theater.[1] The hope mainly emanates from experimental student and community-based productions, grounded in locality, place, or identity. These community-based productions, which I have both witnessed and helped to develop, reinspire my faith in theater's ability to directly engage and reflect its audience, by integrating local history, concerns, stories, traditions, and/or performers. At the same time, the work raises deeply provocative questions about ethical representation and about how individuals and groups negotiate their identity. Yet, these socially and aesthetically complex productions, affiliated with various twentieth-century theater movements in the United States, remain largely absent from a conventional narrative of American theater. While practitioners have been speaking with each other for quite a while, and, less often, with scholars and scholar-practitioners, a wider audience remains predominately unaware of community-based theater's impact. In order to understand and complicate issues of identity fundamental to the ongoing negotiation of "America," and to apprehend aspects of audience engagement crucial to the vitality of American theater, this field must be more explicitly surveyed.[2]

Staging America introduces aspects of this critical landscape through focus on Cornerstone Theater, a fluid ensemble that has been developing a community-based aesthetic and practice for over sixteen years. Founded in 1986 as a response to the limitations of regional theater in reaching a more broad-based audience, Cornerstone spent five years traveling and producing shows with mainly rural towns in the United States. Since 1992, Cornerstone has been based in Los Angeles, working with and bridging urban communities, variously defined.[3] This documentation and analysis of Cornerstone as a community-based theater details some of the complexities, compromises, and conundrums—as well as the pleasures—that undergird the practice of developing performances with nonprofessionals.

Pleasure tends to be easy to discuss; criticism requires more thoughtfulness. One of the most profound questions confronting community-based theater centers on ethical representations, calling in turn for careful reflection on my own methodologies. How do I begin to responsibly survey the field to include its multiple aspects of historiography, practice, criticism, and theory? How do I do so in a way that moves between evaluation, appreciation, and documentation? While no survey of this growing and shifting terrain can be complete, I choose to organize this study through a constellation of strategic methods, including cultural and performance studies as well as theatrical critique. In addition to these frameworks, I also ask questions about critical ethics, embracing what Elaine Lawless terms "reciprocal ethnography."[4] Lawless addresses the quandary of professionalized distancing rhetoric found in most ethnographies, separating the subject of study from authoritative interpretation. She suggests that a more inclusive, ethical, and complex hermeneutic strategy would incorporate the interpreted subjects' interpretations as well as her own, often unmarked, scholarly voice. Thus, my accounting of Cornerstone and community-based theater strives to be at least partially polyphonic, including Cornerstone members, participants, and critics, as well as my own personal experience. "We are obligated," Lawless proposes, "to present ourselves in our texts as we are in our work: humans seeking understanding, engaged in dialogue and interpretation with other[s]."[5]

Attentiveness to rhetorical multiplicity serves a form grounded in intimately linked oppositions: aesthetic and social, hope and disaffection, fragmentation and unity. My attraction to the field as a scholar and practitioner is rooted in these binary bedfellows, beginning with a dysfunctional relationship to theater as a college student. This relationship did not always bear an association of dread. Like many practitioners and scholars, I was initially drawn to theater as a performer, by the twin pleasures of display and camaraderie, of individual achievement and social bonding. The journey from belting out "Ain't it Swell! Ain't it Grand!" in the sixth-grade chorus of a Tom Sawyer musical, to working as a professional dramaturg in regional theaters, to creating performance projects with Balkan youth has been marked by ongoing hunger and dissatisfaction. At Dartmouth College in the mid-1980s, initial delight in the applause received for my performance in Ira Levin's *Deathtrap* shifted to questioning the less delighted audience reception to Bertolt Brecht's *Man's a Man*.

Something seemed awry in this audience response. Studying Brecht in the classroom revealed his passionate belief in the power of theater to engage an audience—to awaken them from a haze of bourgeois sleep. Brecht wrote of yearning for theater that had the impact of a sporting event, claiming "A theatre which makes no contact with the public is a nonsense."[6] Unfortunately, our production, labored over with great diligence and intelligence, seemed a nonsense. We generated a response closer to pre–Tiger Woods professional golf than to the smoke-filled boxing event that Brecht had imagined. A disconnect yawned between the stage and the audience, who seemed inattentive to the production's clever use of *verfremdungseffekt* (the set came apart piece by piece until the actors stood on a bare stage, underlining the constructed nature of theater!). A play that in its content and theory expressed a profoundly moving analysis of war's impact on individual humanity landed in our theater with an unresonant thud.

Meanwhile, outside of the theater building, student radicals protested the college's investment in South Africa and the lack of attention to women's voices on campus. Tampons bloodied in Kool Aid and thrown upon spectators at a football rally, and students living in simulated shanties on the college green, prompted a more engaged (if mixed) response from an attentive audience than had our play. While using the signs of theater—fake bloodied props and constructed shanty sets—the real bodies of protesters asserting emotionally committed, if not always unscripted, dialogue seemed to more effectively "awaken" and provoke the audience.

In his engaging, wide-ranging book, *The Radical in Performance: Between Brecht and Baudrillard,* Baz Kershaw locates this performative effectiveness in the difference between the discursive limits of theater and the expressive excess of performance.[7] According to Kershaw, the commodification of theater, of most theater-in-a-theater-building, limits its potential to provoke reflection and change. Like Kershaw, though, I maintain a "pathological hope" in theater's potential.[8] So, despite the failure of the Brecht production in comparison to campus protests, I retained faith in theater's power to provoke and engage. I was rewarded for this faith in a senior year acting class with the discovery of activist artist Augusto Boal and his *Theatre of the Oppressed.*[9] Through Boal, I relearned how theater could more directly reflect on and enact social change. Our assigned weekly newspaper theater playlets encouraged students to perceive and enact a closer connection between performance and events outside of the building. Further reading on

Boal asserted the impact of his work with nonperformers. Once again, theater designed less for consumption than for provocation, with "ordinary people" rather than professional actors, seemed to me more effective, affective, and engaging.

These somewhat unformed revelations remained with me as I began a year-long internship with the Actors Theater of Louisville in 1988. I knew that the history of regional or resident professional theater in the United States followed an initial trajectory of artistic hunger and dissatisfaction with a centralized product in New York. But after several years of generous funding in the 1960s and 1970s, mainly from the Ford and Rockefeller Foundations, regional theater in the 1980s had come to rely on subscription audiences and local corporate sponsorship to survive institutionally. The best of intentions—a commitment to artistic excellence, to creating thought-provoking as well as entertaining theater in decentralized locations across the United States—could not forestall theater that seemed to me unreflective of the city I walked through every day. The theater also played to a statistically and visually homogeneous audience, again, unaccountable to the diverse region in which it was located. Thus, despite an espoused rhetoric and deep belief in the potential for performances to reach across difference, material and socio-structural constraints limited this regional theater's audience to a mostly white, middle-class base.

Amidst this growing dissatisfaction with regional theater as a representative, reflective, politically invested, or creative space—particularly given the many world-shaking events of 1989—I first heard of Cornerstone Theater. Robert Coe wrote an evocative analysis of the company's mixed-race adapted musical production of *Romeo & Juliet* with a small Mississippi town in *American Theater*.[10] Though lacking the production values of regional, professional, or even academic theater, the show played to packed, enthusiastic houses in a local movie theater. At the same time, while successfully building an audience, and animating the town, the process also revealed fragmentations in the community, its internal boundaries of difference. Cornerstone's production process brought together the aesthetic and the social, reminiscent of my Brechtian, Boalian, and social protest ideals.

As I moved to manage the Organic Theater's literary office in Chicago, I continued to track Cornerstone's travels through mainly small town USA via my friend Patty Payette, who had left the Actor's Theater of Louisville, where we had both interned, to become Cornerstone's company manager. Soon afterwards, I grew discouraged by the financial and artistic limitations of even an experimental regional theater, where I spent several months collecting unemployment checks while working as a grant writer/dramaturg/

waitress. I followed the path of many a frustrated artist and enrolled in graduate school in 1991. In 1994, I began dissertation field research with Cornerstone in their new Los Angeles home, working as a dramaturg for part of the company's year-long residency in Watts. Since 1995, I have published several articles on Cornerstone and community-based theater, while also creating theater with Balkan youth across ethno-religious boundaries.[11] I have also taught numerous courses in performance and social change and community-based theater. As an audience member, scholar, teacher, and practitioner, I assert the vitality and complexity of a form rooted in a century of disaffection and hope in the United States.

A century is a long time to navigate through any theatrical form; as with all surveys, *Staging America* has its limits and boundaries. The book does not offer a comprehensive historical account of community-based theater or an authoritatively complete chronicle of Cornerstone Theater. Nor does it propose that Cornerstone functions as a teleological endpoint for community-based theater, or that the company in any way stands in for this complex and vitally diverse set of practices. And, despite its title, *Staging America* resists asserting that Cornerstone is some kind of über national theater, or that community-based theater in some way serves this end. The "staging" of the title intimates the playfulness of performance, in which all terms remain under revision. Staging also emphasizes the importance of the sign and of embodied representations in making meaning. In short, *Staging America* describes one set of parameters for a field that remains largely uncharted, examining how community-based theater contributes to an investigation of social identity and to an animation of both theater and community. With an emphasis on inclusive ethnography and critical historiography, I try to strike a balance between the material and theoretical, Cornerstone and community-based theater, stability and play. An event that occurred during my work with Cornerstone in Watts perhaps illuminates some of these many hopes and caveats.

Early in the Watts residency, I was awaiting community auditioners with several ensemble members and deaf guest artist C. J. Jones. To pass the time, Jones began teaching us words in American Sign. He had shown the signs for several nationalities—a helmet for "Germany" and horse riding for "England"—when I asked to see "America." Jones interlaced his fingers and circled his hands perpendicular to his chest. "Ah," I exclaimed, "the melting pot." Reading my lips, Jones shook his head to correct me. He explained that his moving hands represented not the motions of a stirring pot but a large cabin with what looked like a lot of people sticking out of it.

This correction of my assumptions about American Sign serves as a resonant metaphor for the way that Cornerstone helps to redefine "American" theater and the communities that construct America. Cornerstone's community-based productions presume an America that is not a melting pot producing homogeneous common culture but rather a matrix of localized cultures—a cabin with a lot of people sticking out of it. What at first glance looks like an image that encloses, derives from an image constructed *by* people. This image of America as a matrix of identities grounds Cornerstone's project of working with diverse communities across the United States in an effort to create theater with an "American identity." In thinking further about this metaphor, however, the American Sign Language (ASL) sign seems more elusive. One cabin is not large enough to contain or be constructed by all of the diverse communities of America, nor does the sign mark the problematic nature of a term, *America,* that at least linguistically colonizes two continents. *Staging America* thus engages with and challenges the metaphor by asserting the negotiable nature of an American identity as well as that of the communities with which Cornerstone works. At the risk of overburdening this poor metaphor, one more point strikes me: the cabin moves. Examination of Cornerstone's productions suggests that identity may be more dynamic than rooted, exemplified in movement rather than locality.

While movement and dynamism exemplify much of Cornerstone's work, the company's production history can also be traced to a tradition of locally grounded grassroots performances, particularly those invested in identity formation via theater. Community-based theater and its affiliations encompass a rich and complex tradition of grounding identity through group building and mythmaking. In the early twentieth century, pageantry and industrial dramas inscribed a particular capitalist and colonial history onto the bodies of immigrants, creating through narrative a more unified notion of America than actually existed. In contrast, the Workers Theater Movement of the 1930s suggests a different notion of community, one grounded in class interests rather than geography or national ideology. In the 1960s, groups such as El Teatro Campesino and Free Southern Theater contributed to the ongoing dispersion of community-based theatrical practice, as well as to the discourse of identity associated with the practice. Both companies saw theater as a way to resist assimilation, and, respectively, to unify Chicano farmworkers and rural Southern African Americans through performance. Contemporary community-based performance tends to continue this movement towards the representations of the local—animating groups who live together and, therefore, share a supposedly common history, interests, and/or set of values. Oral history, storytelling, and textual adaptation emphasize and embody local practice and seem to enliven as well as to create a sense of commonality among participants and audience members.

Anthropologist Victor Turner describes this enlivening of community as "communitas"—a sense of group feeling resulting from performance.[12] This feeling may be temporary, lasting only as long as the process of creating the performance. However, the social and aesthetic exchanges that take place during this event create and enable community, while also illuminating the ambivalent nature of community identity. Yet, social theorists such as Anthony Cohen, Iris Marion Young, and Paul Gilroy propose that the group feeling associated with a perception of commonality is complicated by what it conceals: the fragmented and exclusionary nature of community, and the fact that individuals identify with multiple groups.[13]

Cornerstone Theater embodies both the animating cohesion and perturbed dynamism implied by these notions of community formation, achieved through negotiations of difference, as well as through performances of commonality. The company's sixteen-year history traces a trajectory that maps some of the major movements and issues raised by community-based theater. From its rural beginnings in 1986 to the company's current urban and professional collaborations, to the bridge shows that bring together a variety of disparate groups, Cornerstone's work illuminates and builds on (without standing in for) a history of community-based theater.

Cornerstone's beginning rural years (1986–1991) engage a more traditional notion of rural grassroots community-based theater. At the same time, these early productions arose from transactions between a seemingly stable small town and a traveling company, and between local semiosis and classical texts. A Wild West *Hamlet* in Marmarth, North Dakota, a mixed race *Romeo & Juliet* in Port Gibson, Mississippi, and an adaptation of *The Oresteia* on a Native American reservation in Nevada exemplify these years of cross-pollination. Cornerstone's urban work (1992–present) begins with a more fragmented understanding of community to include aspects such as culture and language (Arab Americans across the city), age (a multilingual senior center), and workplace (librarians and police officers). In 1993, the company also began to collaborate with professional regional theater companies. These collaborations suggest an intriguing reflexivity: Cornerstone had been founded in reaction against the limited audience base of regional theaters, which themselves had grown, in part, out of the more community-based Little Theaters.

Cornerstone's ongoing redefinition models what social theorist Frederick Buell proposes is a particularly American phenomenon: America as a nation is defined by its own continuous self-reflection.[14] *Staging America* thus examines both the literal staging of Americans that Cornerstone enacts through its diverse rural, urban, and regional collaborations across the country, as well as the more ephemeral staging of "America" as a contingent ever-fluctuating social formation. This redefinition of America includes aspects of a largely unknown history of community-based performance traditions, as well as ongoing questioning of "community." To survey the American performance experience, it is essential both to mark prior omissions as well as to suggest that the map-making process itself can never be completed. Thus, strategies of interpretation include elements of cultural studies, anthropology, and sociology as well as theater studies.

Methodologies and Strategies

> There has been a sea change in our notion not so much of what knowledge is, but of what it is we want to know.
> —Clifford Geertz, "Blurred Genres"

Ethnographer Clifford Geertz's insight in "Blurred Genres," an article in *Local Knowledge,* grounds this detour, which further details my strategies of surveying.[15] Like Cornerstone and community-based theater generally, Geertz focuses on the local and specific rather than the universal or abstract; philosophical notions of epistemology (what knowledge is) become less important than local knowledge (what it is we want to know). Community-based theater demands a shift in what theater scholars and practitioners in the United States want to know. This shift in content requires a change of perspectives, a movement away from aesthetic critical analysis towards a spectrum of approaches rooted in performance studies, ethnography, and cultural studies. A breakdown of these approaches, and the terminology of "community" and "culture," clarifies this strategic deposition.

In his seminal book *Performance Theory,* Richard Schechner posits a performance field that includes "the entire constellation of events that take place in/among both performers and audience from the time the first spectator enters the field of the performance—the precinct where the theater takes place—to the time the last spectator leaves."[16] This investigation reaches even further than Schechner's interpretive field to embrace text and community selection, rehearsal process, spatial analysis, marketing, and reception as well as to trace aspects of community-based theater history in twentieth-century United States. In each of these sites of inquiry, performance studies serves as a key method. Performance studies situates theater as a cultural practice rather than an artistic phenomenon, concerned with the way that performance animates the networks of social relations rather than with formally assessing the resultant *mise-en-scène*. Focusing less on textual or production criticism, and more on how performance functions as an expressive device, this interdisciplinary field encourages an investigation of community and culture as well as theater.

Both "community" and "culture" bear a complex history of use and meaning, and thus merit further exploration. Sociologist Raymond Williams locates each term as a keyword embedded in a specific material history. According to Williams, community refers to both a social grouping and a quality—a sense of common identity.[17] Yet, the term maintains a connotative fuzziness, serving as a convenient, positively inflected symbol encapsulating a number of contradictory notions. In the 1950s, George A. Hillery Jr. infamously described ninety-four use-definitions of the term, with little in common among them.[18] This ambivalence of meaning is, in fact, an important element of how community functions. In *The Symbolic Constructions of Community,* sociologist Anthony Cohen suggests that "community" operates symbolically to avoid the confrontation of its connotative differences. According to Cohen, "Symbols are effective because they are imprecise."[19] We generally understand community as a function of commonality, whether that commonality is one of location, class, interest, age, or ethnic background. But commonality also implies boundaries, difference, and exclusion. In order for a community to distinguish itself, its members must differentiate themselves in some way from other communities through boundaries of land, behavior, or background. Community thus encapsulates both commonality and difference.

Cornerstone residencies illuminate the challenge of enacting "community," demonstrating that members of a geographically defined community do not necessarily share the same values. A production in Eastport, Maine, included a group of publicly out homosexuals as well as homophobic high school students. In Long Creek, Oregon, community residents performing a version of Brecht's *Good Woman of Setzuan* (1988) disagreed on the definition of a good woman. Cast members of Port Gibson's *Romeo & Juliet* (1989) and Dinwiddie County's *Pretty Much True Story of Dinwiddie County* (1987) differed in their feelings about the appropriateness of depicting interracial marriage.

As well as revealing value differences, Cornerstone residencies also illustrate the multiplicity inherent in defining identity through community. A resident of Maine can simultaneously live in the Eastport area, belong to the Passamaquoddy Indian tribe, identify as a homosexual, and act in a Cornerstone production. These multiple communities do not necessarily cohere. Other residents of Eastport are not identified as Native Americans or homosexuals. Individuals who identify as homosexuals exist outside the Eastport area. Cornerstone's productions demonstrate the difficulty of using the term *community* to imply stability or permanence.

Culture too suggests seemingly contradictory meanings. The variant uses of the term surprised Raymond Williams so much upon his return from service in the Second World War that he constructed an entire disciplinary field based upon its study. Linguistic development over time ranges from reference to crop tending, folk activity, the process of aesthetic development, and a particular way of life. By the mid-twentieth century *culture* had come to suggest both popular forms of expression that identified a social group and works of high art.[20] Both of these uses impact on a study of community-based theater. On the one hand, this theatrical practice often cites a concern with reflecting, animating, or generating a specific culture. These kinds of popular cultural emanations range from an early-twentieth-century civic pageant in St. Louis to the Black Arts Movement's espoused intent to serve as the cultural "sister" of Black Power, to Cornerstone's original production of *Ghurba* with Arab Americans in Los Angeles.[21]

Cornerstone's adaptations also address the high art aspect of culture. While community-based theaters often develop original texts that speak to a specific locality or moment, many of Cornerstone's productions, particularly in the company's early years, adapt canonical works of Western theater. These include Aeschylus, Shakespeare, Ibsen, Chekhov, Brecht, Noel Coward, and Thornton Wilder, as well as some classical Sanskrit and Chinese texts.[22] Intriguingly, this hybridization of the universal and the local provides another site to investigate the very notion of culture, as reframing a text within the specifics of a "local culture" can point out the heterogeneity of community. *The Toy Truck* (1992), a show with the multiethnic Angelus Plaza Senior Center in Los Angeles, exemplifies this dynamic. The Angelus Plaza houses seniors who speak Mandarin, Korean, English, and Spanish; most residents speak one language exclusively. In this site, a univocal mediation of local culture became impossible. Instead, the company worked with residents to develop a multilingual story in which each character spoke his or her native language, while choruses and banners announced translations. The resulting production suggested the chaotic collage of cultures in the Plaza, Los Angeles, and, to an extent, in America, representing both the attempt to communicate common ideas in the ancient Sanskrit text as well as the extreme difficulty of locating this commonality in any one particular context.

In general, I am less concerned with pinning down either "culture" or "community" than with looking at how they are enacted and negotiated

The Toy Truck (1992), a collaboration with the Angelus Plaza Senior Center, which included translations in four languages

through community-based practices. At the same time, a cultural studies analysis offers a way to place these practices within a larger context of power relations, noting how relationships among groups and institutions impact on the meanings and assessment of community-based theater. Thus, a Cornerstone production of *Hamlet* with residents of Marmarth, North Dakota, funded by the state's humanities council, in cooperation with the town mayor, enacts a different set of power relations than El Teatro Campesino's *actos* developed with the Chicano farmworkers' union.

Assessment and documentation of these projects borrows from anthropology as well as cultural studies, as community-based performance functions as a kind of ethnography, or writing of culture. Assessment thus depends upon an understanding of contemporary debates in ethical ethnography. As opposed to late-nineteenth-century "armchair" anthropologists, the ethnographer lives amongst those studied, positing that empathetic understanding arises from the "sheer fact of coexistence in a shared world."[23] But as the 1967 publication of anthropologist Bronislaw Malinowski's surprisingly curmudgeonly *Diary in the Strict Sense of the Term* illustrated, participant-observer fieldwork might be neither transparently objective nor particularly inscribed by empathy.[24] James Clifford proposes that current ethnography is marked by interpretive study rather than objective explication.[25] Interpretive frameworks that write Others, as well as of the more recent phenomenon of native anthropologists, and Lawless's emphasis on "reciprocal ethnography," require ongoing reflection on the relationship between observer and observed, grounded in the terminology of "insiders" and "outsiders."

"Insider" ethnographers and community-based theater makers emerge from within a particular group to consider and document its cultural practices. Members of Roadside Theater in Appalachia have lived and worked with this population since 1975, staging story circles, and developing performances based on oral history of the region. Participants at a Cornell symposium on grassroots theater in 1992 described such a theater as one in which the makers are part of the culture from which the work is drawn.[26] Not surprisingly, critics of insider research propose that it is a deterrent to objective perception and analysis, while supporters argue that insiders are more likely to pick up on nonverbal expressive cues, and more easily establish trust-based relationships.[27]

In contrast, an "outsider" has the advantage of recognizing difference, of viewing a community or culture with critical distance. Anne Elizabeth Armstrong refers to students who she worked with on a community-based project in Williamsburg, Virginia, as "catalysts," who animated the community by virtue of not belonging.[28] Outsider status may also carry distinct advantages to projects purporting to bring together disparate groups through theater. In my work with Croatian, Serbian, and Muslim youth in former Yugoslavia, my status as a relative outsider unaligned with any one of these already problematic markers of identity provides me with a kind of productive mobility. But "outsiders" can be perceived of as cultural colonists, imposing a point of view, a way of working, or a set of values of which they may be unconscious. In an article about the Colquitt, Georgia, production of *Swamp Gravy*, which he directed, Richard Owen Geer relates how he became aware of these outsider impositions. Frustrated with community performers for arriving late to rehearsals, he swore. Unaccustomed to this kind of behavior and language, they left. Geer came to understand that certain ways of doing theater had to be relearned within this subculture.[29] José Luis Valenzuela, UCLA theater professor and director who works mainly with Latinos in Los Angeles, points towards the danger of an artist "coming into a community that they haven't taken enough time to investigate and be inside of." He warns that "paternalism can exist, or the savior idea, or exoticism that communities offer through economic or social conditions."[30] As Geer's story illustrates, and Valenzuela's warning underlines, community-based theater initiated by "outsiders" takes on an animating role and must grapple more publicly with issues of authority, imposition, and protocol, unlike ethnographers, who generally maintain a low profile in the community in which they write.

Still, the insights in both processes suggest that boundaries of belonging, and insider/outsider positions, have a dimension of fluidity that complicates the relationship between community-based artists and participants. As anthropologist John Aguilar explains, "Sociocultural systems are complex. Many societies are fragmented by class, regional, urban-rural, and ideology-related affiliative differences, and all cultures (including subcultures) are characterized by internal variation."[31] Cornerstone, a multiethnic ensemble no longer living directly with small rural communities, focused as much on bridging as on animating community, locates and elaborates on this complexity. Questions about bias and insider status remain, compounded by power dynamics implicit in the competition for scarce arts funding resources in Los Angeles, and by boundary negotiation.

Assumptions of a cohesive individual subject, or homogeneous face-to-face community, have been challenged by postindustrial social dynamics and postmodern thought. In *The Location of Culture,* Homi Bhabha suggests that it is in "the overlap and displacement of domains of difference—that the intersubjective and collective experiences of *nationness,* community interest, or cultural value are negotiated."[32] The negotiation of individual identity and collective experience marks community and nation with more complexity and specificity than stabilizing definitions. Yet, community-based theater often relies on more "essential" understandings of identity rooted in place, class, race, and ethnicity, as well as on disruptions of those assumptions. Gayatri Spivak refers to a strategic essentialism, a conscious choice to assume a temporary unified subject position in order to further a particular end.[33] Cornerstone's production process suggests that community transactions can encompass both strategic essentialism and the concurrent negotiation of multiple sites of identity. In playing a sighted senator in the Watts/Cornerstone coproduction of *The Central Ave. Chalk Circle* (1995), blind African American playwright Lynn Manning slips among multiple subject positions. In the production process, Manning at times foregrounded one of his many subject positions, or aspects of identity; at other times, he was marked by the shifting perceptions of others. As a guest artist with Cornerstone from South Central Los Angeles, Manning also navigated an insider/outsider position with both coproducers. These negotiations, contradictions, and slippages, implicit in community representation and expression, point towards the multiple meanings of community and nation.

In addition to addressing the fragmentation of identity and the writing of culture, cultural anthropology speaks to theater as an expressive site. Clifford Geertz and Victor Turner view culture and society in dynamic performative terms rather than as a static map of relationships and practices. In "Blurred Genres," Geertz locates an increasing interest within sociology in the "expressive devices of collective life."[34] Turner talks about performance as an ex-pression, or pressing out, of a sense of community.[35] Enactment and symbolic communication can enliven a community's sense of identity.

But the communication that occurs in community-based theater moves beyond transmission and expression. Bruce McConachie emphasizes the importance of adopting a critical stance that reaches towards what Raymond Williams terms the "structures of feeling" in a society, including the collective concerns and emotions that activate community.[36] Judgment and pleasure figure as prominently in a discussion of community-based theater as questions of identity and social formation, and we arrive at a literal critical juncture to consider an ethical, appropriate scholarly response to community-based performance.

Some Critical Points

In a response to critical assessment of a Cornerstone production, cofounder and playwright Alison Carey prompts some vital questions about the artist/critic relationship in community-based theater.

> Culturally imperialistic critics, praying at the altar of theoretical and over-simplified radicality, disallow human beings the right to see on stage what they want because it goes against the critic's reductive, knee-jerk, uninformed and appallingly patronizing pre-conceived notion of what [the community needs and what community-based art should be].[37]

After breathing a sigh of relief that one is not on the receiving end of such blunt though deeply felt commentary, a closer look reveals issues that repeatedly crop up in conversations about community-based theater critique. The critic is often perceived to be in a parasitic relationship to the artwork, at once uninformed and overly theoretical, patronizing and confusing, biased and reductive. At the same time, Carey's comments raise the issue of the ethical relationship of the practitioner to the community. How much should the artist allow community-based participants to "see what they want" onstage when it goes against the artist's own beliefs and values? How much is "what they want" influenced by a mediated culture, hegemonic ideology, and/or institutional power relations? Must community-based theater have a "radical" or socially progressive agenda? How reflexive should the practitioner be about the work and its institutional links? What responsibility, if any, does a critic have to point towards those links? Who represents what for whom and in what language? The questions become dizzying in their propensity to self-replicate. And there remain others about the critic's role, responsibility, and relationship with community-based theater. It is difficult to separate out these issues, and to appropriately represent an ongoing and many-sided debate, but I will attempt here to sketch out what I perceive to be some critical touchstones and will outline my own contingent choices.

ARTISTIC ANXIETIES

A number of community-based artists feel strongly that criticism of the process and/or product should emerge from within, from practitioners rather than critics. A report reflecting on building civic partnerships, collated and edited by Linda Frye Burnham, asserts that "critical evaluation of a project is not in the hands of conventional art critics, but in the hands of the participants themselves."[38] At *National Gathering with an Attitude,* Jan Cohen-Cruz facilitated a conversation that evoked similar responses. At this gathering, Mat Schwarzman spoke for many practitioners in articulating his concern about the public nature of criticism.[39] As Schwarzman and others have observed, there remains little space for dialogue or response within a conventional critical form. Pondering a similar issues in *Between Theater and Anthropology,* Richard Schechner explains, "Most artists scoff at critics but accept their praise. These same professionals welcome the criticism of fellow performers when offered in private. What is resented is the public nature of critics' opinions."[40] Schechner further asserts that direct responses that can be acted upon within the rehearsal process may be of the most value to practitioners (an ironic position given his later publication of Sara Brady's critique of a Cornerstone production, elaborated upon below).[41]

While the public nature of a criticism that prohibits dialogue or direct action concerns artists in general, community-based practitioners express additional anxiety about aesthetic critiques that ignore process. Conventional criticism tends to adopt an aesthetic model of evaluation, grounded in late-eighteenth-century Kantian thinking on discrimination, taste, and beauty, which privileges the art object. In community-based theater, however, process remains as essential as product. Speaking of new genre public art, which like community-based theater collaborates more directly with its audience, Suzanne Lacy posits an "underlying aversion to art that claims to 'do' something, that does not subordinate function to craft. . . . That their work intends to affect and transform is taken by its detractors as evidence that it is not art."[42] Indeed, dance critic Arlene Croce infamously lambasted choreographer Bill T. Jones for his "victim art," which she deemed "beyond criticism."[43] This art/social work dilemma can confound even practitioners working with a form that expressly moves between and merges this binary. Yet, practitioners at gatherings such as those cited above seem quite capable of defining parameters that include artistic evaluation as well as ethical assessment of community involvement. Community Arts Network (www.communityarts.net) documents ongoing projects and raises issues of relevance to the artists who contribute to the site, a role often taken by critics.[44]

Given the extent of communication among practitioners, the emphasis on documentation and self-evaluation, as well as on community inclusion in the entire process, one might well ask whether a role remains for community-based theater scholars beyond a kind of freeloading knowledge production. Perhaps not surprisingly, I assert that there is: as documenters, historians, cultural critics, and interpreters and as artistic evaluators.

CRITICAL ROLES

Theater historians, cultural critics, and audiences suffer a loss when traces of certain nontraditional ideas pass away or become overwhelmed by the dominance of the conventional. The logocentrism of theater studies privileges the dramatic text and the written remnants of critical reports, both of which submerge the visibility of community-based theater. Though practitioners try to document their work, it is often too difficult in the moment to step outside the process. Burnham's report cites grassroots scholar-practitioner Robert Gard's lament for the subsequent loss of historical information: "Perhaps because of the demands upon [grassroots practitioners], because of the very complexity of the things they attempted, they did not bring themselves to write down their experiences."[45] While marking what practitioners often do not have the time to attend to, scholars can also look beyond the particularity of the event to connect it to larger paradigms and practices. A critical report may also exceed the descriptive to include analysis and abstraction, rendering criticism communicable beyond theatrical production. Scholars may also be able to offer some evaluative critiques and help to develop paradigms for artistic judgment. As in documentation, some of these criteria might be developed through participation. Otherwise, a critical evaluation runs the risk of assuming conventional aesthetic measures that are themselves ideologically embedded. The lack of objective referent in a postmodern world need not paralyze critical response. Nor should evaluative critique be overly theoretical or obtuse. However, awareness of critical language and intent should be foregrounded by the critic.

I prefer to look for what Ann Bogart refers to as aesthetic arrest—moments in a performance when one is stopped in one's tracks.[46] These moments remain somewhat subjective, but the criterion of arrest focuses on that which, as Suzanne Lacy notes, "results from reassembling meaning in a way that, at that moment, appears *new*."[47] While innovation and imagination may be applied as a measure of quality to any conventional theater production, Lucy Lippard proposes an array of contradictory principles that specifically refer to community-based aesthetics. Lippard calls for an assessment of familiarity and unfamiliarity, evocation and provocation, moments of wonder and critical reflection.[48] My own critical framework refers to attention to innovation and complexity as cited by Lacy, Bogart, and Lippard, with an additional awareness towards representational ethics and a foregrounding of process and participation. I propose a more collaborative approach with practitioners and participants, one that acknowledges the multiple frames of interpretation that designate a project as "good" or "successful."

At the same time, while I have been in dialogue with Cornerstone about the company's process, practices, and productions, I assert my own particular scholarly viewpoints and responsibilities. Neither fear of approbation, nor intimacy of relation, nor a desire for polyphonic interpretation should prevent the critic from expressing what Gilles Sandier refers to as the "right of indignation."[49] These rights can extend to an assessment of process and power, as do José Luis Valenzuela's comments about the dangers of paternalism in community-based performance.[50] Questions should also be asked about the extent to which an event succeeds at animating and including community participants, about the appropriate representation of traumatic events, and about institutional relationship to power. The key concern in an ethical practice, however, remains how best to communicate critical discomfort. I submit that this may be better accomplished in relation with rather than in opposition to community-based practitioners. This calls for an in-betweenness of the scholar-practitioner that respects the expressed goals of practitioners, asserts the responsibilities of the critic to express indignation, and attends to the voices of community participants.

CRITICAL NEGOTIATIONS

In order for indignation to have impact, a space must be found for practitioners and scholars to speak with each other about process. Moving between the experiential and the analytic can enhance both the practice and process(ing) of community-based theater. Many scholars associated with the community-based theater already work in the field.[51] Jan Cohen-Cruz in particular continues to address questions about the scholar/artist relationship.[52] While it is certainly possible for critics to address a production without reference to process, as David Román astutely does in his review of *A Beautiful Country*, an essay by Sara Brady in *TDR* raises evaluative as well as ethical questions through its critical strategies.[53]

"Welded to the Ladle: *Steelbound* and Non-Radicality in Community-Based Theatre" critiques the process of collaboration between Cornerstone, Touchstone, and the community of Bethlehem, Pennsylvania, a process in which Brady participated.[54] In her detailed assessment, Brady questions the inclusion of Bethlehem Steel in the performance-making process, which she claims led to censorship. Brady suggests that an evaluative approach of community-based work should center on the admission of "failed radicality of the work without sentimental discussion" (67), proposing a thorough abandonment of the conflation of community-based theater with theater for social change (52). Yet, Brady assumes this conflation in order to refute it, while concurrently critiquing the process for its "failed radicality."[55] The impact of funding and ideology on the community-based production should be examined, as should the paradoxes of inclusivity. However, as a participant in the process, who for various reasons voiced most of her criticism after the fact, Brady undermines the article's effectiveness as community-based scholarship.[56]

Though I disagree with Brady's methods, I appreciate her work for its value in helping me to articulate my own critical beliefs and choices. Community-based criticism should generally refer to how a producing group identifies itself. Since Cornerstone does not promote itself as "radical" in content, a critique should at least acknowledge this fact.[57] Secondly, as with reciprocal ethnography, critical work should engage in dialogue. If directly involved within the performance-making process, a critic should attempt to express his/her concerns to the producing company. Thirdly, in writing about a production after the fact, the scholar should endeavor to understand the process and to converse with the producing company about his/her responses. While these guidelines need not apply to all production critiques, they foreground strategies of engaged criticism that may ultimately help shape the future of the field as much as ongoing practice. As someone with experience in both criticism and production, often moving in between the two, this engagement and reflection is doubly essential.

As a scholar, I feel called upon to question, to critically summarize and situate gaps, to theoretically contextualize the performance-making process, to expertly document certain moments in theater history. As a community-based practitioner, however, I feel a responsibility to express my less cynical responses to the project participants' expressed hopes, to evoke what Cornerstone's *Good Person of New Haven* participant Brian Olivieri termed "the beauty and dignity and passion" of the process, as well as its gaps and contradictions.[58] Throughout my witnessing and practice of community-based theater making, I have been struck by the capacity of participants to celebrate and critique their own experience. These voices are indispensable in asserting the validity of individual experience alongside structural and aesthetic critique. In tracing a history and practice of community-based theater, I strive to keep these voices in play with more conventional historiographic accounts. In keeping with this task, I offer the following organizational points of entry.

Points of Entry

In its methodology, rhetoric, and organization, *Staging America* acknowledges multiple approaches and perspectives. The chapter headings thus submit various sites for the reader to engage with community-based theater, depending on interests in practice, historiography, or performance and identity. While reading these chapters consecutively offers a cumulative account of Cornerstone and aspects of community-based theater, each can stand on its own as a depiction of past traces, current practices, or ongoing reevaluations of community and performance. In terms of methodologies, or ways of exploring how to approach community-based theater and scholarship, each chapter restages the question "How do I talk about this?" and responds in a slightly different way. This variety of approaches results in distinct conversations, as well as manifold imaginings of Cornerstone, community-based theater, and America.

The next chapter, "Identity Traces: Historiographic Perspectives on Cornerstone and Community-Based Theater," proposes a genealogy of community-based theater in the United States, locating the field as a vital yet largely unwritten performance tradition participating in the ongoing staging of America. Community-based theater shares affinities with early-twentieth-century pageantry, Little Theaters, workers theaters, grassroots, identity-based, and social protest performances, among others. While each tracing bears vital distinctions, these theaters and movements emphasize the integration and expression of the "local," variously defined as regional, class based, or ethnically specific. Performances highlight social and aesthetic representations that embody, enact, and mythologize community. While much has been written about these theaters individually, this chapter explores the relationship among various movements and moments, particularly noting their self-identification as "American" theaters. "Identity Traces" also looks more closely at Cornerstone as a fluctuating community, exposing various layers in the company's development as an ensemble, an institution, and a producing organization. Depictions of this sixteen-year-old company as a traveling collective working with rural communities, and later as a diversified Los Angeles–based company bridging urban communities, provoke further reflections on performance making and social identity.

Chapter 3, "Perfor(m)ations: Cornerstone and Transactions of Community," reintroduces Cornerstone as a particular site through which to investigate contemporary community-based performance. This more explicitly theoretical chapter details the social and aesthetic interactions that define Cornerstone's work with communities, which both creates community and perturbs the notion of "community" as fixed or univocal. Details of Cornerstone's production process—selection, auditions, adaptation, performance, response, and aftermath—illuminate the complexities and fragmentations beneath the surface of even the most seemingly cohesive community.

Chapters 4, 5, and 6 reexamine some of the previously introduced observations and interpretive frameworks through in-depth, differential analyses of three collaborative sites, configured in rural, urban, and regional spaces. Each site study takes on a particular documentary practice, dependent upon discrete critical inquiries, archival selections, and the depth of my direct involvement with the performance process.

Early practitioners of grassroots theater, such as scholar-activist Robert Gard, advocated for theater linked to the "earth"—meaning its regional locality and its physical audience base. Chapter 4, "Rural Routes," situates Cornerstone's work via its affiliation to grassroots and folk theater, exemplifying and perplexing this connection. This chapter explores negotiations between insiders and outsiders and Western classics and local interests, by focusing on *The Winter's Tale: An Interstate Adventure,* which capped Cornerstone's first five years of community collaboration. From 1986 to 1991, the company traveled to various small towns developing adaptations of classical texts with local communities. *The Winter's Tale* staged America by reuniting performers from previous rural residencies, traveling across the United States in performance, and by exploring some of the archetypes that unify America as a mythic site. The company's rehearsal process illuminates the tensions within rural communities through interactions with various classical texts and with a mobile group of "outsiders." The rehearsal process magnified the difficulty of negotiating this mythic America through a diverse and mobile cross section of individuals from across the United States. The production asked the question "What does it mean to be home?" addressing this query from Long Creek, Oregon, to the Walker River Paiute Reservation in Nevada, to the Washington, D.C., mall.

Urban sites trouble the notion of community as rural, local, or unified. Yet, within the urban field thrive a number of communities of ethnicity, interest, and orientation. Chapter 5 investigates the implications of staging community within the city. While "Rural Routes" examines the performance of America via a matrix of dispersed rural communities, "Urban Revisions" considers the ongoing restagings enacted in a more densely populated site. Cornerstone's transition from a nomadic ensemble to one based in Los Angeles further illustrates the complexities of staging and defining community, and of enacting this staging through adapted and original sources. This phase of the company's work, from 1992 to the present, self-consciously reexamines "community" as a nongeographical site while also expanding the diversity of source texts. Productions with Arab Americans, a multilingual senior center, civil servants, and Angelenos sharing the same birthday explode notions of "community" and of "classics." Cornerstone also continues the practice of crossing community boundaries through bridge shows, such as *The Winter's Tale*. These bridge shows culminated in a December 2000 production at the Los Angeles Mark Taper Forum, with an adaptation of John Fletcher and Francis Beaumont's *Knight of the Burning Pestle,* bringing together all of the urban communities with whom Cornerstone has worked over the past nine years. Attempts to bridge cultural, ethnic, linguistic, and geographical borders in Los Angeles suggest the im/possibility of staging America. As a dramaturg and assistant on three shows in Watts, I respond to the production process mainly as an ethnographic participant-observer.

Chapter 6, "Regional Returns: A Tale of Two Collaborations," steps away from the city, and towards a more spatial and sociocultural examination, to critically reflect on two provocative collaborations between Cornerstone and regional theaters. Cornerstone's movement represents a paradoxical return for the company, which was formed in reaction to regional theaters. While regional or resident theaters have roots in the early-twentieth-century Little Theater Movement, professionalization in the 1960s often distanced the theaters from a diverse audience base. By the 1980s, regional theaters statistically served a narrow, white, middle-class audience, leading to Cornerstone's foundational opposition to the theaters. In the 1990s, Cornerstone's professional coproductions confronted the narrowness of this audience base and the notion of "professionalism" in relation to community. In 1993, the company coproduced an adaptation of Charles Dickens's *Christmas Carol* with one of the country's oldest regional theaters, Arena Stage in Washington, D.C. Developed with East of the Anacostia River (EOR) participants, *A Community Carol* brought into and onto the stage a section of D.C. that had felt previously excluded from the Arena. Collaborations with and questionings of regional theaters continued with Long Wharf Theatre's collaboration on *The Good Person of New Haven* (2000). While both productions performed for and staged an audience community not traditionally served by either theater, each coproduction raised distinct questions about the limits of inclusion in community-based theater.

Staging America concludes by re-viewing community formation via Cornerstone's sixteen-year history, embedded in the lengthier genealogy of community-based theater, and by suggesting how this examination offers new ways of conceptualizing social identity and community-based theater. This chapter also looks back at the historical site of affiliated practices, and the questions that these practices raises about theater, aesthetic engagement, and the negotiation of nation through performance. Finally, *Staging America* proposes that Cornerstone's work can be viewed not only as a site of instability and negotiation but as a way of thinking more generally about the relationships among performance, social identity, and the nation.

I have subtitled this introduction "Surveying the Terrain," which connotes efforts to both examine and mark the field of community-based theater, while keeping open the possibilities for new structures to be built, and for variegated responses to engage in dialogue with mine. I recognize that the landscape I am surveying remains under construction. As I continue to develop my interpretive strategies, and to include some interpretations of those interpretations, I acknowledge that the company I began writing about and the field of community-based theater itself will have changed—perhaps in part due to the writing itself. I welcome all ongoing revisions.

2

IDENTITY TRACES: HISTORIOGRAPHIC PERSPECTIVES ON CORNERSTONE AND COMMUNITY-BASED THEATER

If you would judge beforehand of the literature of a people that is lapsing into democracy, study its dramatic production. . . . No kind of literary gratification is so much within the reach of the multitude as that which is derived from theatrical representations.

—Alexis de Tocqueville, *Democracy in America*

Sophomoric, amateur, insulting. Gordon [Davidson, artistic director of Mark Taper Forum], how could you use this at the Taper?

—Anonymous Taper subscriber responding to Cornerstone's *For Here or To Go*

Community theater has an image problem. Or perhaps it is a semantic problem. For what has emerged in the past twenty years as "community-based theater" bears little resemblance to the images conveyed by the term *community theater,* at least in the United States.[1] Prior to the addition of a hyphenated base, borrowed from public funding language and popularized in the 1980s, theater scholars and professional practitioners tended to refer to community theater and its antecedents in pejorative terms, conjuring scenes of Mickey Rooney and Judy Garland rummaging through Granny's trunk in the barn, puttin' on a show. John Anderson's 1938 dismissal of early-century Little Theaters as an "abortive" and "rather silly national excursion into the drama" is typical.[2] And despite a wide range of ongoing practices and developing scholarship, contemporary attitudes towards community-based theater can echo Anderson, as witnessed by the regional theater subscriber cited above. The subscriber's comment, with its implicit focus on the difference between good (regional, professional) and bad (community, amateur) art, exemplifies a prevailing critical distinction.

But as Terry Eagleton and Pierre Bourdieu have pointed out, aesthetic critique and taste cannot be divorced from power and ideology.[3] John Malpede, who creates theater with LA's transient population, explains further: "Everybody pays lip service to community art, but it's a code word for 'bad art.' And art is about hierarchy."[4] Indeed, canon formation, aesthetic critique, and history making are always in part conventional—either establishing or following guidelines for inscribing value-laden narratives onto fragmented and dispersed events.[5] History making in particular tends to stabilize and valorize particular practices or events. I hope in this chapter to do neither.

But I am begging a few essential questions. What's so wrong with writing the unwritten and making some sense of the past? And on the other hand, why include a chapter on history at all, given my resistances? Let me begin by admitting that the tactics I lay out in this chapter are on the whole more mercenary than missionary; I am more concerned with notions of staging America than with archiving community-based theater as a whole.[6] Scholars who document the relatively marginal can bear a crusading quality—marching boldly into the mists of historical obscurity to return with a grail-full of new narrative. Seeing a defenseless and marginalized set of vital practices, the historian attacks the available archive, discovering, unearthing, un-marginalizing a history. Such a practice is admirable, and I don't evade a critical examination and contestation of traditional history. Convention might then call for me to demonstrate that community-based theater has always existed in some form, and has simply not been considered worthy of historical record. This important work may grant the field some canonical traction, as witnessed by historical revisionings that have made such artists as Aphra Behn and the African Grove Theater more visible. Why not simply follow these important precedents? While I do wish to assert the field's vitality, and combat the tendency to collapse community affiliated performance into an undifferentiated and somewhat distasteful mass dismissed as "community theater," I don't want to risk ignoring the historical specificity of various theatrical moments to fit them into a narrative progression culminating in Community-Based Theater or in Cornerstone Theater. Neither depends upon proof of lineage for its current vitality.

So I am mercenary. I focus on those practices that inflect the definition and negotiation of American identity. These associative threads open up ways of thinking about Cornerstone, as I examine the methods, missions, and complexities of previous moments, not behind but beside Cornerstone. In doing so, resonant questions emerge about Cornerstone's own mission and methodology, rather than a progressive accumulation of past moments that culminate in the present.

Decentralized Scholarship

> History is a form within which we fight, and many have fought before us.
> For the past is not just dead, inert, confining; it carries signs and evidences
> also of creative resources which can sustain the present and prefigure
> possibility.
>
> —Louis Althusser

Given an understanding of the relationship between historical selection and
authority, I align this chapter's historiography with Michel Foucault's writings on the genealogy of knowledge, asserting the importance of articulating "the singularity of events outside of any monotonous finality."[7]
Grounded in affiliations rather than continuities, and emergences rather
than progressive forces, this approach counters more conventional historical narratives. While not on a mission to displace these narratives, I am
prepared for engagement, fighting within the form that Althusser delineates.

A dominant account of American theater history is not difficult to discern. One of the first explications that includes the early-twentieth-century,
John Anderson's *American Theatre,* offers a strictly progressive chronology
favoring individual exceptionalism. In Anderson's chapter headings, colonial birth pangs give way to apprenticeship and finally reach maturity, culminating in the authentic American voice of Eugene O'Neill.[8] Other mid-
century renditions of American theater history follow suit.[9] Oscar Brockett's
prodigious *History of the Theater,* initially published in 1968 and currently
in its eighth edition, remains an impressive presence in undergraduate theater education.[10] Embracing European, American, and, in later editions,
Asian and African theatrical forms, the text seems all-encompassing. But a
largely positivist approach to theater history, concerned with names, dates,
and cause and effect relationships, submerges the influences of community
performance in America over the century, while claiming a nonideological
point of view.[11] The most recent edition summarily collapses the Little
Theater Movement and community drama into two paragraphs, situating
both as inheritors of a specifically European tradition and as forerunners
to the off-Broadway and regional theater movements.[12] Brockett gives some
attention to El Teatro Campesino and the Free Southern Theater as part
of a social change initiative in performance; however, his historiographic
practice largely depends upon naming predominately male individuals and
particular theaters, rather than identifying collective initiatives.[13] The Cambridge Guide to *American Theatre* and the more expansive *Cambridge History of American Theatre* refer to less conventional movements and events,
but neither explicitly includes nor defines community-based theater.[14]

While these richly detailed sources offer varying degrees of cohesion in their narratives of American theater history, they focus in general on what Felicia Hardison Londré and Daniel J. Watermeier refer to as the "mainstream" with some attention to "tributaries."[15] Other scholars have proposed entire supplementary renditions of American theater history.[16] Yet, their status as alternatives indirectly underlines the normative position of the more progressive "great man" (playwright, producer, actor) versions of theater history. More theoretical approaches to American theater, such as Loren Kruger's *National Stage* and several articles in Jeffrey Mason and J. Ellen Gainor's anthology, *Performing America,* explore the role of performance in fabricating national and social identity.[17] These examples of rigorous historical scholarship on community-based theater are unfortunately few and far between. There remains a gap between firsthand accounts of twentieth-century practices and interpretive assessment, though scholarship on contemporary and recent historical practices is increasing through journal articles and anthologies as well as oral history transcriptions, surveys, and artist gatherings.[18]

Like those movements and productions that can be identified with community-based practices, the scholarship of American theater has begun to decentralize. What follows is less a synthesis of ongoing scholarship, and more a tracing of emergent modes and methods, focusing on the struggle to redefine American theater ideologically, regionally, and aesthetically. I locate four historical moments that characterize distinct relationships among participatory representational practices, politics, and American identity: 1) progressivism and pageantry; 2) representation and grassroots theater; 3) socialism, identity politics, and community specific theaters; and 4) radical coalition building and the American Festival Project. Each of these traces has resonance with Cornerstone's practices, and I conclude this chapter with a closer look at the company as a shifting ensemble-based community. Like Cornerstone, these categorizations are neither fixed nor complete. My temporary divisions propose one way of locating the trends and complexities I perceive in interactions between performance and identity in staging America, particularly those that resonate with Cornerstone's sixteen-year production history.

PROGRESSIVISM AND PAGEANTRY

Progressivism refers to early-twentieth-century theater's participatory aspects as well as the limitations to that participation, particularly emphasizing the pageantry expert's tendency to formulate notions of citizenship for a nation striving to assimilate an influx of immigrants in the wake of a world war. While nineteenth-century practices, such as public schools taught in various immigrant's native languages, tended towards cohabitation rather than assimilation, progressive era politics and educational reform emphasized Americanization, often defined in a top-down manner. Anxieties about a labor force with increasing leisure time additionally contributed to the development of a pageant and civic theater movement, exemplified by a piece such as *The New Pilgrims* (1918).

Constance d'Arcy Mackay's play presents a vivid pageant scenario for an "Americanization Festival."[19] The brief text includes sing-along patriotic tunes, an allegorical representation of America, and a chorus of foreign-born citizens reciting and enacting pledges of allegiance. At a central point in the pageant, New Pilgrims wearing their "immigrant costumes" and carrying native flags, enter and place the flags at America's feet, receiving an American flag in return.[20] The Pilgrims then distribute these flags to the audience, who raise them at America's cue. Everyone joins in singing the National Anthem, as a soldier and sailor "in contemporary uniform" enter to stand at either side of Liberty and the crowd disperses to the strains of John Philip Sousa's "Stars and Stripes Forever."

Though perhaps overdetermined in its Americanizing practices, *The New Pilgrims* presents a fairly typical example of civic theater pageantry, with formal emphasis on symbolic enactments and community embodiment, and rhetorical focus on assimilation and allegiance. Thus, while the pageant seems to enact a participatory practice by including the bodies of immigrants, it also reformulates those bodies, adding American flags to their "immigrant costumes," and suggesting a more appropriate "uniform" look in the outfits of the soldier and sailor. But a closer look at this movement's practices and documentation suggests a more complex paradigm for negotiating early-twentieth-century American identity. While often linked to Christian values and targeted Americanization, and cited as oppressive to industrial workers through its practice of constructive leisure, civic theater may illuminate the process of community and nation building through the very obviousness of its rhetoric.[21]

At its core, civic theater must grapple with the paradox of mandated democracy, recognizing the easy slip from inclusion to compulsion. According to many of its practitioners, civic theater exemplifies and enacts a uniquely American form of participatory democracy. However, this democratization often presumes and regulates a certain kind of American citizen— one who is well-behaved, rooted in one place, and Christian. Additionally, "participation" often translated to embodiment, as pageant experts determined the staged and textual enunciations of participants. One of the foremost and prolific pageant experts, practitioner and theorist Percy Mackaye (no relation to Constance Mackay), foregrounds these links between theater and progressive democracy in his writings and speeches. Mackaye proposes that civic theater involves "the conscious awakening of a people to self-government in the activities of its leisure."[22] The kind of "active citizenry" Mackaye envisions, however, is implied in his reference to "self-government," suggesting not only civic participation but also behavioral control.

This presumption of moral citizenship can also be perceived in the sometimes hyperbolic rhetoric espousing civic theater as a panacea for ills ranging from alcoholism, worker inefficiency, and moral depravity to disenchantment with one's hometown, the challenge of assimilating immigrants, and the challenge of negotiating home economics. Following the United States' entry into World War I, Mackaye adopts combat rhetoric to propose the creation of "a new kind of army—a new kind of community in arts for the attainment of democratic world-freedom."[23] But civic theater has roots in progressive era socialism as well as Christian morality and patriotic allegiance. While critics of civic theater and community drama point towards its ultimate ineffectiveness and forced idealism,[24] proponents such as Louise Burleigh contrast the activating potential of civic theater with the passive consumption of more commercial arts.[25] The negotiation between anticapitalist participatory embodiment and moral coercive elements in civic theater can also be discerned in its contradictory affiliations with Christianity and Marxism.

Religious overtones quite literally announce themselves in civic theater's texts and theories. Pageant author Mary Russell claims that "dramatizations used in the Church school will make it possible for the children to know the stories of the Bible and the truths of Christianity."[26] Mackaye refers to community drama as "the ritual of democratic religion," and to its motive and method as Christian neighborliness.[27] Yet in the same address where Mackaye speaks of this Christian neighborliness, he cites the value of Karl Marx as a philosopher who synthesized a vision of social democracy.[28] Mackaye's drive to reconcile labor with joy in civic theater implicitly refers to Marx and Hegel's theories of workers alienated from their labor. Unfortunately, as Hiroko Tsuchiya notes in his astute analysis of the Industrial Drama Movement, recreational drama could be exploited by corporations attempting to pacify and unify workers, and occupy their leisure time, thus preventing congregation at working-class sites of amusement doubling as union meeting halls.[29] However, neither Mackaye's optimistic nor Tsuchiya's more critical view suffices to fully explain the power of civic theater as an expressive and coercive medium. As Tsuchiya suggests, the pageantry format could be co-opted as a medium of control. But expressive diversities could also be manifested, particularly in the link between civic theater, citizenry, and nation building.

In *The Civic Theatre*, Mackaye relates how a theater artist "reconciled the petty feuds of six districts of doubting Thomases, and united the township of Thetford [Vermont], after a century's schism, in the cooperative pleasures of pageantry."[30] This local self-development and unification, Mackay asserts, "may well be directly applied to the constructive solution of an American problem,"[31] integrating an immigrating population perceived by Mackaye as "ignored or stamped out by ignorant derision."[32] Mackaye believed that the joy of creating together an imagined vision of integration could actually manifest that vision. While community drama encompassed a number of forms—including church festivals, playground associations, and outdoor plays—civic pageantry most clearly expresses the link between progressive era politics and Americanization.

Often performed on holidays, such as "community anniversaries" or the Fourth of July, pageants like *The New Pilgrims* embodied and enacted potentially achievable myths of an assimilated America.[33] Cast directly from the participating community, pageants could draw crowds in the tens or even hundreds of thousands, or speak directly to a specific community of town citizens or churchgoers. In most of these divergent cases, pageant directors explicitly linked these "idealized community epics" to the process of Americanization.[34] Despite sometimes simplistic dramaturgy, this process has its complexities. Mary Russell's *Columbia's Concern for Her Country* (1923) and Mackaye's *New Citizenship* (1915) contrast distinct tactics for staging America.[35]

More overtly Christian in her focus, Russell is also more expressly ideological in her rhetoric of pageantry's application to citizenry: "The duties of American citizens are to correctly interpret American ideals, laws and customs to these foreigners. . . . action, costumes, tableaux and processions transmit the message better than do words."[36] Even without a vivid description of costumes or tableaux, Russell's text for *Columbia's Concern for Her Country* clearly communicates a need for educational reform that would embrace a recent influx of immigrants. Allegorical figures, such as Prosperity, Religious Education, and Truth, debate the current state of the nation before an enthroned Columbia. Despite overtly Christian rhetoric—Religion asserts that men are free to worship God as they please, and Truth replies that not every American is yet Christian—Russell's text also enacts a socialist sympathy.[37] Responding to Education's overblown assertions of her impact in America, Truth offers a stern corrective: "If a child is born in a wealthy section he is carefully educated. . . . If he is born in a section less supplied with natural resources he is denied even a grade school education."[38] Russell's staging of American ideals and critiques accompanies an embodied processional staging of Spirits of Uneducated Boys and Girls, Scouts, and Ministers, drawn directly from the participating community. Thus, *Columbia's Concern* literally embodies the community in its performance—a community figured as potential Americans when offered access to appropriate education.

Percy Mackaye's approach to Americanization pageantry in *The New Citizenship* qualitatively differs from *Columbia's Concern* or *The New Pilgrims*. Mackaye includes fewer allegorical figures, instead textually integrating historical documents such as a Woodrow Wilson speech that encourages immigrants to import and impart to America a renewal of their belief in her potential.[39] The incorporation of Wilson's speech characterizes Mackaye's take on inclusion as potentially transformative of that within which one is included. Rather than staging a ceremony of assimilation to a flag-happy America, or of allegiance to an enthroned Columbia, Mackaye's pageant presents an image of immigrants coming forward to express themselves individually via artistic means appropriate to their national identity.[40] Mackaye favors diversity over homogeneity, specifically stating,

> Here is the most inspiring occasion for revealing the multiform meanings of America, and for giving scope to those enlightened ideas of the new citizenship which stand not for the leveling away of all world-cultures to leave bare an American mediocrity, but for the welcoming of all world-cultures to create an American excellence: not for a national melting-pot.[41]

Mackaye's idea of diverse American excellence seems surprisingly and perhaps anachronistically multicultural, underlining the potential heterogeneity in any staging of America. These stagings may at the same time embody ideological control, participatory diversity, and animating unity—all elements which continue to merit more rigorous assessment in contemporary community-based theaters such as Cornerstone.

For the most part, civic theater in its many forms illuminates the ideological constructions of citizenry in early-twentieth-century America and the limitations and possibilities of participatory inclusion. Embodied and rhetorical stagings propose a heterogeneous insight into negotiations of nation and community. Large-scale examples of civic theater, such as the St. Louis Masque or Mackaye's *Caliban* in Central Park, brought together urban dwellers in celebratory and, perhaps, coercive pageantry. At the same time, regionally dispersed community dramas, in churches, schools, and small towns, animated community while often regulating behavior. The various stagings of America enacted through this drama were mainly ideological, though also locally diffused. In contrast to this primarily ideological focus, grassroots, Little, and folk theaters propose a decentralized representative regional federation as another way of staging America.

REPRESENTATION AND GRASSROOTS THEATER

The Little Theater Movement (approximately 1915–1930) and ongoing grassroots and folk theaters initiated in the early 1900s, attempted like the rural Cornerstone projects to define an American theater through a matrix of geographic localities. Proponents of both movements identified them as essentially American in character, in contrast to the more commercial, irrelevant theater believed to dwell on Broadway's stages. Robert Gard eloquently locates the Little Theater impulse "to be an integral part of the native American scene [responding] to the call of Emerson to produce an art that might be essentially American."[42] Regional dispersal and rootedness were essential to this call, as was an impulse to create theater with direct relation to the lives of everyday people, in the places that they lived. "It is the theatre of the whole vast United States," writes folk playwright Paul Green, "built and created by people themselves for their own needs, their feelings, purposes and vision."[43] For Green, and many founders of the Little Theater Movement, "the people" had no space for this expressive need in America's Broadway and touring theaters.

Scholars such as Alexander Drummond, Robert Gard, and Frederick Koch all advocated a decentralized system of theaters in the United States that would, according to Drummond, "start from the ground up and organize theater on another basis than the commercial one, to keep the theater experimental, native and alive."[44] Koch, founder of the Dakota Playmakers and the Carolina Playmakers, dreamed of a native theater that would "extend its influence throughout America."[45] Koch aggressively documented the folk plays that emerged under his tutelage between 1906 and 1941, including titles such as Paul Green's *Lost Colony,* set in North Carolina, John Philip Milhous's *Davy Crockett—Half Horse, Half Alligator,* from Tennessee, and Rietta Winn Bailey's *Mourners to Glory: A Negro Ritual Drama,* from Georgia—a veritable federation of folk. These folk plays, mainly located in the American here and now (at the time of their writing), were crafted in resistance to those more stylistically indebted to European influence. Koch notes that the plays are spatially localized, with characters "indigenous to the life they portray."[46]

Writing about one's "indigenous characters" does not, however, guarantee ethical and inclusive representations, and Koch can romanticize the plays' subjects. He enumerates "the folkways of our less sophisticated people living simple lives not seriously affected by present-day complex social order,"[47] and the rural zest for living close to the earth, engaged in communal tasks. He additionally celebrates the "gentle Mormon people" and "child-like, excitable Mexicans" portrayed in the included dramas.[48] While these renditions of "the people" are mainly well intended if simplistic, some folk plays practiced a more extreme form of erasure. In Fred Eastman's *American Saint of Democracy* (1942), the historical Quaker John Woolman challenges the capitalist morality of a local businessman. Due to Woolman's influence, the businessman eventually frees the slave he had intended to purchase. Yet, the slave herself has few lines, most indicated in stage directions calling for her to sink to the floor moaning "O Lawdy, Lawdy!" for the bulk of the short play.[49]

Despite this tendency towards oversimplification, grassroots theater saw itself as inclusive and relevant. In response to what he viewed as theater that had no relation to the lives of everyday people, Allen Crafton founded one of the first rural Little Theaters, the Prairie Playhouse in Galesburg, Illinois, in 1915. Like Cornerstone, Crafton felt that in order for theater to be meaningful to a local audience, it must spring from the people. He explains, "We tried to make this everybody's theatre, and asked help from everybody and anybody."[50] True to his word, Crafton's theater involved community residents in all aspects of production. A former Cultural Minister to Denmark and his wife served coffee at intermission. A local physics professor sold the theater rheostats for lighting dimmers at a greatly reduced cost. Actors included a banker's wife, preachers, shop girls, teachers, and a delivery boy, who Crafton cites as "one of our best character actors."[51]

Locally inclusive and reflective, Little Theaters blossomed in the years from 1915 to 1917. However, as the young men who established them were drafted for the First World War, many, including The Prairie Playhouse, dissolved. Others, suffering from financial instability, institutionalized their organization, often at the expense of the involvement of the community, as the theaters hired "professionals" from outside. Still others transformed into amateur theaters. The evolution of Little Theaters into regional theaters is often celebrated; their deterioration into community theater disparaged. Joseph Zeigler dismisses community theater as a "lowercase movement with lower case ideas."[52] John Anderson writes wittily if scathingly of "the movement's rosy promises, which sound now as if they must have been made under powerful narcotics." While his comments seem at first dismissive, Anderson also proposes an incisive critique of the Little Theater Movement: "Instead of becoming a pioneer in production, instead of devoting its attention to the possible local development of playwrights, instead, in fact, of doing anything at all constructive, it became a frank imitator of Broadway theatre."[53] This "frank imitation" is ironically lauded in historical accounts of the Little Theater Movement, many locating its emergence in companies such as the Washington Square or Provincetown Players. This history tends to privilege those theaters that developed into professional off-Broadway or regional fixtures, rather than the grassroots rural theaters located outside of major metropolitan regions. These rural theaters did in fact devote attention to the development of local playwrights. Though sometimes romanticizing the folk about whom they wrote, grassroots theaters that remained grounded in and attendant to their local audiences flourished. On the other hand, efforts by professional theaters to capitalize on the folk aesthetic fell into troubling representational traps.

Many folk theaters and Little Theaters enacted unconscious exclusionary practices. Indeed, as discussed in this book's introduction, community requires exclusion. But a more conscious and blatantly hypocritical exclusion is starkly evidenced in the professional production of a folk play by a theater claiming to be grounded in a particularly "American" aesthetic. As an ensemble dedicated to the production of plays without regard for their local resonance, the Group Theater does not follow the paradigms defining community specific work. I cite their production of Paul Green's *House of Connelly* (1931) not to exemplify participatory practices but to illuminate the emergence of more self-conscious fragmentation in community specific theater.

SOCIALISM, IDENTITY POLITICS, AND COMMUNITY SPECIFIC THEATERS

In the early-1930s, the Group Theater attempted to produce shows resonant with an American as opposed to European aesthetic.[54] *The House of Connelly* did indeed present "American" issues, exploring the growth of the country from an agricultural to industrial society. Yet, the Group explicitly denied membership to the play's two black actresses, Rose McClendon and Fannie Belle De Knight. Producer Cheryl Crawford's description forty years after the fact (in 1973) remains crass at best: "We had to take two black actresses with us because they played important parts in the show. The rest of the people comprised this new company."[55] The Group's understanding of an American theater seemed based more on thematics than inclusive representation.

This kind of subgroup erasure, of class, race, ethnicity, and gender, generates a conscious fragmentation in participatory theater practices. Embodied representation and the development of identities separate from that of a unified America characterized such movements as the Workers Theater Movement of the 1930s, and the Chicano Theater and Black Arts Movements of the 1960s. All three movements arose from specific political circumstances and developed artistry that responded to those conditions. The Chicano and Black Arts theaters proceeded from the civil rights and identity movements for Chicanos and black Americans, respectively, foregrounding separate aesthetic practices linked to those movements.[56] The workers theaters generated a class-based aesthetic and practice, emerging from efforts to unionize workers. The particular theatrical practices that ensued cannot be divorced from the specific sociopolitical circumstances and goals that informed them.

Socialism and the workers theaters. The workers theaters emanated from several intertwined goals: to educate workers, to support unionization and strikes, and to further the development of a working-class culture. At its height, the League of Workers Theater included four hundred members producing mainly agitational-propaganda plays at strikes, at rallies, and in union halls. These collectively generated performances often featured the mass as a hero, with choral chants reinforcing didactic messages. Workers theaters were local, political, presentational, collective, and mobile as opposed to universal, existential, psychological, individually generated, or stably located. Sometimes dismissed for their simplistic style, the theaters' goal-oriented focus produced a unique and effective aesthetic practice. The importance of communicating a clear message to a targeted audience with minimal funds dictated a presentational, locally specific style that emphasized imagination.

In the early-1930s, a number of workers theaters staged a piece by Langston Hughes entitled *Scottsboro Limited* (1931). The play told the story of nine Alabama black boys unlawfully accused of raping a white woman. The mobility of the theaters called for the transformation of iconic objects. Through the context of the piece, a nondescript chair became a judge's seat, an electric chair, and a platform from which the boys issued a final cry for freedom. The chair's transformation, through the context of performance, established a powerful and occasionally ironic connection between judge and jury that would not have been available with more specific representational objects. The piece also called for one white actor to play all the white roles, signaling that racial and class signification was more important to the story than the development of psychologically differentiated characters.

Another initially working-class theater, El Teatro Campesino (The Farm Workers' Theater), also developed a condition-based aesthetic within an environment of political activism, exemplified by the 1962 founding of the United Farm Workers. Often linked with Luis Valdez and the *commedia* style he brought with him from his year with the San Francisco Mime

Troupe, Yvonne Broyles-Gonzalez's revisionist history focusing on the Campesino ensemble underlines the artistic influences of Mexican oral culture and Teatro storytelling traditions.[57] Both physical and oral elements are visible in El Teatro Campesino's political performances. *Actos,* signifying both one-act and taking action, featured physically exaggerated, masked characters such as the pig-faced *Patron* (Boss) and were performed off of flatbed trucks or at strike rallies. Like the Farm Workers' theater performances, *actos* were designed to be simple rather than simplistic. Rather than fixating on virtuosity and the uniqueness of the individual performer's talent, the theaters emphasized collective replicability. This repeatability was essential to a movement ultimately less concerned with aesthetic practices than with the power of theater to agitate for change in the conditions of the working class. Rather than seeking to enact a representational cultural politics, the workers theaters sought large-scale social change. But the political atmosphere of the 1960s differed radically from that of the 1930s, when socialism and even communism seemed a viable political option for America, at least from the point of view of the labor force. An emerging emphasis in the 1960s on civil rights and cultural representation situates a shift from socialism to identity politics in community specific theater practices.

Identity politics, Chicano theater, and the Free Southern Theater. The practice of collective creation forged by El Teatro Campesino continued in the 1960s and 1970s with the emergence of a more broad-based Chicano Theater Movement, associated with the Chicano civil rights movement, *El Movimiento.* Theaters such as El Teatro de la Esperanza (Theater of Hope) performed for targeted audiences in Chicano schools and communities. In these theaters, social commentary and explorations of a Chicano identity emerged alongside calls for more direct political action. One of Esperanza's founders, Jorge Huerta, identifies this growing body of work as people's theater, enacting through performance a specific cultural and political identity separate from either Mexico or the United States.[58] Ethnically based performance is certainly not a new phenomenon in the United States; Yiddish and German theaters influenced early workers theaters such as Artef. The development of a theatrical form designed to formulate a *new* hybrid identity within America distinguished the Chicano Theater Movement.[59]

Formal and cultural separation from "White America" also characterizes the Black Arts Movement. Though varied in its artistry, and regionally dispersed, the movement sought a distinct Black aesthetic divorced from White or Western forms. Amiri Baraka describes the need for a national consciousness "where a people come to see themselves in contrast to their oppressors, and their lives and laws. Where they climb back into the stream of history."[60] As LeRoi Jones, Baraka had earlier called for "poems like fists"—art as a weapon in the revolution for Black cultural separatism.[61] Like the Civil Rights Movement, Black Arts traced a trajectory of initial integration with liberal whites, followed by independent cultural nationalism. The Free Southern Theater, founded in 1963 and given a New Orleans jazz funeral by John O'Neal in 1985 to mark its 1980 death, exemplifies this trajectory.

Eventually based in New Orleans, the Free Southern Theater traveled extensively in rural Mississippi hoping to educate and unify as well as to entertain rural black communities. Founded by black student activists Gilbert Moses, John O'Neal, and Doris Derby at Tougaloo College in Mississippi, funding to support the idea grew with the participation of Richard Schechner, then a professor at Tulane University in New Orleans. Initial supporters included Langston Hughes, Paul Newman, and Barbara Streisand. Early performances embraced both black- and white-written plays, including Ossie Davis's *Purlie Victorious* and Samuel Beckett's *Waiting for Godot,* and featured integrated casts. A history of the theater edited by Schechner, Moses, and Thomas Dent characterizes the Free Southern Theater as enacting Southern black experience supplemental to the Civil Rights Movement.[62] As the Movement shifted, however, so too did the theater.

Black Arts poet Larry Neal has described the Free Southern Theater as less a theater than a "history of the thinking of black nationalists."[63] In 1965, the theater reflected the increased activism of the Civil Rights Movement and a more participatory community-based aesthetic by introducing improvised performances from the audience playing themselves as civil rights workers, police, or judges. Further inclusion increased with the introduction of Black Arts South in 1967, encouraging the local development of performance poetry. Then in 1968 the company began to ask questions about its focus. Should they emphasize education or the language of the streets? Regional theater or street theater? A split erupted over differences in artistic direction, and the Free Southern Theater emerged as a locally grounded black organization. Jackson Hill specifies this shift in his brief history of the theater, which indicated that the company no longer imported actors but instead established a training program to teach and develop local people. The company also set up a writing workshop and strengthened its community theater program.[64] The Free Southern Theater continued bringing together black nationalist aesthetics with community-based ethics and programming through the late 1970s. O'Neal even planned the jazz funeral to coincide with "The Role of Art in the Process of Social Change" conference held in 1985. Explaining the theater's eventual demise, O'Neal notes that sociopolitical conditions changed, and "the broad-based social movement that gave rise to the Free Southern Theater now lies fallow."[65] A shift had taken place; the conditions allowing for a certain kind of theater dropped away or were perhaps absorbed into the culture at large. O'Neal recognized that this changed set of circumstances required a different praxis.

The social circumstances that supported the Free Southern Theater and various Chicano theaters shifted in a variety of directions, including critiques of gender bias in the black nationalist and Chicano (rather than Chicano/a) civil rights movements. Theaters developed that served ever more particular communities: feminist, lesbian, queer, disabled, Latino/a, and Asian American among them. Alongside these theatrical developments, a paradox emerges: In the quest for group identity, performance is seen as both a manifestation and formation of culture. Identity then is not pre-formed but performed, essential but not essentialist. At the same time, some activist individuals realized that split political focus contributed to the decreased effectiveness of a "broad-based social movement." bell hooks refers to this revised activism as "radical postmodernism." This radicality relies less on the performance of a cohesive social subject position, less on prescribed core group unity, and more on the building of empathy—creating ties that will, according to hooks, "promote recognition of common commitments and serve as a basis for solidarity and coalition."[66] From these particular conditions, a fourth contemporary and more specifically "community-based" theatrical trace emerges, focused on forging links across a variety of communities.

RADICAL COALITION BUILDING AND THE AMERICAN FESTIVAL PROJECT

Even before John O'Neal had ritually buried the Free Southern Theater, he had begun moving away from work geared towards a specifically African American audience. "The reason I perform for white folks [now]," he explains, "is that I came to realize that you can't change the black condition without the support of the majority of the population."[67] O'Neal's less explicitly theoretical enunciation supports hooks's appeal for a politically aware postmodernism that "calls attention to those shared sensibilities which cross boundaries of class, gender, race."[68] This renewed vision of community-based theater is less grounded in assimilated unity, socialism, or identity politics and more in strategic bridge building. As part of Junebug Productions, the theater he founded following the demise of the Free Southern Theater, O'Neal joined a coalition of artists working under the umbrella of the American Festival Project. Along with such other associations as Alternate ROOTS (Regional Organization of Theaters South) and the

Community Arts Network, individual artists and groups have begun to collaborate as a way to decrease cost, increase artistic and organizational support, and generate new ideas about building cross-cultural bridges, and, in the process, question essentialist cultural identity. These coalitions propose a new way of staging America—as an ongoing exchange.

Based in Whitesburg, Kentucky, through Appalshop, the same organization with which Roadside Theater functions institutionally, the American Festival Project is rooted in the belief that cultural exchange can provide a context in which "diverse peoples can begin to understand and respect one another."[69] The festival brings together companies and artists such as Roadside, the Los Angeles Poverty Department, Junebug, and El Teatro de la Esperanza to develop community collaborations across the United States. The project claims to build coalitions and dialogue, catalyzing long-term community interaction and transformation. Representative exchanges include a celebration of Appalachian and Chicano cultures in Whitesburg and San Antonio, a three-year interaction between African American and Haitian American communities in Miami, and a lengthy environmental justice project with Junebug and New Orleans–area activists.

What occurs in these exchanges? What can they reveal about the contemporary nature of American identity? Certainly fragmentation is visible. In order to build bridges, there must be some differences to be bridged. The artists and theaters involved also emphasize participatory performance, a kind of democratization. But the American Festival Project relies less on federated unity, less on large scale nation building, than on providing a platform for asking questions and making discoveries about differences and links. It is a project that is always incomplete.

The Environmental Justice Project continued for five years with Junebug and various arts and community organizations participating. The amount of collaboration and actual progress achieved was astounding and ongoing. Yet, early in the process, tensions erupted between organizers and artists. Some community organizers felt that the artists were focused upon more short-term projects and did not have as much of a commitment to community building. Pat Bryant of the Gulf Coast Tenants Association expressed concern about the outreach aspect of artistry and its impact on self-reliance: "People—especially African Americans—have been taught to rely on outside experts, as opposed to people in their community [so] we don't need any 'artists.' We need workers. They must participate as regular people."[70] O'Neal agrees, noting that the Justice Project's focus on direct action allowed him to reconnect with his geographic and cultural roots in New Orleans and his organizational roots in the Free Southern Theater.[71]

Despite O'Neal and the Festival Project's commitment to more long-term transformational projects, theaters involved with collaborative work have critics across the political spectrum. Professedly conservative theater producer Martin Platt questions the ethics of "subsidizing [Roadside's] folk art taken out of the hills for export."[72] Believing that *Hamlet* speaks as clearly to a Southern audience as Appalachian storytelling, Platt challenges both the community-based aspects and coalition building drive of Roadside's work with the American Festival Project. An anonymous participant in Cornell's symposium on grassroots theater offers another skeptical point of view, questioning the value of cross-cultural bridge work when a community feels disempowered: "We have to be very careful. We say we want to break down barriers between us, but sometimes I want barriers. Sometimes I want to feel I have an identity that everyone else cannot buy into, have, co-opt."[73] Coalition building requires tricky navigation—respect and recognition of attachments to what might seem to be more transitory community identities. Despite poststructural efforts to point towards a destabilized subject, despite community-based productions that illuminate the construction and multiplicity of identity, it remains a privilege to select one's identity, to remain unmarked by the differences that a dominant culture can marginalize, erase, or appropriate.

Within this discursive environment characterized by critical tensions between associations and distinctiveness, between bridge building and boundary construction, Cornerstone emerges—not as an endpoint but as an exemplary site of ongoing negotiation amongst these various tensions. Founding members locate direct influences in the "truck theater" of El Teatro Campesino, the ensemble structure of the Group Theater, and simultaneous production within the Federal Theater Project, which emerged during the height of the Workers Theater Movement in 1935. Rather than simply providing a historical context for Cornerstone's contemporary projects, however, these and other past traces propose sites of inquiry about the relationship among ethics, performance, and identity.

The complexities of producing civic theater prompts questions about how a community-based company navigates between coercion and participation, particularly when working with a diversity of individuals holding different values. The frustrations created by subgroup erasure and hypocritical "representation," in such productions as *The House of Connelly* and *The American Saint of Democracy*, provoke considerations about parameters for ethical representation that allow for cultural coalition and exchange. Zooming in on the functional dynamics of one particular company also allows for more minute queries about organization and process. How does a community-based company concerned with inclusion organize itself institutionally? How does funding impact the organization and its values? What does the artistry produced say about the company and the communities it purports to work with and represent? How does this artistry move between expression and control? Between art and social service?

While many of these questions will be addressed in the following chapters, which focus on Cornerstone's coproductions, the remainder of "Identity Traces" looks at Cornerstone as a collective, ensemble-driven entity that is itself in flux. A magnified lens heightens the ongoing changes present, but often smoothed over in more summary accounts of long-term organizations. Over sixteen years and three mission statements, Cornerstone has undergone innumerable modifications and transformations, now no longer identifying itself as a specifically American theater. In this kind of representative institutional shift, along with changes in personnel and aesthetic redefinition, the ever-transforming "Cornerstone" offers further insights into the complexities of community and nation formation.

Cornerstone as Community

When you become a part of Cornerstone, you create what it is.
—Ensemble Member Page Leong, Durfee Oral History

Then new ensemble member Page Leong uttered the above comment during a 1994 oral history retreat funded by the Durfee Foundation. As a midpoint between Cornerstone's founding in 1986 and ongoing work in 2002, the retreat offers a fascinating look into how the company reconstructed and envisioned itself structurally, conceptually, and artistically. At the time the retreat took place, half of the original company had resided in Los Angeles for two years, after five years of working as a nomadic, institutionally undefined collective of artist-administrators. Since arriving in Los Angeles, a number of key changes had taken place. The company had committed to diversifying its ensemble, which had to that point consisted mainly of white Harvard graduates. Bold artistic choices had also unfolded. Shishir Kurup, who later became a core ensemble member, directed a show with Arab Americans citywide that enacted several firsts for the company: The production was company-devised rather than adapted, directed by someone other than cofounder Bill Rauch, and created with a nongeographically defined community. Cornerstone had also recently concluded its first regional coproduction with the Arena Stage, requiring participating ensemble members to join the Actors Equity Union. Financial restructuring and input from new members brought changes in artistic production methodology as well. Rather than adapting only classics of Western theater, the company produced adaptations of Sanskrit, Chinese, and African texts and commissioned original plays. Cornerstone also developed more ensemble-only shows, bridge shows across communities, and institutional and artistic collaborations. As the company continued to experiment and diversify, its identity transformed.

"Cornerstone" embodies several shifting identities. The name connotes both foundation and building, suggesting stability and growth.[74] It is, additionally, a sign with multiple signifieds, including an ensemble-based institution and collective of individuals, and a producing organization whose methodology and artistry remain fundamentally inclusive. This very commitment to inclusion raises issues of ethical representation and accountability for continuing community involvement. What does it mean to be a part of Cornerstone? What is Cornerstone's responsibility towards former community partners? How does the company grapple with the fact that inclusion may threaten core values? Over the years since attending the oral history retreat, I have addressed these questions to ensemble members, community participants, and collaborators and have scrutinized legal documents, transcriptions of company meetings, newsletters, audience response surveys, program notes, and reviews. I have also witnessed numerous ensemble and community-based shows (and even participated in one). The following analysis proposes a way of looking at Cornerstone as a continuously morphing and intertwined ensemble, organization, and producing company.

Ensemble and Organization

As a collectively run company, Cornerstone joins a tradition of ensemble theater in the United States that includes the Group Theater, El Teatro de la Esperanza, the Wooster Group, and Dell'Arte Company. Founding ensemble members note that this collective tradition initially held far greater influence on Cornerstone than companies emphasizing community-specific practices.[75] Not all of these ensembles enact community-based practices, but they do share a resistance to the hierarchical organization found in most professional theaters, and the consequent problems of balancing artistry and administration. The struggle to grow artistically, while remaining connected to foundational inclusive values, defines many of Cornerstone's challenges in Los Angeles.

Before moving to Los Angeles in 1992, resolving tensions between artistry and administration seemed less of an issue. In Cornerstone's early years, artists were intimately involved with the company's administration—to the extent that there was one. Producing shows comprised most of the company's work, and the group seldom planned productions more than a few months in advance. While the company and its members remained relatively young, this informal system functioned adequately. Cornerstone's office equipment consisted of little more than an answering machine stored in the Rauch family home and a computer and printer on the road. Financial operations involved appealing to donors, writing grants, and balancing the company checkbook, or making cuts in weekly salaries when the checkbook couldn't be balanced. Company members arrived at administrative decisions as a group, took on some specialized roles (as actor, designer, or composer), and worked together on other tasks, such as running auditions, hanging posters, and striking the set. A three-member board of directors composed of cofounders Bill Rauch, Alison Carey, and their mutual friend R. J. Cutler met as seldom as was legally necessary in the company's first year. Beyond a requisite mission statement, Cornerstone codified little of its structural organization.

Institutional shifts resulted from an effort to stabilize financially. The company's initial goal of diversifying the theatrical audience base led eventually to a free or pay-what-you-can admission policy. Cornerstone's earned income thus hovered between 5 and 15 percent of its annual budget. In 2000, the percentage of income earned from ticket sales constituted approximately 1 percent of the company's operating budget, while earned income remained at about 10 percent. Outside funders make up the balance, which in 2001 included a five hundred thousand dollar endowment. At first, funders encompassed mainly state arts and humanities grants and individual donations. As the company grew and required a larger financial base, they hired a full-time managing director in 1989 (Alison Carey managed the company's early seasons). But difficulties separating administrative and production roles continued. Patty Payette, company manager from 1989 to 1990, expressed frustration that her administrative work did not receive the same kind of respect as the company's productions.[76] Stephen Gutwillig, managing director from 1991 to 1995, also had a difficult time avoiding getting "sucked in" and ended up running a complex sound plot for Cornerstone's first Los Angeles production.[77]

The company's attempt to better separate administrative and artistic roles ran into difficulties, perhaps for the better. A 1990 study in *American Theater* suggests that longer running collectives, such as Mabou Mines, the Wooster Group, and Theater X, have survived due to the fact that their ensemble artists also administer the organizations.[78] Artists involved in the day-to-day operations of an organization recognize the context for admin-

istrative decision making, and administrators who work as artists may identify to a greater extent with the organization. Though Cornerstone members have specific jobs, such as artistic director, managing director, or producer, and the company employs an office staff that includes a grant writer
and marketing consultant, major administrative and policy decisions are
arrived at through ensemble consensus, established in 1988.

Consensus requires every member of the group to agree with policy, though
individuals may abstain from a given decision. Driven by the inclusive input
and investment of the individuals who make up the group, this collective
model encourages creative decision making about complex issues. But consensus may potentially reinforce homogeneity and repress dissent. Studies
show that while collective leadership supports creative problem solving,[79]
consensus may also lead to interpersonal tensions and power struggles.

In his analysis of British alternative theater groups, Steve Gooch cites the
difficulties of negotiating unofficial management or unacknowledged leadership structures within a collectively run organization.[80] Some former
Cornerstone members claim that these invisible structures inhibited their
work with the company. David Reiffel explains:

> I was pretty burnt out on the way that the collaboration was going. I was
> finding it very frustrating to be a part of it, because of what I saw as a lot of
> sort of unofficial . . . unofficial sort of channels of power and influence that
> kept some ideas from fruition. Ultimately the collaboration was just too
> hard, and had too much frustration in it in terms of sort of getting, saying
> what I wanted to say. What I felt needed to be said.[81]

Reiffel felt that he was unable to articulate his dissent and compromised his
values. Bill Rauch maintains that Reiffel's problems may have had as much
to do with the "official power" that Rauch and Carey possessed as cofounders.[82] Yet, other members who remain affiliated with Cornerstone also expressed their sense of "inner" and "outer" circle power dynamics, which may
not have been clear to those "inside."[83] Amy Brenneman reflects on her
initial misunderstanding when an "outsider" depicted this exclusivity:

> [He] would go on and on sometimes about, you know, "You don't under-
> stand. There's this inner circle and you're in it, and you can't see it," and it
> was extraordinary. And I didn't understand. And I do a little bit now—a
> lot more now. Not really because of anything I've been through, but it's like,
> oh, of course. I was smack dab in the middle of it, I couldn't see it.[84]

Brenneman suggests that the boundaries of inclusion within Cornerstone's "inner circle" may be difficult to permeate, partially because they
are not obvious to those within the circle. Responding to Brenneman's

comments in a later interview, Bill Rauch proposes that "inner and outer circles" may also have referred to Cornerstone's lack of clarity about ongoing employment with the company: "There was an unspoken separation between those who had confidence about their on-going employment (mainly its founding members) and those who felt that they had been hired on a contract basis."[85] In order to clear up this ambiguity, Cornerstone formalized a permanent company of core members before commencing *The Winter's Tale* tour in 1991. When only half of this permanent company moved to Los Angeles, remaining members renamed the core the Ongoing Ensemble, additionally distinguishing between active and inactive members.

Both of these decisions amounted to striking shifts in the company's institutional development. For the first time, membership was codified. This codification resulted less from assumptions about organizational effectiveness than from the anxieties of those who worked with Cornerstone about their relationship with the company. While grappling with this challenge over relative inclusivity, a new problem emerged—the ensemble's homogeneity.

Consensus requires some degree of value cohesion in order to reach decisions, and Cornerstone's all-white company reflected a particular kind of homogeneity prior to 1992. Members had touched on the need for diversification from as early as 1986, when a teacher in a mixed-race Virginia school had asked in front of the student body why Cornerstone had no black members.[86] In a 1988 newsletter, Alison Carey pondered the issue and its ramifications:

> We are an all-white organization, which is a source of confusion for all of us. It's sort of how Cornerstone started: a bunch of white, middle class kids [but] we realize that we're not kids anymore, we are visiting artists who, simply by virtue of our visibility can unintentionally communicate "this business is for white people."[87]

While Cornerstone worked on the road, however, diversification proved difficult to prioritize.[88] Finally, at a 1992 retreat in Los Angeles, the company resolved to work towards more variety in its membership. Cornerstone's ensemble is now multiethnic, embracing members who self-identify as Latino, African American, and Asian American. The ensemble has also included two former community participants, Damion Teeko Parran, who acted in Cornerstone's Arena Theater collaboration, *A Community Carol* (1993), and Gracy Brown, who participated in *The Good Person of New Haven* (2000), a coproduction with Long Wharf Theatre and New Haven residents.

Constructive conflict within Cornerstone continues, as dissent is embedded in diversity, though this commitment to difference may run contrary to the consensus impulse. Enforcing consensus may lead to the stifling of dissent that Reiffel describes.[89] Additionally, some ensemble members remain more invested in administering the group than others. And as the ensemble grows and younger members join, the group has confronted issues such as differential compensation, which recently took the better part of a year to resolve. In 2000, Cornerstone eliminated life-time tenure, a difficult decision that ensemble members believed would prioritize the long-term heath of the company over individual employment.[90] The ensemble now operates on a one- to three-year contract basis, balancing membership flexibility with stability.

In addition to ongoing challenges of maintaining a diverse and expanding, consensus-driven ensemble, Cornerstone must also function as a producing organization in a nonprofit arts world. Resources other than ticket sales support most of the company's operations, and the constraints of this funding reverberate in its structure and programming. Despite a collective ensemble base, a board of directors legally runs the nonprofit Cornerstone Theater Company. Though supportive of Cornerstone's mission, and inclusive of several ensemble members, tensions invariably erupt between the majority-ruled board and the consensus-run ensemble about the long-term goals of the company. At the same time, funding can influence programming in positive and more challenging ways. Grant opportunities impacted the hiring of artistic collaborators between 1996 and 1998, leading to some tensions between hiring innovative artists and supporting Cornerstone's fundamental values. Yet those values have, in some ways, always been under construction. Production methodology and aesthetics define another essential though evolving trace in Cornerstone's identity.

Producing Cornerstone

What might seem fundamental to Cornerstone members at any one time derives from years of developing work in directions shaped by opportunity and funding as well as by goal-driven initiatives and philosophies. Founding members instituted Cornerstone as a way to diversify the audience attending theater through collaborative productions. With financial support from the Virginia Commission for the Arts, Cornerstone members began residency work directing Virginia schoolchildren in plays and leading improvisation workshops. While this work nominally supported company members, they aspired to work with adults as well. In collaboration with a community center run by Joe Stevens in Newport News, Cornerstone cast its first full-length production, *Our Town* (1986).

A number of members had trepidations about whether this collaborative production would actually work. Alison Carey feared that she had romanticized Cornerstone's goals and that the company would be perceived

Cornerstone's first full-length community collaboration, *Our Town* (1986). Unlike most Cornerstone community-based productions, the text was not adapted. Photo: Lynn Jeffries.

as a bunch of "snotty Harvard assholes."[91] Douglas Petrie adds, "I had thought very much like we're gonna be seen as intellectual snobs, 'get outta here,' we're gonna be rejected."[92] Yet, *Our Town* engaged the community in unexpected ways, allowing for the kind of mutual transactions between Cornerstone and community participants that remain fundamental to the company's method. Petrie details his discovery about how Cornerstone's collaborative vision might function:

> I was technical director for Cornerstone and I was working on this outdoor stage building a platform. . . . And these three kids, big adolescents, came over on bikes and were just kinda checkin' me out. They talked amongst themselves, and one of them approached me and he said, "Hey, man, do you need some help?" I said, "Yeah, yeah." And these three guys helped me build this platform. It kind of got me thinking, people love this, people need this, people want this. . . . And, in fact, people are so hungry for it. That was something that I was not expecting at all.[93]

Lynn Jeffries follows up with an equally resonant, if varied, account of this story:

> I was there and they weren't adolescents, they were ten years old. He came up on his bike and he sat there and looked at us for ten minutes. And he

said, "What y'all doin'?" And we said, "We're building a set for a play." I felt like I was speaking Chinese. And then he didn't say anything for another ten minutes, was just watching us and watching us, and then he said, "Do you need help?" And that was where it all kicked in. In fact, every day more kids came. . . . the next day there were four, and the next day there were ten. We had the whole neighborhood coming over every day before we got there . . . they'd be like sweeping the stage. Little tiny kids, like four year olds who really couldn't actually do anything, they'd kinda take some paint and paint the wood scraps—it was extraordinary.[94]

Initial fears proved unfounded in large part because of a *de facto* method— establishing a spatially accessible project (working outside) and accepting offers of help. Cornerstone's goals implicitly and explicitly emphasize collaboration rather than service. Through work on the production as actors, technicians, and set builders, painting wood scraps, or sweeping the stage, Newport News participants could claim partial ownership of and, thus, accept and invest in *Our Town.*

These social exchanges remain fundamental to Cornerstone's work. They have continued to evolve since the company's first residency project outside of the East Coast. The Marmarth, North Dakota, project in 1986 initiated Cornerstone's early nomadic as well as its adaptive work with a Wild West musical *Hamlet.* At that point, the company felt the time was ripe to establish a national audience base. Based on the notion that a true expansion of the American audience required a leap into the unknown, members decided that they knew least about the state of North Dakota, and that they should therefore go there. They called the state historical council, who eventually led the group to Marmarth Mayor Patty Perry, and the company departed for the Badlands in the fall of 1986.[95]

Future residencies developed according to the working and funding pattern established in Marmarth. Cornerstone members would decide on a region of the country they knew little about or an economic base, such as mining or logging, that they were interested in exploring. Members contacted state historical societies (who often had information about buildings as possible performance sites) or wrote to small towns, or reservations in the case of Schurz, Nevada. Someone eventually contacted a community leader, and if performance space and housing could be arranged, the residency proceeded, often funded by state arts and humanities councils.

In early rural years, the company focused on adapting classical texts of Western theater for a number of material and ideological reasons. As graduates of Harvard, a university without a theater department, these were the literary works company members had studied and produced, believing them

The final duel scene in Cornerstone's first adapted production, a Wild West musical, *The Marmarth Hamlet* (1986), produced with the town of Marmarth, North Dakota, population 190. The photo features Cornerstone ensemble actor Christopher Liam Moore as Hamlet *(left)* and Marmarth resident Rod Prichard as Laertes *(right)*, both blindfolded. Photo: Benajah Cobb.

to be complex stories of common human struggle. Written prior to the enforcement of copyright laws, these texts also required no royalty payments, nor permission to rewrite. Text selection additionally attracted support from several state humanities councils. Given time and funding constraints, adaptations also proved more feasible to produce than original works. Finally, adaptation enacted a philosophy of artistic inclusion; company members felt that locating classical texts within a contemporary, local setting allowed community participants to reclaim these stories.

In addition to establishing strategies for initial contact and textual adaptation, the Marmarth residency also set precedents for transactions within the production process. The nature of Cornerstone's work in Virginia, in schools, with an established community center, and with a town in which they spent several months, allowed for ease in garnering auditioners. In North Dakota and following residencies, members discovered that they had to do more than announce their presence to engage local participants. In Marmarth, this entailed hanging out at the local bar. Ensemble member Christopher Moore recalls: "They didn't really buy [the Cornerstone project]. But they were a little bit tipsy. . . . they saw we weren't leaving and they got curious."[96] Social interactions and introductory periods thus became as important to successful collaboration as the involvement of local leaders such as Mayor Patty Perry.

Following initial engagement of community members, a successful, well-attended performance run required a continued collaboration through publicity, marketing, and other social transactions. Weekly newspaper columns from Marfa, Texas, Mayor Jane Shurley demystified the production process and continued to establish *That Marfa Fever* (1987) as a coproduction with the community. In Marmarth, the local bar owner sent copies of production posters to bars around North Dakota via a statewide beer delivery truck. In rural residencies, local and regional press and word of mouth often led to sold-out productions. Program notes from community members and local participants working at the box office continued community collaboration and publicly displayed this collaboration. Local businesses bought program ads and occasionally supported the group by sponsoring funding events. "Roping nets $1,200 for theater group" read one headline in Long Creek, Oregon.[97]

The details of engagement with a community shifted dramatically upon Cornerstone's move to Los Angeles. A sprawling urban center could simply not sustain as much word-of-mouth advertising, even in smaller communities within the city. The company therefore initiated long-term bridge-building projects linked to advisory boards. A fifteen-month project in Watts preceded a three-year "BH residency" (with communities such as Boyle Heights and Beverly Hills), a two-and-a-half-year New Haven project, and a several-year Faith-Based Theater Cycle, commencing with weekly dialogue meetings in early-2001 and designed to run through 2004. Cornerstone also began to rethink the nature of "community" as geographically based, initiating residencies with police officers, people sharing the same birthday, and a senior citizens center.

While expanding and diversifying its ensemble and productions, the company began to feel the strain of dissipation. José Luis Valenzuela, an artist, activist, and general supporter of Cornerstone's mission, expresses some concern about their tenure in Los Angeles:

> When Cornerstone got to LA, I was excited, because of the work they were doing. My feeling was—great they were inside the community, they lived with the people, they researched—from that experience a production will come out. I thought that was fantastic work. My feeling though, is that it has been dissipated because they have been moving so much—into so many different areas.[98]

While Cornerstone no longer "lived with the people" in a small geographically defined location, Los Angeles did offer possibilities for enacting the radical postmodernism called for by bell hooks. Still, Valenzuela's questions about Cornerstone's long-term impact in Los Angeles joins an array of internal and external challenges to the company. At its core, Cornerstone continues to develop projects based in mutual transactions, adaptation, and cross-community bridging, while grappling with the challenges of a growing, diversified ensemble and board, and the responsibilities of maintaining relationships with community participants. As with its potential for dissipation, this relationship building gratifies, humbles, and haunts the company.

In letters to Cornerstone, numerous participants cite the experience as empowering and confidence building. Dyann Simile of Montgomery, West Virginia, claimed that she stopped being such a "couch potato."[99] In Marfa, Texas, district judge Bill Earney spoke of keeping active, Jessica Carrasco asserted that she overcame her nervousness, and Bruce Aguilar broke out of "the usual rut of 'school, friends and sleep'" by acting in the production.[100] Rod Prichard in Marmarth declared that he had learned to express himself.[101] Schurz student Ramona Dewey spoke of learning to talk to people: "I never used to talk to people. I hate talking to people. It's helped me to, just be myself."[102] Waitress Wanda Daniels in Montgomery simply felt recognized. In *Cornerstone*, a documentary of *The Winter's Tale* tour, she comments:

> All my life, I was just one of the Howrey girls, that's my maiden name, and then when I got married everyone knew me as Herschel's wife. It was like I didn't have an identity. But now I do have an identity. People know me as Wanda Daniels, not so and so's this or so and so's that.[103]

Under-recognized individuals, such as Daniels, can be appreciated through public performance. In Schurz, Mayor Collins claimed that no one in the community had realized that teenager Ramona Dewey had such a beautiful voice before the production of *The House on Walker River*.[104] Ostracized individuals can also be reperceived and embraced by the community. Rod Prichard had been referred to as the local bad boy prior to his performance as Laertes in *The Marmarth Hamlet*.[105] Port Gibson, Mississippi's Edret Brinston, known only as a functionally illiterate track star, astounded local participants by learning his part of Romeo before anyone else in the cast, and later passing his high school literacy test.

Part of Cornerstone's ideology resides in allowing local participants to be themselves, or more accurately, to perform themselves through the production process. This process may offer participants the opportunity to reconstruct their public as well as private identity. Prichard's focus, Dewey's vocal expression, and Brinston's applied skills, enacted in a public forum,

Ramona Dewey as Electra in *The House on Walker River* (1988) in Schurz, Nevada. In a letter to Cornerstone, Dewey noted, "It's helped me to just be myself." Photo: Lynn Jeffries.

reconstructed their identity. The confidence built by public acceptance may also have helped to reconstruct their private identity. Through participation in a communal event, Dewey learned to "just be herself."

While affirming Cornerstone's process, the testimonials may elide further tribulations. Moments captured in testimonials often recall the most positive experiences of a residency. In the more objective context of an oral history, Cornerstone members acknowledge the problematic nature of their work with individuals and communities. While Prichard remained sober during the rehearsal process of *Hamlet,* he returned to drinking after Cornerstone's departure. Brinston landed in jail twice for stealing cars. Ramona Dewey did not have the emotional stability to finish a tour with Cornerstone in 1991. These facts attribute less to Cornerstone's "failures" with individuals than to the limitations of theater, and to the complex nature of identity construction. While Cornerstone cannot remake individual identity, the company can and does make an effort to follow through with their work in communities, though at least one community sponsor expresses a lack of confidence in their effectiveness.

Anne Cavalier, vice president of West Virginia Institute of Technology in Montgomery, critiqued Cornerstone's visit as a "one shot cultural vaccine," prior to their arrival.[106] Company members were taken aback, though many had already recognized that the temporary nature of their presence in a community could cause feelings of abandonment following the company's departure. In the early rural years, Cornerstone members would leave behind a portion of box office receipts towards the foundation of a local community theater.[107] Workshops, correspondence, simultaneous productions, and a rethinking of their mission and organization followed. Many rural towns continued producing theater following Cornerstone's departure. After a decade of productions, Eastport, Maine, residents even returned their five hundred dollar seed money to Cornerstone. Yet, some urban residents expressed indignation at what they perceived to be demeaning, colonial gestures. During *Ghurba,* an Arab participant found Cornerstone's five hundred dollar seed money offer insulting. "Some Arabs resisted and asked why don't we do our own work? Why should Cornerstone come in and do it?" explains Cornerstone's collaborator Fadwa El Guindi.[108] One participant in *Magic Tricks* (1998), a coproduction with the largely African American neighborhood of Baldwin Hills, expressed frustration with the temporary nature of Cornerstone's project, pointing out that sociocultural problems objectified in the script remained unresolved in the community.[109]

In order to better attend to community participants in affecting policy as well as theater, in the early-1990s, Cornerstone invited former community participants to serve on the company's board. The eventual presence of Ron Temple from Kansas and Toni White-Richardson from Washington, D.C., additionally maintained for the company a national presence and identity as an American theater. Ongoing debate among board and company members about their commitment to the Los Angeles community later challenged this representation. Late in 1994, the board agreed to centralize by focusing on a Los Angeles member base. This decision destabilized Cornerstone's identity as a national presence, at the same time as it reinforced commitment to community, specifically to the communities in its own backyard.

Members now acknowledge that the continued success of community theaters depends on the communities' organizational skills and infrastructure as well as their own contributions. Thus in Los Angeles, the board expanded to involve representatives of organizations active in building and bridging communities including at various points, Bill Martínez, former executive director of Community Youth Gang Services, Debra Padilla, the executive director of Social Public Arts Resources Center (SPARC), Shana Waterman, New Haven project coordinator for Cornerstone's collaboration with Long Wharf Theatre, and Alejandro Nuño, founder of the Watts/ Century Latino community organization. Coalitions with board members and their organizations have directly contributed to Cornerstone's community-based theater projects. Nuño recommended and organized the initial efforts towards Cornerstone's Watts residency. SPARC cosponsored Cornerstone's "random community" birthday show, celebrating their tenth anniversary in 1996 by working with a community of individuals united by a June 30th birthday. Board members such as Padilla, Nuño, Waterman, and Martínez legitimate Cornerstone's presence in communities like Watts, while also creating a Cornerstone identity that is greater than its ensemble members. By working directly on restructuring the organization and administration of Cornerstone, board members become a part of the changing identity of the organization.[110]

Efforts towards organizational diversity in its ensemble and board, building relationships with individuals, community leaders, and activists, and a production methodology that emphasizes collaboration and exchange—with attendant complexities and developmental shifts—continue to characterize Cornerstone in 2002. However, most of these efforts remain less visible to audience members and critics in a large urban center, where production aesthetics primarily define a company's public identity. Since the Marmarth *Hamlet*, most ensemble and community-based productions have relied upon contemporized textual adaptations that reflect and formulate community identity. Like other elements of Cornerstone's identity, this aesthetic is interactive and evolving. While the following chapters examine these aesthetic interactions in greater detail, "Identity Traces" concludes with a look at a Cornerstone ensemble show, an adaptation of Garcia Lorca's *Shoemaker's Prodigious Wife*.

Ensemble members initially developed shows such as *I Can't Pay the Rent* (1986), *A Midsummer Night's Dream* (1988), and *Slides from Our Trip* (1988) to introduce themselves and their work to communities. While working within a transactional context, these productions did not reflect the community-based aesthetic of Cornerstone's work. *The Video Store Owner's Significant Other* (1990) became the first ensemble show to grapple with the issues of Cornerstone's aesthetics, ideology, and identity as a community.

In 1990, Cornerstone organized the February Festival, a celebration of different community-based productions produced simultaneously. Based on the model of the Federal Theater Project's openings of *It Can't Happen Here* (1936) around the country, the company organized community adaptations and simultaneous openings of Lorca's play, chosen by the vote of producing communities. Six communities developed locally specific adaptations of Lorca's text. Resultant adaptations ranged from *The Barber's Misunderstood Wife* (Marmarth, North Dakota), to *The Saddlemaker's Wife*

(Long Creek, Oregon), to *The Cowpoke's Persnickety Spouse* (Schurz, Nevada). As Cornerstone members began to develop their adaptation in concert with communities, they realized that the process raised a number of issues related to the group's own identity.

The primary concern of the company centered on situating themselves as a community in order to determine the context of the adaptation. As a transitory collective from all parts of the country, no specific geographical setting could ground their adaptation. One thought was to set the piece in a theater company. Another, to establish Washington, D.C., the performance site and nation's capital, as their setting. Finally, the company decided to locate their adaptation in a "generic American setting," a mall video store.[111]

For many Cornerstone members, the mall represents the archetypal American community, the national agora of modern times. As a site that provides social congregation and cultural reproduction, the video store seemed its cultural center.[112] Everywhere the company traveled in America, introducing live theater to new audiences, members commented that they could always locate a video store or video rental area within a grocery store (with greater ease, sometimes, than they could locate an audience). Cornerstone has since developed several productions in actual malls including *Everyman at the Mall* (1994), *California Seagull* (1995), *Mallière* (1996), an evening of Molière one-acts, and *Foot/Mouth* (1999), integrating Luigi Pirandello's *Man with the Flower in His Mouth* with Samuel Beckett's *Footfalls* for viewers tuned in to the appropriate radio station. Initially, establishing this iconic performance setting for *Video Store* did not, however, complete the adaptation process. Deciding on how to represent relationships in the adaptation proved more challenging.

Cornerstone members experimented with developing the adaptation through consensus, thus integrating organizational with aesthetic identity. A number of participating members had problems with Lorca's depiction of the relation between an older man and his young wife. Additionally, a number of gay members wanted to explore what often remained closeted in Cornerstone's community collaborations. Discussing the company's rural work, Christopher Moore confesses, "I felt that I should have been more out and regretted that I hadn't been."[113] After much dialogue and trepidation, the group arrived at an adaptation in which the gender, age, and sexual dynamics of this relation continuously shifted. Characters rotated to represent the relationship as that between an older heterosexual man and his young female companion, an older gay man and his young lover, a lesbian couple, and an older heterosexual woman and her young male significant other.

While this rotation proposed a diversity of relationships in contemporary American culture, a few reviewers bridled at the suggestion that homosexual and heterosexual relationships could interchange so easily. Noel Gillespie of *The Washington Blade* warned, "Gay and Lesbian relationships are presented not as alternative lifestyles, but as very minor variations on the heterosexual theme—a very debatable premise."[114] Though the production received generally positive reviews, and several award nominations, for Gillespie at least, the adaptation neglected differences among and within particular communities.

Grappling with subject matter remains a challenge in developing community-based productions, particularly navigating between artistic freedom and sensitivity to community concerns, issues that continue to emerge in Cornerstone's rural and urban work. Ensemble members also debate relationships among accessibility, complexity, and innovation when discussing aesthetics and style. Shishir Kurup and Cornerstone Associate Artist Sabrina Peck have more darkly humorous, politicized visions than the stylistic vividness characterizing Bill Rauch's directorial work. Some visiting artists have trouble integrating their more individually derived artistry with Cornerstone's inclusive aesthetics. While most of the time the company can include a number of artistic visions, Armando Molina wonders how to keep the work populist as well as innovative, asking "When is the work calculus and when basic math?"[115] Questions of style and context impact those viewing productions as well those who develop them. Audiences for Cornerstone's community-based shows differ from ensemble-only shows. The broad style of *For Here or To Go* (2000) and *The Good Person of New Haven* (2000) turned off a number of Mark Taper Forum and Long Wharf Theatre patrons (while delighting others). Ensemble shows tend to draw fewer audience members from former collaborating communities. Trying to embrace the variety of ensemble members' artistry and values may lead to the sense of dissipation that some members have felt in the past and that Valenzuela points towards.

CONTINUITIES

The question remains whether Cornerstone as a collective of individual members, and Cornerstone as ideology and aesthetic process, can or should be viewed as completely separate aspects. Joan Shigekawa, formerly of the Nathan Cummings Foundation, once posed the question, "If [cofounders] Bill Rauch and Alison Carey were run over by a truck, would Cornerstone continue to exist?"[116] Responding several years later, Carey notes: "Well, I think the company is clearly sustainable without me, because I've been slowly leaving. Now the bigger question is, and I think it always has been, about Bill."[117] Rauch initially found the query difficult to address, as it uncovered both foundational and personal differences about how Cornerstone should be defined and the degree of institutionalization desired. Some members yearn for the financial and structural stability of institutionalization. Others believe that Cornerstone's identity should reside in its ever-changing collective of individual members. Rauch himself at one point referred to Cornerstone as an idea as much as a collective. In this vision, interested communities and theater artists could potentially reconstruct little cornerstones throughout the country, "like McDonald's," he smiled, half-serious.[118]

Cornerstone as an idea, residing in a foundational ideology of engaging more Americans in theater through direct participation, represents only one organizational facet. Rauch's 1995 McCornerstone vision presumes that the identity of "Cornerstone" is not dependent on the individuals who construct the ensemble, including Rauch himself. Comments from ensemble members as well as community participants challenge this notion of an idea-based Cornerstone, explicitly referring to their experience in terms of the individuals within Cornerstone, particularly Rauch.

In discussing her reasons for joining Cornerstone's *Winter's Tale* tour, Rosemarie Voorhees writes about "being reunited with her Cornerstone friends" and "being directed by Bill Rauch." Douglas Casement states as his reason for joining the tour, "Bill called me and offered me the part." Ron Temple adds that "'if anybody but Bill Rauch had asked me to do this [tour], I would have told 'em where to go.'"[119] As Cornerstone's cofounder, most prolific production director, company artistic director, and frequent institutional spokesperson, Rauch maintains the most public visibility. He and cofounder Alison Carey, along with founding ensemble members Lynn Jeffries, Peter Howard, and Christopher Liam Moore, also embody a historical continuity that balances ensemble turnover and diversification within Cornerstone. Certainly Cornerstone is now identified with longtime ensemble members Leslie Tamaribuchi, Armando Molina, Shishir Kurup, Page Leong, and Geoff Korff, as well as newer members such as Damion Teeko Parran, Chris Acebo, Paula Donnelly, Paul James, Bridget Kirkpatrick, and Mark Valdez. However, by the time this book is published, some may no longer be ensemble members because of the recently adopted shorter-term membership contracts. While ensemble turnover may well increase in the future, Cornerstone's longevity as a company is in part dependent upon the ongoing association of founding members, many of whom remain connected to the company as board members, guest artists, funders, and audience members.

Rauch, however, expresses optimism about Cornerstone's continuance in the absence of its founding members, noting that students at Yale started up an organization, the Open Door Theater, founded on Cornerstone's ideological praxis. Due to funding and personnel dynamics, however, the organization soon discontinued its operations. Comments and experience thus seem to suggest that Cornerstone's founding members should stay away from oncoming traffic, that individuals construct Cornerstone as much as its foundational ideology.[120] But in the years since Shigekawa first posed her query, Cornerstone has diversified its artistic and organizational leadership. In 2004, Rauch will take a six-month sabbatical, providing further opportunity for Cornerstone to assert independence from its founding members.

Negotiations between individuals and ideology, structure and chaos, continuity and change, remain at the crux of Cornerstone's identity. Dialogue among individual founding members, about what theater should and shouldn't be, shaped Cornerstone as idea and organization. A balance of collective and individual decision making arose from experience over time. Though I have suggested the elusiveness of locating a Cornerstone identity through a depiction of these continuous negotiations, one idea has rooted the many tensions defining Cornerstone. The notion of collaborative exchanges, among all of Cornerstone's members, including community participants, and between often classic texts and contemporary contexts, stabilizes Cornerstone aesthetically, structurally, and ideologically, at the same time as those transactions themselves continue to re-form Cornerstone.

Cornerstone in 2002 is no less dynamic an entity than in 1986. Despite a process of ongoing reflection, financial stabilization, and physical growth, the company is not progressively shedding the conflicts that define its youth but rather negotiating new challenges that coexist with these prior tensions. The unfolding of new challenges energizes and complicates perspectives on the company, rendering ineffectual any kind of evolutionary history, and thankfully so. The continuously shifting layers of individual and social identity that the company's work exposes—the very failure of any possible stabilization of community, Cornerstone, or America—remains an attractive aspect of interpretation and analysis. For this destabilization paradoxically arises from a desire to discover, to reflect upon, and to represent as fully as possible a particular moment in a specific community. Meanwhile, the tensions within the company arise from its very ethics of inclusivity. "When you become a part of Cornerstone you create what it is." Just as in Woodrow Wilson and Percy Mackaye's philosophy, "new citizens" transform that which they become citizens of. Inclusion is transformative.

At the same time, the desire to communicate more directly, to a larger, more diverse American theatrical audience, requires translations, exchanges, and further transformations. Because translation implies both the desire and the impossibility of communication, no performance can ever fully reflect, represent, or manifest community. Cornerstone's unflagging drive to continue in the face of impossibility cracks open assumptions about community, culture, ethics, and power.

3

PERFOR(M)ATIONS: CORNERSTONE AND TRANSACTIONS OF COMMUNITY

> To see the thing grow, you know, this is what fascinates me, because this is like planting a crop. If you harvest wheat and you harvest milo and you have a good crop, why then it's exciting. You don't mind working long hours if you reap something from it. And I expect this is kinda what the play is; it's gonna be a harvest. I hope it's a good one.
> —Ron Temple, Kansas farmer and Cornerstone actor

A t 6' 9", farmer Ron Temple tends to tower benevolently over other people. He surrounds himself with vastness—from the acres of fields that he cultivates to his performance as Orgon, the largest speaking role in Cornerstone's 1987 *Tartoof*. It is fitting then that Temple's eloquent simile, equating *Tartoof*'s production with harvesting, heightens and enriches a discussion of Cornerstone, community, and culture. Apropos of Temple's farming metaphor, "culture" has etymological roots in crop cultivation. Over several hundred years the term's connotations have shifted to embrace a complex of meanings, ranging from high art to everyday practices, from social relationships to institutional power dynamics, from wheat farming to theater.

Cornerstone's collaborative projects bring together complementary and clashing aspects of culture production. As Raymond Williams has elaborated, performance manifests culture by integrating modes of production (making things) with symbolic systems (representing things).[1] When individuals like Norcatur, Kansas, residents come together to create something that signifies themselves, as they did in the adapted *Tartoof (Or, An Imposter in Norcatur—and at Christmas!),* they produce community through both social and symbolic systems. When "outsiders" like Cornerstone initiate

Ron Temple as Orgon in *Tartoof* (1987), produced with the town of Norcatur, Kansas. Photo: Lynn Jeffries.

performances via often canonical source texts, they complicate the community-making process in intriguing ways, uniting ethnography and theater, high culture with local culture, Molière with milo. Through collective engagement, and the clashes resulting from efforts to represent community, an intricate meaning-making process ensues. Harvesting may not adequately convey the self-reflexive aspects of this process. Perhaps Clifford Geertz's image, of the "webs of signification" creating culture, can supplement this chapter's investigation. Geertz proposes that culture relies upon these webs of meaning making that recursively shape the individuals who spin them.[2] This Möbius strip–like image suggests a process that folds back upon itself, similar to the way individuals who work with Cornerstone continuously reshape the company. A closer look at Cornerstone's collaborative productions details the overlapping oscillations of symbolic weaving and unraveling that produce culture and community, through dialogue, participation, and adaptation. This more explicitly theoretical chapter details the social and aesthetic interactions that define Cornerstone's work with communities, interactions that both animate and disrupt community in an ongoing process of reweaving.

Cornerstone's community-based process arose initially from a loose thread, or resistant strain. In 1986, a group of recently graduated Harvard students grew frustrated with what they believed to be a limited idea of national identity, as defined by the American Repertory Theater in Cambridge. Cofounders Alison Carey and Bill Rauch felt that, despite its title, this theater's white, upper-middle-class audience base did not in fact represent America. Former ensemble member David Reiffel explains: "We were hearing a lot of rhetoric about American theater and about America. And that was something that was beginning to sound like a lot of bullshit, because people weren't going to it and it was incredibly expensive."[3] Rauch, Carey, Reiffel, and other founding Cornerstone members decided that if they wanted to engage a truly diverse American theater audience, they needed to travel beyond the geographic and economic confines of East Coast regional theaters.

Cornerstone's inception thus resides in two central idea(l)s: that an American identity can be discovered through creative exchanges with local cultures, and that exciting theater is more likely to occur by working with a community rather than for them. In initial discussions about how to discover and create new audiences for theater, Alison Carey explains, "We thought we'd bring a show to a community and ask them what they thought of it through discussions."[4] Further thinking about the creative transactions and the dialogue that they desired led Carey and Rauch to decide that "if

we were sincere in our desire to learn from people what makes good theater and whether theater is important, then we had to be in the trenches
together."[5] Cornerstone's shows thus involve the community in every aspect of production, from planning to adaptation, to publicity, rehearsal, and
performance. This chapter's analysis of Cornerstone's production process,
through cultural and performance studies, details how the collaborative
process builds, performs, and ultimately destabilizes community, while
continuing to raise rather than answer questions about American theater.

Social Transactions

Stimulating Community

The social transactions engaged by Cornerstone's performance process animates a sense of community structurally, interpersonally, and through the
process of shared meaning making—the "making things" aspect of culture
production. These interactions begin long before auditions, rehearsals, or
even text selection, in some instances, as contact with collaborators rein-
forces leadership structures while enabling dialogue among residents of a
town or members of a community. On the Walker River Reservation in
Schurz, Nevada, Tribal Educator Lucinda Benjamin acted as Cornerstone's
local liaison. Auditions then linked the school board with tribal elders,
enacting structural interchange. In Marmarth, North Dakota, the State
Historical Society connected Cornerstone with Mayor Patty Perry, and
planning sessions took place in Marmarth's one bar. These conversations
eventually drew community participants into the process, many of whom
frequented this local social hub. Conversations (outside of bars) also facilitated Cornerstone's most recent Faith-Based Theater Project. Along with
the National Conference for Community and Justice, in early 2001 the
company initiated "Weekly Wednesdays," conversations with Los Angeles
religious leaders, artists, and members of the general public interested in
interfaith dialogue.

These interactions are more complex than they may at first seem, moving between systems and individuals, stimulating dissent as well as consensus, and raising questions about the dynamic link between community leaders and participants. Cornerstone's Animating Democracy grant proposal
for the Faith-Based Project aspires towards conversations that eschew "po-
lite dullness" in order to "get at our differences in a way that wakes people
up," according to Salam Al-Marayati at the Muslim Public Affairs Council.[6] Even when dissent is less desirable, the production process kindles interactions between people and systems. Individuals like Lucinda Benjamin

become engaged through their social roles and ties and are often contacted through a larger governmental organization, such as the state humanities council. As an individual operating at the nexus between native and state, Benjamin offers access to two systems of social organization—the school board and tribal elders. Additionally, Benjamin, Al Marayati, and Mayor Patty Perry are all local leaders, an essential consideration in establishing a shared production process.

Beginning with their first collaboration in Newport News, Virginia, through to the Faith-Based Project, Cornerstone continues to find that effective partnerships depend upon involving community leaders. Cornerstone recognized the importance of these leaders early in their Marmarth residency. Explains ensemble member Peter Howard: "It was certain that [Mayor Patty Perry] was gonna be in the show right from the start. She kept saying no, but it was certain in our minds."[7] Perry played the grave digger, and her presence was instrumental in getting residents off bar stools and onto the stage. In Schurz, Nevada, Tribal Chairman Wayne Johnson's acceptance of a role lent similar validity to *The House on Walker River,* an adaptation of *The Oresteia.* Lucinda Benjamin concedes: "I must admit there was some reluctance surrounding the project. . . . certainly the boost was when the Tribal Chairman auditioned and was cast in one of the leading roles in the play."[8]

Saul Alinsky and Anthony Cohen each propose a contextual rationale for the success of these collaborative engagements, based upon their respective experiences as community organizer and sociologist. In *Reveille for Radicals,* Alinsky warns that equitable, effective relationships can only be achieved when a community and its leaders participate directly in the organizational process with an outsider.[9] Cohen's ethnographic studies further propose that if "outsiders" intervene or attempt to solve perceived problems, the community retaliates by reasserting its exclusionary boundaries.[10]

While local leaders can boost participation and collaborative involvement, Sara Brady critiques a process that she perceives of as dominated by more dynamic community members. According to Brady, the involvement of local leaders may actually prevent a community from fully asserting or animating itself.[11] Brady's assumptions neglect the presence of participants such as Rod Prichard, Ramona Dewey, or Edret Brinston (discussed in chapter 2), none of whom could be considered local leaders prior to their participation in a Cornerstone production. At the same time, Brady's critique deserves consideration, as it raises questions about what it means to "animate community" through performance. In fact, this animation centers less on community itself than on a feeling of community. Emotion as well as structure figure in community building, and animation suggests an enlivening of that which already exists but requires movement to be recognized. While a local leader can stimulate relationships, an active response must arise from a larger group of participants.

Thus in Norcatur, Kansas, the mayor called an initial meeting to discuss Cornerstone's proposed arrival, which involved the entire town in the decision to sponsor the project. A number of town members then worked together to transform the local high school to Cornerstone living quarters.[12] Eighty-year-old cast member Dorothy Kelley details how the production process further animated Norcatur in program notes to *Tartoof*:

> Since the Centennial celebration in 1986 the town has been in the doldrums, coasting along with nothing specific needing to be done and consequently not doing anything. . . . [Cornerstone's arrival initiated] a big clean-up day, and everyone helped to make a good impression. So old tree limbs were hauled away, vacant lots were mowed, everybody tried to put their best foot forward.[13]

The theatrical event provided an occasion for the town to "do something specific," precipitating an activation of social networks involving everyone in the town. Working together also reinforced a commonality of purpose for Norcatur residents. In various other towns, introductory events such as potluck suppers, lemonade socials, and church breakfasts brought residents together, once again reinforcing the social bonds that can constitute community.

Transactions between Cornerstone and communities include labor as well as social exchanges, involving aspects of production that emphasize its materialism. Following Raymond Williams, Bruce McConachie elaborates on these aspects of theatrical production. According to McConachie, the use of "production" to refer to a theatrical process and its outcome emerged in the late-nineteenth century, embedded in an industrial discourse emphasizing relations of labor, capital, and profit.[14] While Cornerstone's community-based productions develop in an explicitly nonprofit milieu, labor and material transactions certainly drive the company's collaborations. In Dinwiddie County, Virginia, a local brownie troop finished painting the set for *The Maske Family Musical* to earn drama merit badges, and in Nevada, a bomb factory donated lumber in exchange for program credit.[15] Rural community hosts offered living and performance space, local businessmen and women supplied door prizes and props (such as a fifty-pound bag of fertilizer in Dinwiddie), and members of the community provided the casting pool and backstage crew. In return, Cornerstone proffered theatrical skills, advertising space, and sometimes a labor exchange, as in

Marmarth, where company members tended bar and milked goats so that local actors could rehearse *Hamlet*.

In rural settings, these transactions seem divorced from profit-motive and economic drives. But a number of sites belie this reading, particularly in urban environs, where the ability to volunteer anything suggests a certain privilege. *A Community Carol* actor Toni White-Richardson explained: "The community people are not coming in to make a living. They bring a sense of dedication. But sometimes they can't put [the show] number one all the time. Sometimes it had to be number four or number five. A lot happens in people's lives that takes priority."[16] Upon their move to Los Angeles, Cornerstone members began to question the ethics of paying themselves salaries of several hundred dollars a week and asking community participants to volunteer time and labor. The company now reimburses participants for performances, bridge shows, and for backstage work on ensemble shows, though the question of equitable compensation remains at issue. In fact, their fourth-wall breaking citywide bridge show *For Here or To Go* (2000), which brought together participants from fourteen Los Angeles communities, directly reflected on issues of compensation and volunteering.

In the original 1613 text by Francis Beaumont and John Fletcher, *The Knight of the Burning Pestle*, a grocer and his wife interrupt the stage action of a typical early-seventeenth-century city play to complain about its representational oversight: No grocers appear onstage. To correct this omission, they send their apprentice Rafe onstage. As the eponymous knight, Rafe sincerely enacts what emerges as a parody of the romantic escapade, simultaneously perforating, commenting upon, and occasionally intertwining with a conventional tale of star-crossed lovers. Cornerstone's freely adapted version of Beaumont and Fletcher's play, staged at Los Angeles's premiere regional theater, the Mark Taper Forum, accentuated the company's inclusive ethics while poking fun at their own excesses and omissions. Early in the performance, a Burger King owner and supposed Taper subscriber, played by Beverly Hills resident Bruce Freidman, interrupts the stage action to complain about the play's portrayal of fast-food restaurants. Like the grocer in Beaumont's original, he sends his worker Rafa onstage, much to the chagrin of characters involved in an entirely different story line, and to the surprise of a largely unsuspecting audience. After a great deal of chaotic hijinks ensues, "Bruce" insists that the "director," played by Cornerstone's Shishir Kurup, allow him stage time to defend his business. He and Shishir are soon embroiled in an argument about fair labor practices, which transforms into a Cornerstone self-critique:

Bruce: We have a high turnover rate because people learn how to do an honest day's work for an honest day's pay and then move onto other opportunities.

Shishir: Just because people are just starting out doesn't mean they shouldn't earn a living wage.

Bruce: Oh, yeah? How many people did you employ last year at a living wage? I heard that crap you said at the beginning. You work with "community volunteers." Which means you get grants to pay the company employee salaries and everybody else gets squat.

Shishir: You don't know anything about how we work with communities. We have stipends.[17]

When I attended the production, Kurup's comment provoked outbursts of laughter, particularly among former community participants in the audience, including myself. As I know from having performed in one, stipends amount to five dollars per show. (Though bridge shows do pay substantially more.) Beyond reference to compensation, *For Here or To Go* addresses critiques that have arisen from former ensemble members and participants as well as other artistic professionals in Los Angeles: "You get grants to pay the company employee salaries and everybody else gets squat." While participants in community productions do not often voice this sentiment, outsiders to the process can be critical about what they perceive as cultural colonization. A newspaper critic in New Haven rigorously questioned Cornerstone's perceived invasion of the city. In several articles previewing *The Good Person of New Haven,* produced with Long Wharf Theatre and city residents, Christopher Arnott wondered whether New Haven really needed Cornerstone (though after seeing the show, he retreats from his position).[18]

In fact, early Cornerstone rhetoric betrayed some insensitivity to the power dynamics implicit in a group of Harvard graduates initiating productions of classical texts with small rural towns. Company members initially referred to these projects as "bringing theater to the culturally disadvantaged."[19] After some years of experience and dialogue, Cornerstone members revised these assumptions. Bill Rauch noted to a local reporter in Dinwiddie, Virginia, "Nobody wants to see a theater company, especially one that is northern-dominated, come down here and give a lesson."[20] Some community residents still expressed wariness. "People around here don't just jump into things," explained one actor in Eastport, Maine.[21] Like John O'Neal's work with the Environmental Justice Project in New Orleans (see chapter 2), Cornerstone members recognized that they had to overcome apprehensions about their commitment to each community. Without devaluing their own craft and experience, company members had to acknowledge that community participants brought skills and insights to the process that would foster collaboration.[22]

Still, different degrees of community involvement persisted, particularly in comparison between rural and urban residencies. Throughout their work in small towns, Cornerstone members found it relatively easy to engage community participants. Marmarth, North Dakota, and Norcatur, Kansas, both towns with populations of around two hundred citizens, appear in Cornerstone's collective memories as "golden" residencies.[23] After some initial caution, Marmarth residents, along with busloads of folks from across North Dakota and Wyoming, flocked to *The Marmarth Hamlet*. Wary Norcatur residents pulled together after a town meeting to greet Cornerstone with their warmest welcome yet, including a "Welcome Cornerstone" sign, pancake social, and full refrigerator. In these smaller communities, collaborative productions involved a greater percentage of the population, leading to a generous amount of local publicity and responsiveness. The press in Norcatur and Marfa, Texas, provided residents with weekly updates on the progress of the production. Press coverage in Marmarth led to full houses, with audiences driving in from three states, including a busload of dignitaries from the state capitol in Bismarck, five hours away. The success of Cornerstone's Norcatur residency encouraged company members to return to the town on several occasions, and some even purchased houses and lived there for a time. "We all still talk about it," comments Dorothy Kelley a few years later.[24]

In contrast to the numerous transactions and interactions that occurred in these small-town residencies, one early urban project turned out to be Cornerstone's biggest failure in terms of generating audience and finances. The company's attempt to deal with the AIDS crisis in Miami with *The Dog Beneath the Skin: An Epidemic Epic* (1987) proved frustrating throughout the production process. The health center sponsoring the company, reasonably more concerned with the AIDS crisis itself than Cornerstone's theater project, did not find housing or performance space for the group. The company had to pay its own living expenses in hotels and did not locate a performance site until weeks into their residency. After a difficult rehearsal period, enormous effort on the part of Cornerstone and local actors, and good press coverage, audience response remained feeble. Though community participants had a positive experience, ensemble members later posited that the failure of the residency to attract participants and audience resulted from the fact that "the community identity that usually gives us our participants and audience [was] infinitely diffused."[25] The complexities of engaging community in an urban setting will be further explored in later chapters. But even in rural areas social identity can be diffuse and complex. Community implies difference as well as commonality, and Cornerstone's productions complicate assumptions about homogeneity even in small towns.

DESTABILIZING COMMUNITY

While stimulating the social networks that animate community, the production process can also expose exclusionary internal boundaries. Sometimes such divisions are clear upon Cornerstone's arrival, as those between Mexican and European Americans in the border town of Marfa, Texas, blacks and whites in Port Gibson, Mississippi, or between established African American and newly arrived Latino residents in Watts, California. In other residencies, Cornerstone members encountered less visible divisions among community members. Subtle class issues emerged in Montgomery, West Virginia, where the proverbial railroad tracks separated college students and faculty from the rest of the town. In Eastport, Maine, Cornerstone members worked with residents of the nearby Passamaquoddy Native American tribe[26] but were surprised to hear from an Eastport waitress that they had not succeeded in casting any "natives." Apparently, non-Native American residents of Eastport who had lived in the area for more than fifty years distinguished themselves in this way from the "from aways," who had moved to town more recently. These less visibly perceptible differentiations point towards the difficulty of performing a cohesive performance adaptation.

Residencies have also shown that members of a geographically defined community do not necessarily share the same values. Participants in New Haven disagreed profoundly about the effectiveness of a former mayor. Residents in Long Creek, Oregon, either went out to bars Saturday night or to church on Sunday morning.[27] Members of Marmarth's historical society disagreed about language use. "They got into a big debate about whether or not they used [profane language]," explains Bill Rauch. "They decided the men did and the women didn't. But then the women said, 'that's not true.'"[28] As well as pointing out internal differences in values and perceptions, community collaborations also illuminate the multiplicity of identity, where individuals may associate with numerous social roles more complex than ethnic or racial ties. Civic leadership, religious affiliation, and alignment with various values affect the ways individuals perceive and identify themselves. Production work on the whole underlines the difficulty of using "community" to imply stability or permanence. When Cornerstone and production participants speak of the work as celebrating community or unifying the community, it is essential to bear in mind the unstable and temporary nature of this community.

Cornerstone can operate with a healthy idealism about the purpose and affective impact of their work, with productions often expressing the bonds formed during the process. Many shows end with a moment in which all the characters join onstage and sing. In *The Pretty Much True Story of Dinwiddie County,* director Bill Rauch composed a progressive unity through his casting of choruses. The first-act chorus consisted of elderly white males played by friends who met daily to converse at a local store (they brought the table they talked at to each performance). A chorus of black churchwomen commented on the second act. Rauch envisioned the third-act chorus as a multiethnic family of man, and the play ended with the cast gathered around this family's dinner table singing a hymn. In one way, the progression towards integration represents a triumph for the company's mission of bringing people together. Rauch notes, "Back during the casting process we had been warned not to let our Family suggest interracial marriage, but we never heard another word about it after the [play]."[29] However, this performance of inclusiveness, according to former ensemble member David Reiffel, concealed the difficulty and complexity of differentiation highlighted in the rehearsal process:

> I felt there were things that needed to get said that weren't. That resolution is not always possible. The endings of our shows were going more and more toward a sort or resolution; everything was okay, everything has been resolved there. And that wasn't happening in my life, I wasn't seeing it happening in the lives around me, and it seemed like a false—It seemed false to end as we did a lot of shows, you know, glibly, I say, with a group hug.[30]

The difficulty of performing differentiation as opposed to "a group hug" resides in the negotiation of agency between Cornerstone and community members. As outsiders to the community, Cornerstone members may notice issues that community members interpret from their own perspective, or simply do not wish to perform. Cornerstone's Port Gibson, Mississippi, production of *Romeo & Juliet* exemplifies the difficulties inherent in attempting to rehearse and exorcise community conflict.

After choosing the text in consultation with Cultural Crossroads, Cornerstone's sponsoring agency, ensemble members decided to experiment with their tradition of inclusive casting by reflecting, through the casting of the Montagues (blacks) and Capulets (whites), what they perceived as a division in the town in which schoolchildren were effectively segregated.[31] Patty Crosby of Cultural Crossroads, an organization promoting the integration of blacks and whites, expressed reservations towards this depiction of division. Many of the white cast members, on the other hand, asserted their discomfort with an interracial bedroom scene. Following a rehearsal period that had been characterized by uneasiness, as well as optimism, the company held a post-show discussion. Though the process had been about bringing blacks and whites together, and while the final moment of the play showed the opportunity for reconciliation in a more subtle way than many Cornerstone shows, the discussion revealed some cynicism about long-term results. Cast member Mary Curry noted

> that her son Allan and another 10-year old cast member, Athena Hynum, a [white] Academy girl, may be playing together now, but as soon as the show is over everything will return to normal—whites will once again pass black people in the streets without so much as a hello.[32]

While other cast members spoke with hope about the experience, the show provoked dissent within the town as to its authenticity and effectiveness. Curry and other black cast members accepted the adaptation's premise of racial division but questioned whether the project would lead to permanent change. Port Gibson Mayor James Beasley challenged the show's depiction of racial division itself. The white mayor, who pointedly did not see the production, conveyed his belief to a local reporter that the townsfolk had lived together in racial harmony for twenty years, thank you, and chastised Cornerstone members for representing a contradiction to this belief.[33]

Curry's and Beasley's responses to the production underline that boundaries of exclusion within a community are perceptual. Whether Port Gibson is, as Mary Curry suggests, a town marked by racial division or, as Mayor Beasley insists, a harmoniously integrated community, this difference in perspectives illuminates the difficulty of defining a single view of the community. Through the Port Gibson residency, Cornerstone members became more aware of the political nature of performing local adaptations; they discovered that the inclusive quality of performance does not necessarily erase differences in perceptions and beliefs.

At the same time, the production had resonance not initially perceived by the company. Port Gibson citizens have since noted that *Romeo & Juliet* did indeed inspire communication across color lines. Three years after the production, the town was honored for having the most racially integrated board of over four hundred Main Street USA communities. Participants have reported that these relationships grew directly from rehearsal and post-performance dialogue.[34]

Through these various perceptions and accounts make it difficult to discern the "real" Port Gibson, they also suggest that there may be no single

Amy Brenneman and Edret Brinston in *Romeo & Juliet* (1988) in Port Gibson, Mississippi. Photo: Benajah Cobb.

authentic vision of the community. Given this multiplicity of visions and values, the question of how best to represent a community through locally situated adaptation remains thorny. Cornerstone members often find themselves negotiating between standing by their values and respecting the beliefs of community members. Conflict in values in turn leads to a verbal or symbolic articulation of the bounded nature of the community—a statement defining who is considered inside and who is considered outside of a particular community. Cornerstone member Ashby Semple describes a conversation she had with a rancher in Long Creek, Oregon, about the morality of premarital sex. They disagreed, and Semple discovered that the fresh milk that had been delivered to her doorstep each morning ceased to arrive. Meanwhile, Bill Rauch and Christopher Moore, a same-sex couple who lived together but did not at the time make public their relationship, continued to receive milk. When the rancher perceived an explicit challenge to his value system, he enacted exclusion through selective milk delivery. This relative exclusion of Semple and the inclusion of Rauch and Moore, of whose relationship the rancher was unaware, again suggests the perceptual nature of value boundaries. These boundaries may be redrawn if a more inclusive enabling device displaces the impact of contradictory values. In this case, the performance process acted as an enabler, and as the production of *The Good Person of Long Creek* approached, Semple began receiving her milk again.[35]

Symbolic Systems

Producing Culture

The social transactions that build and complicate community stem from initial contacts, grow through labor exchanges, flourish in conversation, diversify through dissent, and formally emerge in production. Images of the resultant production are manifold: a well-earned harvest, an occasion for celebration, a group hug concealing difference, a hopeful portrait of unifying potentials. Polyphonic utterances from former and active Cornerstone members, community participants and observers, and an engaged critic cannot untangle the webs of signification woven in storytelling about productions. How then can a play artfully capture the image of a community? In Raymond Williams's terms, how does representation intersect with production? The final product, often written down after performances, stabilizes an entity that is profoundly dialogic in its growth, and dependent upon embodiment and spatial significations for its meaning. A closer look at these symbolic interchanges highlights interwoven aspects of cultural and community production in Cornerstone's theater making.

Community participants impact the development, focus, casting, behavior, and language of Cornerstone texts. Through personal oral histories, Arab participants in *Ghurba* contributed to the basis and creation of the production's script and story. Interaction with residents of Norcatur convinced Cornerstone to refocus the theme of *Tartoof* to domestic rather than spiritual concerns. The company at first thought to emphasize religious issues in the piece, picturing Tartuffe as a midwestern televangelist. Recasting Ron Temple's Orgon as a farmer shifted the play's dynamics. More recently, Hmong residents of Fresno urged director Mark Valdez to rethink moments that seemed unrepresentative of their culture in Bernardo Solano's original play *Growing Home* (2001). These interactions reveal as much about how external perceptions construct community as how individuals within that community represent themselves.

At the same time, the adaptation process can say a great deal about how culture gets negotiated. Working with residents to identify local behaviors, idioms, and values engages a potential audience, who become coproducers of the play's meaning. The production grounds this "everyday culture" in the tangibility of a lamp shaded with a miner's cap in West Virginia, or the smell of eggplant grilling onstage in *Ghurba*. The adaptation and staging process also frames local rituals and behaviors. Daily delivery of fresh milk in Long Creek, Oregon, led to milk exchanges between neighbors in *The Good Person of Long Creek*. Amy Brenneman gutted a fish to highlight one ballad in Eastport, Maine's *Pier Gynt*. These details reflect and reaffirm the distinctness of local culture, while grounding production aesthetics in an imaginative exchange between a historical text and contemporary setting. Within these interchanges, marked by clashes as well as insights, Cornerstone and community collaborators weave another web of signification, through the activation of the symbolic systems that constitute culture production.

The adaptation process originated in Marmarth, where auditioners pushed for specific textual updates. Mayor Patty Perry had invited Cornerstone to Marmarth on the assumption that the company would be producing dinner theater. She and other community members soon learned that Cornerstone instead envisioned a radically cut, but textually unchanged, Wild West version of *Hamlet*. That, claimed one local rancher, would go over "like a turd in a punchbowl."[36] "No tights," came the message from Perry, still unclear about Cornerstone's purpose.[37] Despite some cynicism, and after promising to keep the costumes tights-free, Cornerstone members recruited a company of local actors from the local cafe, grocery, bar, and even the mayor's office. But residents had difficulty with language they found arcane and requested contemporary translations of the text in auditions. "I remember the day . . . we decided to do it," recalls Bill Rauch, "we actually said that to rewrite Shakespeare is blasphemous, but what the hell?"[38] David Reiffel recollects, "It was 'the shit we take from assholes'" that Cornerstone members substituted for "the proud man's contumely," thus somewhat profanely initiating the process of textual adaptation.[39]

Further community reaction and involvement complicated the adaptation process. Marmarth participants voiced concerns about what they perceived to be too many "bad words" and blasphemous references in the adapted text. Members of the community asked that the phrase be changed to "the crap we take from assholes." In an emergency meeting called by the

Marmarth Historical Society, Cornerstone, community actors, and several members of the local church sat down with the script and discussed each textual problem. The meeting revealed to Cornerstone members that their word choice reflected Harvard's urban collegiate rather than Marmarth's rural ranching culture. The residents asked that the language be changed so that it sounded "more like us and less like you," explained Alison Carey.[40] The committee reevaluated, for example, the phrase "downright prick" and changed it to the more locally acceptable and accessible "horse's rear end."[41] Through this interaction, Cornerstone members and Marmarth residents began to understand that resonant contemporary references are often locally specific. The adaptation allowed for further collaboration with residents as well as yielding a play that more fully engaged its audience. Contrary to the expectations of the skeptical rancher, after viewing *The Marmarth Hamlet,* one local cowboy nodded, "Yep. A guy should see it twice."[42]

Cornerstone's interactions with Marmarth illustrate how a symbolic system, language, was renegotiated to more accurately reflect the writing of a culture. These exchanges reoccurred throughout Cornerstone's rural residencies, reflecting and framing distinct idiomatic expressions. In West Virginia, historian Otis Rice refined Cornerstone's translation of Chekhov's line "Thanks to Father, I and my sisters know the French, German, and English languages." The original adaptation read, "Dad taught us how to fish, hunt, and hike." Rice proposed instead, "bark a squirrel, dig out a groundhog, run a trot line." Wanda Daniels, also of West Virginia, recommended the phrase "dog drunk" to replace "falling down drunk."[43] In Eastport, Maine, it became a pastime for community residents to come up with idiomatic expressions. One man ran up a hill after Cornerstone's Ashby Semple shouting, "Theater! Theater! It should be 'bilge water'!" in response to an earlier request for a phrase to replace "Poppycock."[44] In developing these textual adaptations, community participants functioned in many ways as ethnographic informants, relating key behaviors, expressions, and values to Cornerstone's outsider observers. At the same time, these informative collaborations emphasize how Cornerstone and local residents coproduce community meaning, in a way that is neither necessarily definitive nor stable. These kinds of negotiations continue throughout the production process, where the physical bodies of participants prompt further rethinking of source texts and stories.

The talent displayed in auditions does not necessarily reflect initial casting concepts. A higher proportion of female auditioners in Port Gibson led to the reconception of the Capulet family as a matriarchy. The company turned *That Marfa Fever* into a musical after discovering gifted singers in

Marfa, Texas. The casting of these self-named "Canasta Tea Gals" also initiated a Cornerstone practice of creating choruses in many of their productions, allowing for greater inclusion in the casting of shows. Cornerstone has also created special parts for talented individuals. Auctioneer Bob Jones's role was developed especially for him in *Tartoof.* Cornerstone reconceived the role of a bartender in *The Dog Beneath the Skin* for a blind bartending actor. After auditioning everyone from the landlord to the Federal Express deliveryman, Cornerstone cast Suzanne Pollastrini in an initially unwritten role in *Three Sisters from West Virginia,* responding to her breathtakingly choreographed clogging.

Suzanne Pollastrini clogging in *Three Sisters from West Virginia* (1989). Photo: Benajah Cobb.

In addition to rethinking casting to reflect available talents in West Virginia, participants there encouraged Cornerstone to rethink the setting of *Three Sisters from West Virginia.* While most community-based productions are set locally, Montgomery's *Three Sisters* emphasized a nostalgic longing for the West Virginia country. In Cornerstone's adaptation, the family left West Virginia after a local coal mine had shut down, and relocated to a trailer park in a working-class Detroit suburb. This relocation, along with idiomatic translations in the text's adaptation, both point towards a paradoxical engagement of the literary with the local. "The whole idea behind a Cornerstone adaptation," writes former company manager Patty Payette, "is to show how classic plays and their issues and concerns can be used to universally reflect lives and issues in the United States today."[45] But the need for adaptation implies both resonance and dissonance, calling for a rethinking of universality.

"They pegged us folks," admits reviewer Cheryl Keenan of *Three Sisters from West Virginia*. "I've been to many parties like the one in the play. I've felt the same despair. I've dreamed the same dreams. Those people were West Virginians. They were us."[46] Keenan compliments the production's local resonance while referring to the framework and affect, the dreams and despair, of Chekhov's story. Several reviewers, scholars, and Cornerstone members themselves refer to this local resonance as accessing something more profound and inclusive. Otis Rice explains:

> In transferring and adapting the basic themes of Anton Chekhov's *Three Sisters* from a Russian to an American setting, the Cornerstone Theater Company demonstrates that good drama can have a universal message that can deepen our knowledge and understanding of the human condition.[47]

The problem with "universality," like "community," seems one of usage. Universality implies access without the necessity for translation or modification. Yet, Cornerstone's shows access the "universal" through specific local references. Writer Robert Coe proposes that this local resonance is in itself universal: "What seemed corny to Harvard graduates had universal meaning [in Port Gibson, Mississippi], and so Queen Mab was pushed aside by Hollywood's dreamtime master [Freddy Krueger]."[48] Coe's comment points towards particularity rather than universality, a particularity that allows audiences and participants to make connections among colliding cultures.

Re-cognizing Community

The clashes that emerge in efforts to reflect and produce culture through symbolic systems, such as language and everyday behavior, are further heightened in performance. Physical bodies of community participants, enacting rewoven stories, in altered spaces, not only perform collaborative co-ownership but also reflect and refract a doubleness of community and performance roles. These performances stimulate additional thinking about how individuals as well as communities negotiate their identity.

The House on Walker River exemplifies this performative doubleness. Bill Rauch describes the adaptation process, in Brechtian terms, as "that which makes the familiar seem strange and the strange seem familiar."[49] Brecht based his ideas on those of early-twentieth-century Russian Formalists who posited that the framing of an object through estranged language rendered it more visible. This defamiliarizing, or, in Brechtian terms, "alienation," compelled an audience to reperceive and historicize the everyday world. The casting of local actors in roles that reflect those that they play in their community familiarizes the strangeness of the cultural context of the source text as well as legitimizing the piece as a community coproduction. A local audience, who may not comprehend how Agamemnon functions in an ancient Greek city-state, understands the role that Wayne Johnson plays as chairman of the tribe. The framing of Johnson as a Greek leader makes the familiar strange as well, reinforcing Johnson's role of leadership within the community. The community becomes engaged in the production as it reflects its own leadership structure and reawakens an understanding of that structure.

Christopher Liam Moore as Orestes *(foreground)* with Schurz resident Joel Hodes as Coyote in *The House on Walker River* (1988). This adaptation of *The Oresteia* incorporated Paiute myth in its retelling. Photo: Benajah Cobb.

Additional de- and refamiliarizations emerge in performance significations. A triumphant return from a warring city in the original text transformed into a pickup truck pulling in from Reno with slot machines tied up in its bed. The familiarity of the slot machines was estranged by a context in which they were also perceived as "war booty" and "a conquered city." The framing of these familiar referents as dangerous booty suggests additionally a subtle cultural critique. Participant Mel Brown comments that "political issues plaguing the tribe made their 'presence' known within the play."[50]

This recontextualizing and consequent reflection of and on the familiar can also be described in Bakhtinian terms. Mikhail Bakhtin proposed that a recontextualization of a linguistic signifier alters its meaning, as meaning is produced through a dialogic interaction between speaker and listener. He explains that a word can invoke a "double-voicedness" when pronounced in a way that comments upon another's usage of that word. For example, the impact of the word *nigger* depends on context. A white woman calling a black man a nigger in the streets of Port Gibson, Mississippi, carries a doubled connotation when that woman uses the phrase "thou art a nigger" in *Romeo & Juliet,* set in a small Mississippi town. The word maintains extremely negative connotations, but framed by a performance, it is contextualized to demonstrate the maliciousness of an interracial feud, while also juxtaposing classical syntax with contemporary jargon.[51]

The physical space of performance can also be read in this double-voiced manner, contributing to the sense that the community has a stake in the artistic product, as well as recontextualizing the familiar.[52] In some instances, the memories associated with a site can add to the emotional resonance of a piece. Cornerstone's coproduction of *Steelbound,* staged in Bethlehem Steel's old iron foundry, held particular meaning for its local audience of steelworkers and their families. A woman standing in line on opening night confessed her heightened nervousness to a friend; her father had been killed in the foundry, and as a nonemployee, she had never before been allowed to enter the space.[53]

As in *Steelbound,* the theatrical site of a production is specific to each performance, while maintaining its local function within the community. Cornerstone's design aesthetics remind the audience of this functional presence. This aesthetic engagement with and framing of the community space reflects an essential difference between Cornerstone's community-based work and most community theater. In general, community theater productions attempt to mimic conventional notions of theater design—the design works to conceal the auditorium-ness, or the city hall-ness of the space. In contrast, Cornerstone designer Lynn Jeffries employs elements of the community space that remind the community audience of its ownership of the space. Jeffries views this approach aesthetically rather than socially, explaining: "[W]e try to take every interesting element of the [home] theater and use it."[54] In Norcatur, Jeffries incorporated a basketball net and scoreboard into the set of *Tartoof*, which was performed in the school gymnasium. Storage space underneath a church auditorium stage provided surprising entrances for the young angels and devils in *Los Faustinos* (designed by Katherine Ferwerda). Jeffries took on the ultimate aesthetic challenge in Long Creek, Oregon, creating a design that worked against the most prevalent of community theater clichés: Cornerstone staged *The Good Person of Long Creek* in a barn. Jeffries framed the iconicity of the setting, working with Rauch and technical director Benajah Cobb to remind Long Creek residents that they actually *were* in a cattle-sale barn in Long Creek. Rauch staged much of the action on a centrally located cattle gate. A rotating stage and a vertically elevated chair, upon which a knitting woman occasionally descended to comment on the action, invited the eye to travel through and take in the entire barn. The imaginative staging that results from working with rather than against the given space suggests a kind of found aesthetic that is less available in either conventional community or regional theatrical sites.

In contrast, when Cornerstone's set does not engage as fully with the performance space, the resultant design suggests a complex and potentially problematic social reading. In Schurz, the company performed *The House on Walker River* in an unused welding shop. Production posters and flyers did not designate the space by its community function, or former function but did so as "the building across from the Tribal Hall." Flyers also refer to how the performance had changed the space: "The pipes and metal junk's all gone, it's cleaned and painted and someone's stuck in these huge wooden rocks. . . . the floor's all swept neat and smooth." In renewing the space for production, the company also removed vestiges of its past performance as a welding site, perhaps erasing some elements of the community's ownership.

In general, the semiotics of Cornerstone's production sites evoke a more inclusive approach to theater. Many rural and middle- to lower-class potential audience members view conventional regional theaters, with their high-priced subscription base and downtown urban locations, as cultural palaces that they feel uncomfortable entering. This discomfort is related to a theater's location in an urban field as well as to the theater's architecture. Louisville's Actor's Theater, located within the city's financial district, and Chicago's Goodman Theater are both removed from lower-income housing. The New Haven Long Wharf Theater and the Washington, D.C.,

The cattle gate incorporated into Lynn Jeffries's design for *The Good Person of Long Creek* (1988). Photo: Lynn Jeffries.

Arena Stage are difficult to get to using public transportation, at least from certain areas of the city. A centrally located and familiar space can invite community members to attend a performance more readily.

The architecture of most conventional theaters may also reinforce divisions between audience and performers that Cornerstone members hope to break down. In "The Semiotics of Theatre Structures," Marvin Carlson describes this conventional theater space as one in which the viewer and viewed are separated by performance and supporting spaces, each of which often maintains a hierarchical spatial division.[55] The backstage area in many theaters is divided into more or less privileged dressing areas, according to size and closeness to the stage. The balconies, boxes, and orchestra pit, priced according to their prestige and distance from the performance area, can socially stratify the audience. Cornerstone's found locations work against these conventional semiotics. The staging and set sometimes surround an audience, as in the production of *That Marfa Fever*. Pay-what-you-can bleacher seating allows for little stratification among audience members. A makeshift backstage area shared by all the participants erases semiotic differentiation among cast members. Ideally, the semiotics of location, space, and architecture work together to invite and include resident audience members as they reinforce ownership and frame elements of the community's cultural identity.

While textual adaptation, design, and spatial (re)signification reinforce, reflect upon, and reimagine what constitutes a community, the performance itself can unite the community through common experience. Anthropologist Victor Turner proposes that narratives, rituals, and performances can structure and create meaning for a society. Experience becomes meaningful and complete when "expressed" or "pressed out" through the performance event.[56] Turner describes the "sense of community" derived through this event as *communitas,* referring to the ephemeral sense of connectedness experienced by a group through the common experience of a unifying ritual. The theatrical event functions as a unifying ritual in Turner's terms, momentarily manifesting and underscoring a feeling of communal identity.

Audience response to local references, issues, and performers underscores this unifying sentiment. When a character in the *Three Sisters from West Virginia* informed the sisters that he used to work in Boomer, a mining town near Montgomery, one audience member shouted out, "Boomer! That's where I'm from!"[57] In the Watts production of *Los Faustinos,* audience members consistently reacted with vocal derision to a giant puppet of then governor Pete Wilson proclaiming his support for the recently passed Proposition 187, which limited immigrant rights. One excited mother, who attended a number of performances exclaimed, "That's my baby!" each time her son sang about television. Perhaps because of this local resonance, and the perception that the community is cocreating the performance, audience members sometimes involve themselves more directly in the performance. During a slow scene change in West Virginia, audience members helped to move the set, receiving a round of applause from those who remained seated. During *The Winter's Tale* tour, audiences helped move the outdoor set to an alternate indoor location in Schurz, Nevada, as a sudden thunderstorm threatened the production.[58] Certainly these experiences do not typify all Cornerstone shows. As further chapters elaborate, audience members also respond with moderation, listlessness, or rejection. A small but vocal number of regional theater audience members at *For Here or To Go* and *The Good Person of New Haven* walked out of productions that I attended. On the whole though, Cornerstone's community-based audiences tend to sit further forward in their seats, linger longer in the space, and respond more vocally to productions than audiences at most theater productions I have attended.[59]

In addition to the group feeling underlined by audience responses, community participants often cite the value of "coming together" when asked by Cornerstone to evaluate their performance experience. Melanie Aragon of the Walker River Paiute Tribe describes the moment "when everyone applauds," observing that "there's a feeling of community and there's a high level of energy."[60] Mel Brown agrees that this feeling of community "knit together" the spirit of the tribe.[61] As Anthony Cohen points out, however, this sense of community or *communitas* may operate only symbolically to unite a group of people whose values, beliefs, and backgrounds do not necessarily cohere.[62] As Cohen suggests and David Reiffel echoes, *communitas* may conceal difference.

On the other hand, the performance-making process may allow for a more complex negotiation of relationships than the performance itself. Cornerstone participants cite the process as one that gives "a name and face to the other."[63] Hirsch Griffith of Dinwiddie observes: "The first week or so I was cast with a black lady playing my wife. After that she was just Judy, a very talented actress."[64] Several participants in Port Gibson noted that *Romeo & Juliet* allowed blacks and whites to work together, for the first time in some instances. Alison Carey avows, "The first time black and white people were on stage together in the history of Claiborne County [Mississippi] was at our Christmas sing-along."[65] An astonishing moment occurred during *For Here or To Go* rehearsals when a former felon and several Los Angeles police officers, who sang together onstage, shared their experiences and fears with each other. These examples remain instants of potential enacted between individuals rather than institutional shifts. As such, they might conceal the very real constraints of power and privilege that can divide people. But when recognized as the beginnings of social exchange, rather than as metonymic embodiments of social change, these lived occurrences possess real power.

The negotiation of social relationships and the co-ownership of artistic elements such as production, acting, and performance space work with Cornerstone's initial goals of engaging the community and the audience in the process of creation. A result that is not articulated by Cornerstone members, but nonetheless arises from the work, is an awareness of the dynamic interplay between culture and identity. The fact that community performers are generally untrained in the "method" of psychological realism keeps them from disappearing into the characters that they play. As reviewer Steve Vineberg notes of a production of *The Winter's Tale*, "Every time these actors opened their mouths, they told us, 'This is who I am.'"[66] Vineberg proposes that the community actors remain present in performance. Wayne Johnson does not "become" Chairman Agamemnon; he presents the character and remains recognizable to the community as Wayne Johnson. By remaining just slightly outside the roles that they perform, these actors call forth the constructed nature of character and the instability of representation.

In various mission statements, Cornerstone members articulate their efforts to include, to perform, and to build community. Yet, the gaps and lacunae of community performance, the holes in the self-made webs of cultural signification, suggest a more fluid notion of identity. Community actors remain more present as both actor and character, community member and artist. This very presence suggests absence. By never fully "disappearing" into the role of Agamemnon, Wayne Johnson remains present in performance. Yet, in his performance as Agamemnon, Johnson temporarily disappears from the *performance* of his role as tribal chair. This kind of double presence might seem to occur in other representational situations. Mainstream cinema relies on our desire to see Julia Roberts or Bruce Willis present as "themselves" within their performances. Yet, for most of us, knowledge of "Julia Roberts" or "Bruce Willis" remains confined to carefully controlled and mediated public constructions. The impact of community-based theater depends upon a sense that the audience often "knows" the individual performer through daily interactions, while discovering something previously unknown through performance. Social formation and reformation in the process of theater making heighten this sense of instability, even as participants feel that the process brings them together, reflecting and stabilizing a sense of community. This paradox of identity remains at the heart of Cornerstone's work, and rightly so. The space of "not quite" allows for the possibility of continuing to reimagine community.

Cornerstone members founded the organization as a way to engage an American audience and discover an American aesthetic. In the process, the group uncovered the elusiveness of this American identity, or indeed, of the identity of even the most cohesive rural community. The production process illuminates the fluidity and multiplicity of social identity. The performance itself, while enabling and expressing a moment of community cohesion and suggesting potential sites for a community to express identity and ownership, also opens up another realm for the exploration of the constructed nature of individual identity.

To examine the nuances of these ongoing reconstructions requires more focus on singular moments in Cornerstone's production history. The following chapters investigate these singularities through a variety of means, beginning with the challenges encountered when the ideology of collaboration confronts the reality of individual difference in *The Winter's Tale: An Interstate Adventure* (1991). This production caps the first five years of Cornerstone's work with rural communities. The company's efforts to structure and govern a community sharply illuminates the complex nature of identity and identification, as individuals negotiate their identity as Americans, members of a variety of communities, and their relationships to Cornerstone and each other.

4

RURAL ROUTES

Voices from *The Winter's Tale: An Interstate Adventure*

To be directed by Bill Rauch is an honor, as is traveling and acting with Cornerstone.

>—Rosemarie Voorhees, company member, Schurz, Nevada

The art got homogenized.

>—David Reiffel, former ensemble member

You can't solve every problem with forty people.

>—Larry Tasker, tour bus driver

Who's going to decide when the work gets done? The people who do it or people half my age?

>—Doug Casement, Antigonus in *The Winter's Tale*

I am not a person who "expects" much. But, I was constantly pleasantly surprised by the friends I made. . . . [If I could change anything] I would have been kinder to people and more tolerant myself.

>—Doug Casement, president, Stage East, Eastport, Maine

It was a great, lost opportunity.

>—Alison Carey, Cornerstone cofounder

It was like . . . it was the end.

>—Bill Rauch, Cornerstone artistic director

The world should learn from this tour.

>—Larry Tasker, actor in *The Winter's Tale*

While polyphonic representation of Cornerstone and community-based theater remains a basic tenet of my research and writing, the number and variance of voices associated with *The Winter's Tale,* such as those above, test the limits of this ambition. With hundreds of hours of documentary videotape, reams of oral history, written testimonies from over fifty participants, and the usual production detritus—programs, posters, newsletters, reviews, and grant narratives—multi-vocality threatens to degenerate into chaos—a problem that, not incidentally, plagued *The Winter's Tale* tour. With performers, crew, and guest artists, aged seven to seventy-six, from each of Cornerstone's thirteen rural residencies and various urban sites, in addition to the company's own nomadic membership, all living and traveling together for several months in close quarters, the scale of the enterprise magnified tensions that had remained previously containable. Yet, this very scope and the resultant cracks in Cornerstone's edifice allow for closer examination into the difficult, moving, and potentially regenerative negotiations enacted within *The Winter's Tale: An Interstate Adventure.*

A number of tensions played out in the tour, within the adapted text, and across the bodies of participants, resulting in both the culmination and the end of Cornerstone's traveling, rural performance methodology. Tensions between a grassroots emphasis on locality and a mobile cross-country tour, between a classical text and a necessarily new form of adaptation, and between professionals and participatory ethics all raised questions about the nature and governance of Cornerstone and its efforts to represent America textually, geographically, and through the embodied presence of participants from across the country.

Selecting a point of entry into this cacophony of questions and documents proves as challenging as Cornerstone's selection of participants, production sites, and marketing imagery. I begin by submitting a constellation of three archival fragments to semiotic analysis: *The Winter's Tale* Humanities Flyer, production poster, and Cornerstone's logo, each developed before performances began. Respectively produced as part of government funding, under the auspices of a corporate sponsor, and independently by the company, each fragment offers insight into Cornerstone's publicly projected image, the material contours shaping *The Winter's Tale,* and relationships between the two. Examined together, the items illuminate some of the many, sometimes productive tensions underlying *The Winter's Tale* production and Cornerstone's desire to create a new kind of inclusive American theater.

Signs of Production

As Marvin Carlson points out in *Theatre Semiotics: Signs of Life,* programs, posters, and self-produced articles function as orienting devices, priming a potential audience for the production experience while displaying a company's desired self-image.[1] *The Winter's Tale* Humanities Flyer provided an

occasion for the company to articulate its mission and methods for a potential audience of 150,000. At the same time, the multi-page flyer con-
formed to a particular mandate for government funding from several state
humanities councils, impacting its content, layout, and focus. Articles
emphasize civic dialogue, presenting issue-oriented meditations on topics
such as dysfunctional families, out-migration, and idiomatic language. Text
and images additionally invoke inclusiveness, diversity, tolerance, and
Americanism. Individually, none of these notions contradicts Cornerstone's
self-image. But their juxtaposition underlines some inherent complications
in negotiating national identity, regional difference, and humanistic commonality. These contradictions coalesce in the flyer's front cover, featuring
a production image created not by Cornerstone but by *The Winter's Tale*'s
corporate sponsor, AT&T: *OnStage*.

The poster image features a figure whose high forehead, hairstyle, facial
hair, and clothing call to mind William Shakespeare. Stockings, a velvet
cloak with high collar, and the figure's relaxed pose, one arm akimbo, left leg
delicately crossed and poised over the right, evoke an image of early-seventeenth-century ease. This sense of ease may derive from work well done, as
the figure seems to have recently completed painting. His right hand holds
a wet brush, above which is scrawled in thick lettering "The Winter's Tale."
A white can of paint rests by the figure's feet, adding to the suggestion that
he has recently authored "The Winter's Tale." The paintbrush also points
towards a metal sign immediately below this lettering reading "An Interstate Adventure," written in a style reminiscent of that found on national
highways. The juxtaposition of this classically resonant figure of Shakespeare
with the contemporary interstate sign modifying the authorship of "The
Winter's Tale" alludes to Cornerstone's epic interactions of theatrical classics with contemporary America. The poster seems to effectively communicate this essential aspect of Cornerstone's self-image. But some other core
values are notable for their absence; behind the scenes, anxieties about the
image and its corporate sponsorship emerged among Cornerstone's members.

Prior to *The Winter's Tale* tour, Cornerstone and community residents
had worked together to publicize their coproductions. These efforts had
ensured the development and dissemination of signs emphasizing collaboration and local participation. The scope of *The Winter's Tale* tour required
a larger scale of financial support, hence AT&T: *OnStage*'s involvement.[2]
Because the funding came from the corporation's marketing budget, AT&T:
OnStage financed publicity for the production, hiring an advertising firm
to create the poster image. While Cornerstone members consented to the
poster, many were troubled by the image and its development. The advertis-

The Winter's Tale (1991) poster. Photo: AT&T, *OnStage.*

ing company insisted on foregrounding the playwright, less essential in Cornerstone's ideology and purpose than community collaborations. In addition, the poster production cost twenty thousand dollars, comparable to the budget of some early residencies. Given the tour's later disastrous financial shortfall, requiring the entire company to give up a portion of their already meager weekly income, the poster budget seemed in retrospect even more indefensible, even though AT&T: *OnStage* covered its cost. On top of these anxieties, neither the poster nor flyer effectively oriented an audience of AT&T employees to *The Winter's Tale* production. With no information or briefing on the community-based nature of Cornerstone's work, many members of this audience walked out during a performance in Miami.

While ineffectively communicating some core aspects of Cornerstone's collaborative methodology, the poster and flyer did offer insight into the complexities of building what a recently minted mission statement defined as "a new, inclusive American theater." Flyer articles refer to America as a series of geographical regions, a matrix of specific communities, a large and tolerant community of diverse individuals, and a collage of cultural archetypes. Interactions among these versions of America and their relation to Cornerstone's mission reverberate in the front cover poster image.

In 1990, Cornerstone members articulated one aspect of their understanding of America as a negotiation between the urban and the rural.[3] With "The Winter's Tale" scrawled on the side of a rough-hewn barn surrounded by hay and wheat and set against a city skyline thrusting upwards in the background, the poster image foregrounds this opposition, though again using "Shakespeare" to unite urban and rural icons. Nonetheless, the figure points towards the highway sign, "An Interstate Adventure," proposing that Cornerstone's contemporary adaptation might serve as a vehicle uniting the rural/urban divisions in America. The interstate sign additionally suggests how this uniting might occur—through travel across the regions of America. Text in the upper-right-hand corner of the poster refers to these regions as "the fertile expanse of the Great Plains," the "historically rich lushness of the Deep South," and "the dynamic urban hubs of the East Coast." This text expands and specifies the poster's evocation of "the urban" and "the rural" to include the various regions of America to which Cornerstone will travel.

A contiguous depiction of America as a network of specific communities expands on this image of America as a matrix of geographic regions. A horizontal black band at the bottom of the poster lists thirteen American towns and cities, specifying the "American communities" referred to in Cornerstone's mission statement. These are the communities with which Cornerstone has forged its identity and to which *The Winter's Tale* will travel. While national identity may be fashioned through a negotiation of America as regions and specific communities, the necessarily selective depiction of both aspects suggests what is left out as much as what is included.

The listing of travel through the Deep South, urban East Coast, and Great Plains specifies America as a matrix of regions while omitting the numerous ways that these regions can be redrawn—as the Industrial Midwest, Adventurous Alaska, or the Forested West Coast, for example. Cornerstone's effort to represent itself iconically more clearly marks both presence and absence. A logo created in 1989 for a fund-raiser points out the locations of collaborating communities to which *The Winter's Tale* eventually traveled. The map foregrounds interactions between specific communities and America as a whole. Explains designer Lynn Jeffries:

> We deliberately sought to work in as many different regions of the continental US as we could. By the time we did the *Winter's Tale,* we had worked in the north, south, east, west, and center, and we worked near both the Canadian border and the Mexican border. The graphic shows how evenly dispersed our residencies were while featuring very small towns in a very big country. The relative hugeness of the arrows leading to these little invisible spots on the map was about the excitement of that discovery.[4]

While graphically depicting Cornerstone's accomplishments, its negative spaces also highlight the absence of communities with which Cornerstone has not worked, will not travel to, and will not be embodied in *The Winter's Tale's* representation of America.

Of course, a literal coverage of America is impossible. *The Winter's Tale* did bring together an extraordinary array of individuals, unprecedented in American theater. Depictions of this regional and individual diversity, alongside a conceptual myth of America bifurcated by an urban/rural split, and more profound spiritual questions about what it means to represent America, all communicate and complicate the company's and the tour's desired self-image. The very tensions inherent in attempting to embrace and embody an inclusive American theater, a collaborative corporate-sponsored tour, and a nomadic grassroots theater provide a more complex framework for exploring each Cornerstone manifestation. These manifestations play out in layered rounds of discord and harmony in two distinct sites: in *The Winter's Tale* adaptation and in interactions among members of the producing company.

REPRESENTING AMERICA

Discussions of *The Winter's Tale* in company meetings and later newsletter articles promoted the belief that Cornerstone's collaborative production could re-present America. At a 1990 ensemble meeting, before rehearsals for *The Winter's Tale* had commenced, cofounder Alison Carey spoke with enthusiasm about the tour's potentials: "With this show, we can paint a portrait of a country that has lost faith in itself, but that can awaken its faith through the restoration of tolerance."[5] Carey and others proposed that Cornerstone could recreate an image of America as a broad-minded nation embracing difference through the process, adaptation, and presentation of *The Winter's Tale.*

Representation of an archetypal America through *The Winter's Tale* embodies an inherent ideological contradiction, however. Cornerstone's work up to this point had emphasized the specificity of the community culture within textual adaptation by "writing local concerns into the script, sewing local color into the costumes, [and] by rehearsing local actors into the roles," according to a 1991 Mission Statement. The "locality" of *The Winter's Tale* had to encompass both the matrix of specific and consciously diverse communities with which Cornerstone had worked as well as the whole of America. According to Artistic Director Bill Rauch, Cornerstone hoped to render *The Winter's Tale* adaptation "universally recognizable . . . to people all over the country," while understanding that "instead of the specificity of the host community which usually infuses a Cornerstone script, we found ourselves having to paint portraits of a mythic America, both urban and rural."[6] Lacking the specificity of location, this process strove instead for a "generic American setting."[7]

The adaptation that arose reflects many of the challenges encountered in developing *The Video Store Owner's Significant Other* (1990). Both adaptations had to rely on more general cultural archetypes. *The Winter's Tale* had the advantage of casting community actors as well as Cornerstone ensemble members, and of working with the specificity of community performance arenas as opposed to the more generic theater spaces hosting *Video Store*. The resultant adaptation, derived with input from community participants, thus engages both the typical and particular; focusing on urban/rural relationships in the U.S., program notes propose that the synthesis of urban and rural represents the entirety of America—a position complicated by the diversity of community participants. In contrast, *The Winter's Tale* production settings evoked a sense of America as both binary and multiple, with each act of the play framing and supplementing the other.

Cornerstone's adaptation translates the first act, initially set in the court of Bohemia, to a courtroom in New Urban, transferring the site of power from regal to legal. The set for this location traveled with the production, maintaining a fixed sense of urbanity while pointing towards the transformative possibilities of theater as evidenced by the main set piece, a steel table that alternately served as a dining table, bed, and ping-pong table. In contrast to this relative fixity, the second act set outside of New Rural framed the particularities of each tour site. At the end of the first act trial, a courtroom backdrop was removed, and the tour bus entered between the audience and set as an act curtain.

The bus drove away to reveal a painted backdrop of wheat field and sky and, following intermission, the distinct landscape of the town to which the show had toured. The first few scenes following intermission were site specific. The second act scene thus varied dependent on the location, from

Cornerstone's tour bus, which appeared at the end of act 1 of *The Winter's Tale*, driven by Larry Tasker *(right)*, standing next to Doug Casement. Photo: Lynn Jeffries.

a wheat field in Kansas to a dirt Main Street, to a New York City park, to the Washington, D.C., Mall, with the Capitol Building lit up in the background. The scene change also integrated the bus (and driver) in which the company traveled, a self-reflection on the tour as well as on Cornerstone's previous five years of criss-crossing the country. The presence of the bus also suggests a connection among the various communities to which the show journeyed.[8] In addition to the divisions suggested by the New Urban setting and New Rural locations, a third set emphasized unification through pop culture commonality. A truck stop (featuring dancing gas pumps) reflected on the interstate touring aspects of the production while displaying recognizable commercial icons such as a McDonald's logo.

While site specific, the New Rural settings also conjured a shared national culture, additionally reminiscent of early-twentieth-century pageants. Cornerstone's *Winter's Tale* adapted Shakespeare's sheepshearing festival to a Fourth of July picnic, a celebration understood and shared by the majority of Americans, celebrating their American-ness. Guests at the picnic reflected a number of recognizable figures such as Elvis, Superman, and Uncle Sam. A woman wrapped in an American flag standing next to Uncle Sam reinforced iconic "Americanism," while Perdita, dressed as the Goddess Flora in Shakespeare's original, entered the picnic as the Statue of Liberty.

The Winter's Tale potluck supper with Edret Brinston as Superman, Johnny Bain as Uncle Sam, Jessica Carrasco as Perdita dressed as the Statue of Liberty, and Rod Prichard as Florizel. Photo: Lynn Jeffries.

It is difficult to say whether these icons of Americanism created the sense of common national culture towards which the production strove. Their variety suggests eclecticism as much as commonality. And while most audience members would recognize the characters, this pop cultural identification does not necessarily enact a national identity. In Cornerstone's community-based shows, icons specific to the community evoke a more local identification. Recognizing this tendency towards generalization, the picnic scene emphasized the specifics of the host town as well as common cultural signs. The site-specific scene framed and emphasized the uniqueness of each local setting. The picnic featured a guest artist from the community who entertained the audience, and at the end of the show, a special bow acknowledged the community participants from each locality to which the show traveled. These particular references allowed for the specific community identification emphasized in Cornerstone's previous shows, while also suggesting a greater national common culture.

Both larger cultural and community-specific references work within the Brechtian and Bakhtinian theoretical context discussed in the previous chapter. Through dialogic interactions between the source text and its revisions, contemporary adaptations familiarize the unfamiliar, offering commentary on the connections and disjunctions between the historically distant and the here and now. *The Winter's Tale* adaptation relied on a contemporary theatrical medium to communicate messages of "tolerance" and "transformation" through epic negotiations of language, character, and setting.

As in previous rural shows, textual adaptation grounds Cornerstone's ideology of transcultural interaction through language. "Thou usest eye shadow the color of lime jello," one character hurls at another, invoking a contemporary reference within a classical syntax. The linguistic play suggests that while idiomatic form may change over time, "the insult" itself remains. Negotiations between stability and change also work to great effect in the transformation of a snide comment on Perdita's legitimacy. The original text reads, "This has been some stair-work, some trunk-work, some behind-door work" (3.2:73–75). Ron Temple's Farmer instead comments, "This has been some back-seat-of-the-car work, some parents-away-for-the-weekend work, some stealing-into-home-base work,"[9] at once acknowledging and distancing the transhistorical and transcultural presence of illegitimacy.

Transformations of character and setting present additional interactions between the classical and contemporary, familiarizing archaic references while offering commentary on American culture. Cornerstone's adaptation refers to Leontes as a "prep school friend of Polixenes." Antigonus, a "Lord of Sicilia" in Shakespeare's text, becomes the more locally grounded Chief of Police. Rather than referring to the Delphic Oracle to determine the legitimacy of Paulina's child, Leontes calls in a medical expert to announce paternity test results. Additions to the original text also comment on contemporary American culture. The framing of the play as a courtroom drama and the relaying of information through television journalism reflect a national fascination with the court trial and the prevalence of television as a medium for receiving information. By challenging the truths derived from these media, the adaptation questions the ways we as Americans derive our information.

The casting of community actors in *The Winter's Tale* proffers a more complicated, often double-voiced interpretation. Wanda Daniels plays Hermione as a coal-miner's daughter; Ron Temple's Farmer is also a farmer. These doubled readings also reinforce specific community connections— Wanda Daniels *is* a coal-miner's daughter, and Ron Temple *is* a farmer. Doubling also underlines the social and geographic diversity of community participants, reflected in the working-class industrial background of Hermione Smith and the rural earthiness created by Temple's characterization of the farmer.

In most cases, these translations and adaptations rendered archaic references accessible to a contemporary audience. In some instances, Cornerstone members found it difficult to translate all of the contextual elements of the original reference. Director Bill Rauch discusses one particular difficulty in "Flowers to Taco Pizza: the Evolution of an Adaptation."[10]

In Shakespeare's original, Perdita, dressed as the goddess Flora, hands out flowers to guests at a sheepshearing festival. Flora and Polixenes, the disguised father of Perdita's betrothed, Florizel, strike up an argument about the streaked gillyvor, a crossbred flower that Perdita terms "nature's bastards." Polixenes disputes the depiction, citing the natural artistic skill required by crossbreeding. The scene juxtaposes these arguments about the flower in relation to a later discussion of crossbreeding between the "low-class" Perdita and Polixenes' "higher-class" son. In the later argument, Perdita and Polixenes adopt positions opposite to their points of view on the streaked gillyvor.

Rauch notes that the translation of the sheepshearing festival to a Fourth of July picnic and Perdita's transformation from Flora to the Statue of Liberty worked well but complicated the search for an appropriate adaptation of the streaked gillyvor. At first the company worked with flags, an object that the Statue of Liberty might conceivably distribute; but the flags could not ultimately convey the complicated references implied by the crossbreeding argument. A second draft replaced flags with yellow ribbons. While making a political statement in opposition to the then current Gulf War, and reflecting a specifically American issue, this translation could not capture the personal relevance of the crossbreeding argument. After further reading and discussion among community participants, adapters struck on the idea of a crossbred food—taco pizza. Explains Rauch, "In disliking this combination of Mexican and Italian food, Perdita would be making direct comment on the perils of relationships that cross lines in America: lines which can be economic, ethnic or cultural."[11] The taco pizza substitution captured the personal relevance of the argument without making as direct a political statement as the yellow ribbons did.

Rauch's article conveys some sense of the complexities of translation. Later conversations clarified the larger contextual difficulties involved. Two members of the permanent company had written a song that protested the Gulf War; they felt that the yellow ribbons reference would be an appropriate reflection on the song and recent political situation. Rauch and others expressed concern that this commentary did not serve the larger structure of the play. The songwriters believed that resistance to their ideas exemplified the company's political cowardice. As a compromise, though the taco pizza eventually replaced the yellow ribbons, an edited version of the war song remained in the production. As Rauch and others had worried, the song drew intense negative reaction from some audiences and reviewers, although others were moved.

Humanities scholar Ronald R. Butters, reading an early version of *The Winter's Tale* script, noted that the ribbons seemed "garish" and "too controversial and topical."[12] Reviewer Steve Vineberg felt the war song represented a "concession to political trendiness" that ground the play "to a screeching halt."[13] Efforts to include a variety of voices undermined the impact of the production for some, and in this instance, Cornerstone's inclusive process worked against itself. The company would confront similar difficulties in a later collaboration with Arena Stage, discussed in chapter 6.

In the Arena coproduction and *The Winter's Tale* project, Cornerstone collaborated with East of the Anacostia River communities. With two theaters, an advisory board, and at least one other community-based institution involved, the production process necessarily confronted differences in procedure, priorities, and perspectives. Negotiating these differences within the visible *Winter's Tale* company proved impossible and illuminating.

Community Transactions

Transactions of community began with the establishment of local contacts in each former residency and the recruitment of past participants into *The Winter's Tale* company, all of whom were to be paid at the same rate as Cornerstone members. These transactions, both financial and social, continued in Norcatur, Kansas, which had become a literal and figurative home for many Cornerstone members. The town served as the rehearsal location to which disparate participants came in the late spring of 1991. The company then opened their tour with a performance for Norcatur residents. A local newspaper heralded the performance, and Norcatur's relationship to the company, with the lead "Cornerstone Theater Company came home to Norcatur Friday night with another extraordinary production."[14] The small town had grown in reputation as a local arts center through its relationship with Cornerstone and seemed proud to host *The Winter's Tale* company rehearsals.

Norcatur and Schurz, Nevada, residents also participated in more explicitly financial transactions to support Cornerstone. Due to a funding shortfall on the $750,000 production, in part due to an accounting error, the $225 per week promised to company members had to be reduced to $200 upon the arrival of community participants to Norcatur. The Norcatur Arts and Humanities Council, founded after the Cornerstone *Tartoof* collaboration, invited the cast to participate in "An Evening of Cole Porter." The council then donated gate receipts from the benefit to a general fund supporting cast members less able to cope with salary reductions. Schurz residents donated $150 from local casinos. Additionally, residents of other towns contributed when Cornerstone members passed the hat at the end of each show. In return, Cornerstone kept ticket prices low through their pay-what-you-can admissions policy.

Labor exchanges further involved individuals within host communities. These local contacts measured baseball diamonds, parking lots, and cornfields in order to set up performance sites and located cars to lend for the performance. On Cornerstone's side, Technical Director Benajah Cobb expended great effort talking to state officials, convincing them to parole two company members.[15] During the production, audience members became unconventionally involved, helping to push a stalled Chevy from the stage in Marmarth, North Dakota, and a taxi in New York City.

The production as an event helped to enact community, serving as an occasion for gathering at the performance and surrounding events. In Eastport, Maine, the *Quoddy Tides* invited "everyone in the Eastport community . . . to come to the Christ Church Parish Hall on Key Street on Wed. Aug. 28 at 6 PM for a potluck dinner to welcome back the Cornerstone theater members."[16] The production itself featured a potluck festival during which the company invited audience members to share in the feast and festivities. In return for featuring participants from the community, local papers promoted the production. The performance offered opportunities for transactions with Cornerstone's nongeographic community of funders as well. Cornerstone thanked this community of supporters through free performances in Boston, New York, and Washington, D.C.

While interactions with host communities and audience members strengthened the production's impact, relationships between Cornerstone members and community participants served as a more direct expression of Cornerstone's ideology. Through process and public documents, Cornerstone underlined the nature of the diverse, inclusive community that they worked to build through *The Winter's Tale* production. In various ways the production represented and performed this diverse community. Both performance and public expression also consciously avoided foregrounding the enormous difficulties encountered in attempting to build an inclusive, participatory community of individuals with different backgrounds, values, and interests.

Fifty company members gathered in Norcatur to begin work on *The Winter's Tale*. Guest artists and community participants from around the country joined the thirteen Cornerstone members who had been working to complete an adaptation draft. Participants left homes and families for the five months of rehearsals and touring in exchange for the opportunity to work on the production and receive minimal financial reimbursement. At a weekly art talk, administrators, technicians, and actors met to discuss aspects of the show. In collaborative company meetings, participants enacted an interrelation between art, community, and individuality. Rauch describes this coming together in a Cornerstone Newsletter: "We talked about our beliefs, our homes, our pasts, our interpretations of character and text and our artistic vision."[17] Cornerstone worked to include everyone, to have each company member invested in all aspects of the production. The company even wrote a part for their tour bus driver. Production literature proudly details these aspects of collaboration, underlining the intersection of process with the play's themes of tolerance. Program notes explain, "*The Winter's Tale* could enable us to examine the intolerances of differences within communities [and] argue against it." The program emphasized the equality of individual contributions and importance through an alphabetical listing of the company members.

At the same time as it foregrounded the importance of unity and tolerance, production literature emphasized the individual diversity within the company. In the Humanities Flyer, Cornerstone introduced community participants through an emphasis on their different backgrounds. Individuals became representational types: the "college student from Texas," the "tobacco farmer from Virginia," the "high school graduate from a Paiute Indian tribe," the "freight hauler from North Dakota," the "track star from Mississippi," and "the hair dresser from Maine."[18] At the same time, the article suggested the complexity of diversity defined through differences in class, age, ethnicity, and background.

Company participants cited the value of diversity in evaluation reports written at the completion of the tour. Cornerstone member Ashby Semple noted the importance to her of bringing together professional and nonprofessional participants "on more equal footing." Community participant Jaime Daniels, from West Virginia, talked about her discovery of tolerance: "I never thought when I left that my two best friends on tour would be, one would be gay and the other a Mexican American, two things I had never been exposed to and never would have met [otherwise]." Noting the values of tolerance within diversity, bus driver Larry Tasker stated, "The world should learn from this tour." Company member Tim Banker underlined the notion that the performance event enabled this diverse community, stating, "[A] play is a great place for humans to meet."

These comments, written in the immediate afterglow of a well-received performance tour, reinforce the notion that the production enabled inclusive interaction and the building of community. Other reports from within the process point towards the immense difficulty encountered through the collaborative process, and some inevitable absences within a profoundly diverse production. While Cornerstone strives to illuminate the complexity of multiculturalism through emphasis on geography, age, and class, as well as race, in one instance the company fell prey to a more reductive depiction.

Company members generally recognize that diversity involves more complicated factors than race. Articles, program notes, and biographical text detail this complexity. But company members also understand that performance tends to foreground race and gender as visual markers of diversity. This understanding of the power of visuality led to the exclusion of two white brothers from Mississippi. Bill Rauch explains that although he wanted to invite the boys to become a part of *The Winter's Tale* company, he did not because of "diversity issues."[19] Though the boys, known locally as "white trash," were diverse in terms of their class background, this marker would not have read in performance. Rauch and other company members projected that a racial reading of diversity would better express Cornerstone's efforts to embrace an inclusive company.

Indeed, press coverage of *The Winter's Tale* tended to elide and simplify "diversity," highlighting limited racial aspects of multiculturalism. Bill Gato of the *Miami Herald* cited Cornerstone's company as representative of "Hispanics, blacks and other minorities."[20] Reporter Mary Feuer was "struck by the sight of so many strange partners working side by side. There's an elderly black gentleman assembling bleachers alongside a freckled white boy."[21] Feuer and Gato reduce a "variety of strangeness" to more easily consumed subsets of race and age. American reporting on diversity tends to simplify issues to literal and figurative black and white dichotomies.[22] Cornerstone offers a site at which to negotiate a more complex understanding of the makeup of America and Americans. Although in some ways Cornerstone's casting decisions played into a more reductive understanding of diversity, members did work to create a complexly defined multicultural company.

Through the production process, Cornerstone members also began to understand the more problematic aspects of bringing people of different backgrounds together. Johnny Bain, the "tobacco farmer from Virginia," explained at one point that walking barefoot was easy for him because he had "nigger feet." Cornerstone members, personally uncomfortable with Bain's language, also recognized that Bain's vernacular could be potentially offensive to several other company members. Yet, it would be equally problematic to alter Bain's personal vocabulary. In this case, Cornerstone members tried to explain to Bain that some of his phrases offended them personally and could be offensive to others.

Other incidents moved beyond the more surface political correctness that some critics of Cornerstone believe conceals rather than eliminates difference. Interactions between race and power are highlighted within the documentary created about *The Winter's Tale*.[23] Early in the documentary, Edret Brinston expresses a sense of frustration at being in Kansas among so many white people. Released from county jail immediately prior to joining the tour he comments, "Being out here is like being locked up." Brinston directly ties this sentiment to racial discomfort: "This is my first time relating to a lot of whites. In Mississippi, we didn't, what you call, sit at a table and eat dinner together." The documentary immediately cuts to a local restaurant where Brinston sits with fourteen-year-old Charlie McHatton from Oregon. The scene reads like a scripted dialogue, influenced perhaps by the self-conscious knowledge that the two were being filmed, and framed by clever editing. Whether conscious or not, the scenario illuminates both the possibilities and challenges of bringing individuals together across racial difference.

> *Brinston:* Is this your first time being around a black guy this much—it's a totally different thing for you, right?
> *McHatton:* You just talk weird (laughs). I got a joke to tell you. I've kept it from you for a long time. It's one of my favorite jokes.
> *Brinston:* What is it about?
> *McHatton:* It has a little bit to do with skin color. I just want to tell you, okay? Can I tell you?
> *Brinston:* Yeah, come on.
> *McHatton:* Okay, Cocoa (laughs). Okay, listen. It's a good joke, okay.
> *Brinston:* I'm listening.
> *McHatton:* (drinks water) Don't punch my lights out, okay?
> *Brinston:* Okay.
> *McHatton:* What's a black man with a wooden leg?
> *Brinston:* (rubs nose) Mmmmm.
> *McHatton:* (hands covering face, then opening) A fudgesicle (Laughs. Pause). Do you have any white man jokes?
> *Brinston:* No.

McHatton's joke can be easily read as a derogatory racial slur. But the exchange contains a variety of shifting power dynamics between a younger white boy and older black young adult, including McHatton's efforts to gain Brinston's permission to open up a racial dialogue that he has wanted to initiate "for a long time." Marked by the repetition of questioning "okays," and an invitation for "white man jokes," McHatton's tries to engage a two-way interaction. "You just talk weird," indicates McHatton's willingness to embrace Brinston as what he terms in a later scene "an older friend." But Brinston's short scene-ending "no" (immediately cut away from by the film-makers), implies that more is at stake here than an individual exchange, and that the ability to tell jokes might signal the comfortable power of a dominant culture. In a later scene that highlights these dynamics on a micro-level within the company, Brinston confronts choreographer Sabrina Peck in a firm but friendly manner: "It's what you are in this company. Who would take my word over your word in this company?" Peck is silent and Brinston gently remarks: "See what I'm saying? See, you're left speechless right there, so that answers that question to yourself."

Brinston's comments allude to the invisible hierarchies within Cornerstone that other participants had encountered in the past (see chapter 2). The company reflected on this at a planning meeting a few months after *The Winter's Tale* tour ended, acknowledging, "A lot has to do with people you've been working with for ten years and been acting with for ten years."[24] As in prior rural residencies, the company trusted the collective consensus process to emphasize the importance of mutual respect and open communication. This process, however, had its own difficulties. Cultural difference, added to the emotional stress of the production process, and the filming of the entire event, further challenged collaborative unity in a way that Cornerstone members could not have foreseen.

No Consensus about Consensus

During the rehearsal and performance of *The Winter's Tale,* the company organized weekly consensus-run meetings to discuss tour logistics. Having worked with consensus decision making in their smaller company, Cornerstone members felt that this process embodied the inclusive format that the company championed. The effort to implement consensus into the larger, more consciously diverse company of *The Winter's Tale,* however, proved problematic if not disastrous in both emotional and logistical terms.

Ensemble member Christopher Liam Moore explains the difficulty of working with the full company through a model of consensus forged by Cornerstone members:

> It was trying to foist a model that we had unknowingly crafted over four years of working together; the way we arrived at decisions, the way we created our art. . . . Sometimes I think people wanted to just be told what to do, and didn't want to have to be asked, "What do you think?" and "What is best for you?"[25]

In a 1994 interview, Moore clarified his feelings that Cornerstone's expectations of teamwork were difficult to translate to task-oriented individuals. Doug Casement affirmed Moore's trepidations at a company meeting in Schurz. Casement, an older crew member from Maine, spoke out about his frustrations with Cornerstone's approach: "Who's going to decide when the work gets done? The people who do it or people half my age?"[26] Speaking with reporter Mary Feuer, Jim Carrol seconded Casement's frustrations with consensus: "They have these meetings and they want to do everything by consensus, but it's always the same people talking. Me and Johnny [Bain] just sit there and keep our mouths shut so we can get out of there."[27]

Rather than solving problems by giving everyone a voice in making decisions, consensus increased the stress of the project by pressuring attendance on people who felt as though the process wasted their valuable time. Several participants also criticized Cornerstone members, particularly co-founders Rauch and Carey, for not taking more leadership responsibility. Comments Moore:

> We were supposed to be the experts, and we were bringing together these people, some of whom were incredibly independent and self-sufficient, others who had never ventured outside their home state and were scared and needed a lot of care. At the same time, we were all so overworked, so exhausted, and there was this incredible emotional drain. . . . It was really, really hard. And the schedule was grueling; even though there was a day off built in, there was set-up time. It was just a hugely ambitious undertaking.[28]

Many company members, used to the emotional release allowed by consensus, felt the process to be essential to their sanity. Others used the meeting as a forum to express the painful emotions caused by the stress of the production schedule and the insecurity of being without their support network of close family and friends. In one meeting in Schurz, meant to provide a forum supporting individual insecurities, temporarily disabled Rosemarie Voorhees stated that she felt like a "heavy, ugly prop."[29] At the same meeting, Rod Prichard of Marmarth admitted that he was afraid to get close to people. But as Mary Feuer points out after interviewing some company members, "The airing of grievances and frustrations in the meetings [felt] embarrassing or silly for some who were not used to expressing their feelings in this way."[30]

The conflicting needs of company members caused the meetings to become increasingly emotional and tension filled. Community participants felt unguided as Cornerstone members persisted in working with the consensus model. A brewing storm broke during company meetings held to discuss the firing, rehiring, and eventual return of a hot-tempered crew member. Several community participants and Cornerstone members later commented that Rauch and Carey ought to have stopped the emotional process that pressured company members to express their feelings about the individual in front of him and to have made a firm decision about his firing and rehiring outside of this process. Even bus driver Larry Tasker noted that Cornerstone needed to function less as a therapy group and more as a theater. As Rauch later related, "Larry Tasker said it this morning. 'You can't solve every emotional problem with forty people. You can do theater with forty people. If we want to be in full-time therapy then we should do that.'"[31] Three years after *The Winter's Tale,* Rauch admitted to the failure of the company to deal with the emotional stress of the tour: "In terms of the emotional life of this group of people and our feeling of control and our relationship to our community collaborators, the tour was in many ways a disaster."[32]

At a meeting in Port Gibson, Mississippi, the company attempted to address the difficulties of collaboration through the consensus process, asking everyone to describe their fantasy of how the group could better work together. Although the expression relieved some immediate tensions, it also revealed the incredible diversity of opinions in the company. Strategies ranged from creating "harmony and understanding" (Daniels) and "working together as a group" (Brinston) to the "practicalities of one on one communication" (Petty) and "recognizing individuals by saying hello" (Carey). Some members simply pointed to the importance of "cushions, snacks and holding hands" (Desmond, Rauch, Dewey). Others reminded the company of the importance of listening and respect (Jeffries, Semple).[33]

While all the opinions were valuable, and the advice practical, most comments did not directly address ways to engender "respect," "harmony," and "listening." And while reflecting the diversity of the company, the diversity of opinions illustrated the problems with achieving consensus. Cornerstone members began to understand that the diversity they initially lauded was contributing to intolerance rather than resolving these issues. As stress increased, individuals grew more likely to express this intolerance.

At one company meeting, Rod Prichard grew upset at this perceived expression.

> I don't feel part of the company and I haven't for about two weeks. There's a lot more things going on with me and with other people. I'm gonna speak my mind. There's racial slurs; that's really pissed me off. I know I haven't been no sweetheart. There's just a lot of things that aren't being said.[34]

Efforts to open up discussion through consensus were not working.

While the consensus process both added to and occasionally alleviated company divisiveness, performance reunified the company. Despite the demanding schedule, participants cited the performance itself as a positive moment in evaluations of the tour. In its requirement for commitment and collaboration, performance provided a space for company members to move beyond the emotional difficulties of production. Performance served as a mediator, reminding company members of the reason for committing to the tour. Additionally, the performance of tolerance in *The Winter's Tale* offered a *potential* space to enact compassion and unity. In the November 1991 Cornerstone Newsletter, the company admits to the struggle of process but also emphasizes these redemptive and unifying powers of performance:

> Consensus decision-making with fifty people was grueling and not always successful. People were sometimes intolerant of other's differences in race, political and spiritual views, sexual orientation, age and gender. People fought, people bickered, people cried and some people even left the tour for a variety of personal reasons. But also, people listened and learned from each other. . . . despite the differences the show held us together.[35]

Rauch cites the stresses of the tour as benefiting the artistry of the production. He writes in the Humanities Flyer, "[A]s we became more aware of the differences between each of us on tour and the resultant intolerances we sometimes all felt, we became more aware of the play's themes of redemption and tolerance."[36]

Performance requires collaboration. It serves as a site for company members to negotiate their difference, to forget and forgive by working together. Performance offered a space for *communitas* among company members themselves as well as with the audience. The full company, including crew members, joined together at the end of the piece to sing a song about home, engendering a tremendously emotional moment. Reviewer Steve Vineberg notes of the final Washington, D.C., performance that he had "rarely felt such a close connection between a company and its audience."[37]

Ironically, while *The Winter's Tale* script directly addressed a variety of tensions among characters in the play, and the country they represented, the production could leave an audience and cast members with an overwhelming sense of unity. There is nothing inherently wrong with this feeling; it is indeed essential to company members, moving to audiences, and redemptive of the company's struggles. But this performance of unity may have taken emphasis away from the text's exploration of difference, while obscuring the tremendous difficulty of group governance. While this organizational challenge would be addressed after the tour's completion, during the run of the show, biographies, articles, and oral histories restored

For the final version of *The Winter's Tale*'s "Home Song," the crew, in orange vests, joining cast members onstage. Photo: Lynn Jeffries.

emphasis on community complexity, underlining divisions among individuals while illuminating the difficulty of pinpointing the individual identity from which "diversity" springs.

INDIVIDUAL IDENTITY AND INTRA-COMMUNITY DIVISIONS

Public documents reveal significant differences among groups within the company, reflecting the intra-community divisions discovered in such residencies as Marfa, Eastport, Port Gibson, and Long Creek. Contrary to most media perceptions, however, the most striking divisions within *The Winter's Tale* company were not drawn between those of different ethnic or racial backgrounds but among Cornerstone members, community participants, and guest artists.

This division initially revealed itself at the first full company meeting, at which the company discussed a potential pay cut. Cornerstone members, used to pay cuts already, and feeling responsible for the tour, had no difficulty accepting these cuts. Some community members had problems with the amount of the cut in relation to their personal budgets, and the company later instituted an anonymous salary fund to cover these personal deficits. In opposition to these acceptances, guest artists articulated their opposition to the cuts. Bill Rauch recalls, "I just remember there was a pretty huge schism between the professional guest artists and the community artists."[38] This schism did not go on public record until the company oral history emerged in 1994. Public documents associated with *The Winter's Tale* emphasized the collaborative unity among company members. Yet, one element of the program reveals clear examples of intra-community differentiation. Biographies in conventional theater programs offer an inter-textual reading of artists' works in other venues. Cornerstone's biographies offer inter-textual readings of self-identification. The relative importance of home, age, family, work, and Cornerstone itself underlines distinct differentiations among individuals within *The Winter's Tale* community.

Community participants defined themselves primarily by their hometown, additionally situating the roles that defined their membership in a community. In some cases, what they did literally defined who they were. Johnny Bain listed himself *as* a tobacco farmer and peanut farmer who *became* a real estate agent. Biographies also emphasize connections to a variety of communities including those defined by geography, work, family, and religion.

Like community residents, Cornerstone members cite where they are from as being of primary importance to most, though "home" was an ambivalent notion for some. When asked where she was from in her evaluation form, Ashby Semple noted, "God knows. It's a problem." Many listed their relation with Cornerstone as being of primary importance. The longer they had been with the company, the more likely members were to list Cornerstone's primary importance to their biographical identity. Ten out of fifteen members were equally adamant about citing professional experience outside of Cornerstone, perhaps in an effort to establish their individual artistry without relation to the community of Cornerstone. Not surprisingly, the biographies of guest artists followed more closely the format of conventional professional theater biographies, which tend to discourage personal statements and emphasize the inter-textuality of professional work.

These individual listings suggest the variety of communities to which participants belong, ranging from the geographic areas most often associated with the notion of "community" to communities of profession, age, religion, and family. Biographies seem to fill in for the diversities rendered less visible through performance. No one specifically cites ethnic, racial, or sexual identity, though these seem to be such important markers of community identification to outside observers. Visible identification, textual citations, and self-identification all suggest the multiplicities of communities to which individuals belong and assert the complex nature of identity formation. As implied by the company biographies, identity arises from a negotiation among the various communities to which an individual perceives that he or she belongs. Identifications associating individuals with Cornerstone would soon shift dramatically, as the company underwent a drastic shift at the end of the tour.

Beginnings and Endings

The Winter's Tale reflected and clarified issues of boundary definition, individual and cultural identity, and negotiations between process and ideology. The tour also marked a transition for Cornerstone from a touring company to a more stable resident company in Los Angeles. After five years of travel, the company decided to settle in an urban area and explore the diversity of community formation from a more permanent vantage point.

In a number of ways, *The Winter's Tale* tour led to the ending and new beginning of Cornerstone as a company. As the few ensemble members remaining after the tour note in the company's November 1991 newsletter, "[T]he tour celebrating Cornerstone's first five years almost destroyed it."[39] The emotional and financial costs of the tour halved the company in terms of personnel and left continuing members with a fifty thousand dollar debt.

Cornerstone began in 1986 as both an idea and a community of individuals, most of whom had remained with the company through *The Winter's Tale* tour. Consensus had contributed to the ideological structure of the company and strained it. In the year preceding the tour, the company had collectively decided to move to an urban center. Exhausted by life on the road, the group felt that they needed to settle. Their work in rural areas had also illuminated the complexity of community formation and divisibility, a complexity members thought they could more easily explore within an urban setting. While the company as a whole agreed to the decision to move to Los Angeles, many individuals within the Cornerstone community did not feel that they could make the move.

For David Reiffel, the reasons were both artistic and personal. Reiffel had always expressed difficulty with the decision-making apparatus of the company, and some within the company had difficulty with his perceived resistance to reflect the community in his musical compositions. On his part, Reiffel felt that performed unity concealed struggle and that consensus watered down the art.

> We were sort of jumping to the resolutions . . . and in almost every town that we worked in over the years, we had run into some gay people who were totally closeted. The expression of gayness and lesbianism in the tour show was supposed to be about what we had discovered. At the best, same sex relationships were in the closet in our adaptation of that script. . . . I

thought about the people that I had known who were desperate to see something of themselves on stage and we could give them so little. . . . In our own work, especially in the tour, I felt like there was a desire to express only what could be expressed by consensus. I believe in consensus as a way of running meetings, but consensus got in the way of plurality in the actual show. [The art] got homogenized.[40]

Reiffel's decision to leave was based on this growing level of discomfort with the way the company performed and enacted community. He felt that consensus left no room for dissent or difference. These feelings had been building over the years, but the stress of the tour exacerbated them. He describes his reasons for leaving the company in emotional and artistic terms: "No art was worth it, and certainly it wasn't, I felt, making the art better."[41] Cornerstone had been founded on the dual principles of enlarging the audience base of theatergoers and improving the artistry of its members. Reiffel now felt as though the first goal had superseded the second.

Other members who left the ensemble after *The Winter's Tale* tour departed for various reasons, although for most, the course of the tour solidified their decisions. Anne Beresford Clarke, a guest artist on the tour, later married to a founding Cornerstone member, had both an insider's and outsider's viewpoint on how these decisions affected, and were affected by, the emotional stress of the tour. In the company oral history, Clarke noted that "the consensus process exasperated these stresses" and led to the decisions to leave the company.[42] Clarke posited that the decision-making process became ironically painful due in part to the desire not to hurt anyone's feelings. During a tour in which decisions had to be constantly enacted, the stress grew proportionately.

Meetings throughout the tour gradually revealed that most members were not considering moving to Los Angeles. At a meeting following the final performance of the tour in Washington, D.C., on 14 September 1991, members gave their final decisions. Bill Rauch recalls his growing realization that the founding members of Cornerstone had

> reached the end of our road together, in this exact configuration; and that there was incredible pain and incredible blame and incredible anger and incredible sadness. And I don't think I even began to know it until the meeting in the cafeteria at the Space Museum, when, with cameras on us, like right now, we sat around and acknowledged that it was the end of the line. . . . It was like, it was the end.[43]

For some East Coast–based Cornerstone members, the move to Los Angeles seemed like one more sacrifice that they were finally unwilling to make.

In some ways, however, the reconfiguration and debt engendered by the tour led to a rethinking of Cornerstone's identity and governance structure, marking a new beginning for the company. Remaining members reexamined consensus decision making to determine whether all decisions, especially artistic ones, should be enacted in this way. The company's debt compelled ensemble members to reconceive Cornerstone's organizational structure and emphasize the importance of fund-raising and development work. The departure of founding members also compelled remaining members to reconsider how they worked with and defined communities. "Rather than marking an end to Cornerstone residency work," states the November 1991 newsletter, "this decision reflects our desire to work with communities that are not defined merely by geographic isolation."[44] This rethinking of community also led to a rethinking of the company as an American theater group.

Moving to Los Angeles meant that the group would no longer be traveling across the country. They could therefore no longer define themselves as an American company in terms of geography. How they would maintain this identity, if at all, was at first vague. In the production flyer written even before *The Winter's Tale* tour began, the company stated, "We hope to continue developing and serving an even larger community of citizens who share a faith in an American theater that is of, by and for all the people."[45] The definition of what it meant to be an American theater rhetorically associated Cornerstone with documents laying the foundation for American independence, without yet specifying their tactics for work in LA.

As the company thought through their developing ideology, they began to refine their discussion of community and Americanism. The November 1991 newsletter notes:

> We chose Los Angeles last winter for many reasons. Among them: the diversity within and sheer size of the city, the presence of so many newer immigrants, and perhaps even the fact that the entertainment industry creates so many of the images by which America defines itself.[46]

Los Angeles emerged as an ideological site for the exploration of new ideas of community. America became identified as a locus of cultural images as well as of geographical locales. Finally, on a planning day several years later in Los Angeles, the company began tentatively to favor the idea of building community over the notion of defining themselves as an American company. Meeting notes state, "Alison [Carey] felt that bridge building had become more important to us than 'An American aesthetic.'"[47] As exemplified in Cornerstone's urban work, this bridge building—bringing together divided communities through the performance process—may, in fact, *be* more representative of an American aesthetic.

Ten years after the tour, from the vantage point of a successful Los Angeles home base, Christopher Liam Moore adds to Carey's vision:

> *The Winter's Tale* tour was incredibly emotional, but it really was such a symbol of potential to have all these people from all walks of life, economic background, educational background, and the potential of the whole country really right there and people singing about what home was and what home means to them. And it was incredibly difficult. But so was the experiment of America, and it really was this nation traveling on this bus and working out how to communicate, how do you respect, how do you get respect, how are you heard.[48]

Cornerstone's lack of success at fully embodying the humanist discourse encouraged by government and corporate grant narratives may in fact have vital positive outcomes. Instead of offering a simple image of diverse, inclusive, harmonic America, *The Winter's Tale* detailed the incredible difficulty of day-to-day collaborations across difference. This "failure" to live up to an impossible image offers an encouraging model of America in process.

5

Urban Revisions

Designs, designs all over the place
Tell us about it, doesn't matter what race
Glass and bottles all broken up
To form a design that will not erupt
    —Ebony Morgan, community participant in *Breaking Plates,* Watts, LA

Why did you leave America to go to L.A.?
                  —Peter Zeisler, executive director of the
                  Theatre Communications Group 1972–1995

Cornerstone's first five years, culminating in *The Winter's Tale* tour, incorporated links with pageantry, democratization, and grassroots theatrical impulses, including the drive to ground productions within local space and semiotics, to develop a participatory performance process, and to decentralize American theater. Frequent reference to communal and national holidays, such as Christmas in Norcatur and the Fourth of July in *The Winter's Tale,* reinforced ties among ritual, theater, and community building. At the same time, Cornerstone's productions illuminated the attendant detractions of suppressing difference in community-based work. The company's subsequent movement from a nomadic, mainly rural organization to a more permanent urban site in Los Angeles links Cornerstone with theatrical threads of fragmentation and association, emphasizing collaborations with differentially defined communities as well as coalition and bridge building. Cornerstone's move also entailed revising definitions and boundaries of community within a dispersed urban field, which in turn generated a distinct set of artistic, ethical, and institutional challenges, many of which I experienced personally. My research in this chapter thus undergoes a shift in emphasis as well, from archival interpretation to ethnography.

In the fall of 1994, I worked as a dramaturg, production assistant, and ad hoc flautist for three Cornerstone productions in Watts, while conducting dissertation research on the company. Assumptions about the city, Cornerstone, and my own objectivity were almost immediately upended, and I was continuously compelled to renegotiate my own relation to community and to its research.

I had envisioned "the community of Watts" before entering its geographical terrain, influenced by readings on the Watts riots and media imagery, though I was not consciously aware of these stimuli until confronted by the surprise I felt upon actually entering the neighborhood. In early September 1994, I attended an event designed to introduce Cornerstone to area schoolchildren. I drove with some caution to the Watts Towers, a structure I presumed to be an urban housing project. After locking my car with The Club, I stepped out to view a landscape of single-family dwellings with front yards lining the street and uniformed schoolchildren running around the lawns. The towers themselves emerged as a magnificent artistic structure, a collage of broken plates, bottles, and seashells sculpted into columns, ship masts, and the home of artist Simon Rodia. As I walked inside the Watts Towers Arts Center, a city-run institution maintaining the towers and supporting community art, I was struck by the gospel strains of a young girl singing a song from Cornerstone's latest production, *L.A. Building* (1994). I had at that point never actually seen a Cornerstone production. I had not expected the performance to be so moving and engaging, so "good."

These perceptual clarifications about family dwellings, clothing, urban architecture, and community artistry accompanied a growing understanding of my own subjectivity. I had attended the event intending to observe how Cornerstone members introduced themselves to a community. I instead became involved *in* the event, with little time to ponder my ethnographic stance. Soon after entering the space, Cornerstone board member Alejandro Nuño handed me a knife. A local Subway had donated lunch but had neglected to cut the ten-foot long sandwiches, so we began slicing. I remained through the afternoon helping to clean up and pack food, driving away somewhat stunned. Whether or not I was officially part of Cornerstone, I had at least temporarily enacted belonging. As I became more directly involved in the production process, further interactions complicated my relationship to this and other communities.

On the first day of auditions in the Watts Towers Arts Center, local participants totaled exactly zero. Consequently, director and ensemble member Ashby Semple sent me to the shopping mall to distribute audition flyers. As I later noted in my journal, I felt "very stupid and very white, and clearly *not* a member of the community."[1] I discerned a mass of people involved in lives that couldn't possibly have anything in common with me or with theater. Through participation in the productions, *The Love of the Nightingale, Breaking Plates,* and *Los Faustinos,* my perceptions again changed; I became a part of the production community created through the rehearsal process. Throughout this process, however, I continued to negotiate boundaries of belonging and exclusion, reflecting Cornerstone's own experience in Los Angeles.

Cornerstone Revisions

Cornerstone's roots are rural, in terms of our first five years. We worked in mostly small towns around the country, and we had this just incredible affirmation of the power of the community getting together and telling a story that was deeply rooted in the community. To see the power of that, and then to come back and discover, "Wow, it doesn't work in LA." And, "What are we doing in LA? What am I doing in LA?" And, you know, hating my big, fat, white ass.

—Bill Rauch, speaking at a "Connecting Californians" storytelling symposium

Cornerstone's move to Los Angeles required numerous internal and external revisions of the company, its mission, membership, methodology, and finances. These institutional remappings accompanied shifting notions of community formation and identification. In a city without a clear center, but everywhere influenced by the relationship of urban space to identity, rethinking community nongeographically became a key aspect of how the company reimagined its urban work.

Unfortunately, Cornerstone's rural, nomadic collaborations were fundamental to how external financial supporters envisioned the company. The move to Los Angeles seemed to many an abandonment not only of Cornerstone's mission but of America itself. "It had taken people so long to buy what Cornerstone did," elaborates former Managing Director Stephen Gutwillig.

Now it was like Cornerstone had pulled the rug out from under these people and said, from their perspective, "We're not that, we're this," even though it was so painfully obvious to the company that it was exactly the same thing, just in a different physical environment.[2]

Many supporters also felt that Cornerstone's move reflected a selling out for the fame and fortune of Hollywood. "People did not really understand that there was an entire city here that had nothing to do with making movies," remarks Alison Carey.[3]

Ensemble members believed that their move enhanced the process of engaging a more diverse audience than they had worked with in their prior, mainly rural residencies. But Gutwillig's comment about the company doing the "same thing" in a different physical environment does not adequately convey the level of change initiated by Cornerstone's move, change that encompassed far more than geographic substitution. LA's physical layout had tremendous impact on Cornerstone's work. Even smaller communities within Los Angeles were more dispersed than the majority of Cornerstone's rural residencies. The vibrant urban region also provided more competition for audiences. In Kansas and North Dakota, Cornerstone's coproductions had the full attention of the community and its surrounding areas, for hundreds of miles in some instances. In one of Cornerstone's first Los Angeles coproductions in Pacoima, at the Boys and Girls Club, some club members did not know about the event through the entire rehearsal and performance period. The fact that Cornerstone ensemble members were not living with and continuously interacting with a residency community decreased awareness and a sense of collaboration.

On top of these complications, Cornerstone had to address challenges to its method of community definition and selection even before arriving in the city. Christopher Liam Moore details this discovery made on a scouting trip in the fall of 1991:

> Bill and I had lunch with the people who run the 18th Street Arts Complex [in Santa Monica] where our office was [until 1999]. Keith Antar Mason, who runs an African American male performance collective called the Hittite Empire, was there . . . and we were sort of, you know, talking the Cornerstone talk at that lunch, and saying we'll go into communities that . . . need theater—and he just said, "Whoa, whoa, whoa, what are you talking about? Who are you to say this community needs theater and needs art?" He wasn't unpleasant about it, he was just challenging a lot of the assumptions that we had in Cornerstone. I realized at that one second, well this is going to be really, really different. . . . that issue of ownership and who has the right to create art, who has the right to decide how to define community—it's something that is very much on the city's agenda.[4]

Through their conversation with Mason, Moore and Rauch reconsidered the political nature of defining community and producing theater in an urban environment. Deciding which communities "needed" theater (a verb the company now avoids) implied an authoritative power that Cornerstone professed to resist through its ideals of collaboration and inclusiveness. By defining community, Cornerstone presumed to set boundaries of commonality. To combat this tendency, the company initiated the development of advisory boards, allowing a collective leadership to guide, cosponsor, and legitimate their work with and within communities.

The Watts advisory board served several purposes, practical and symbolic. The board affirmed Cornerstone's collaborative ethics and alleviated the potential for the company to be viewed as an artistic invader. "You have to bring something else into the community than just art," elucidated Watts advisory board member Erik Priestly, "otherwise people will feel like, 'Here comes another group of carpetbaggers.'"[5] During their fifteen-month residency in Watts, Cornerstone members engaged in numerous community activities not directly related to art making. Beyond the usual range of potluck suppers and slide shows, the company held several benefit performances for cosponsoring organizations represented on the advisory board. At one benefit, held at a showing of *The Central Ave. Chalk Circle* (1995), the Watts Health Foundation set up a free clinic. In exchange for Cornerstone's support of community activities, advisory board members guided the company to audition and performance spaces and helped to develop and support marketing, publicity, and public relations strategies.

In addition to involving community advisory boards, Cornerstone began to rethink how they defined community. In their first series of Los Angeles residencies, the company selected three distinct methods—by culture, age, and geography. "We wanted to define community in different ways on purpose," explains Bill Rauch. "We had approached Arab groups during the Gulf War before we moved to LA, we had always wanted to work with senior citizens, and Al Nodal, the Cultural Affairs Department General Manager suggested the neighborhood of Pacoima."[6] In a heterogeneous urban terrain, each residency confronted challenges of how best to represent the participating community, often resulting in artistic innovations. Both challenges and innovations are exemplified in *Ghurba* (1993). Working with an internally diverse Arab and Arab American community, director Shishir Kurup endeavored to move beyond the notion that "Arabs only exist in relation to Jews."[7] The resultant production celebrated and illuminated the complexities of authentically representing this diverse group, though the production's cosponsor, Fadwa El Guindi, expressed some initial trepidation:

> It's a non-community, and they tend to be suspicious of outsiders. . . . I feel as an anthropologist a little worried when people who aren't Arab try to do a piece about Arab identity. It takes years to just scratch the surface of the culture.[8]

Yet, in a few months, the *Ghurba* company dug deep enough to provoke a variety of responses from Arab audience members. The *Beirut Times* included two diametrically opposed reviews a week apart from each other. The first asserts, "*Ghurba* misses [its] target of telling Arab-American experience in L.A."[9] In contrast, Kari Sprowl's later review praises the production's innovative detail, noting that many Arabs she spoke with had attended several times.[10]

Cornerstone members had in fact begun researching the project as early as 1991 and well knew the complexities of attempting to perform any kind of "Arab community." A newsletter article observes, "Arabs share culture and language, though some dialects of Arabic vary so greatly that they are virtually incomprehensible to other Arabic speakers."[11] The article further describes religious differentiations among Arab groups practicing Muslim, Jewish, Druze, and Christian faiths. Even elements of "shared" culture could be variously performed. Arabs from distinct regions argued about the proper way to cook eggplant, drink Jallab, or dance the doepke; but the performance could often offer only one representation of each social ritual. These differences resulted in a combination of compromise and multiplicity.

An actress from Lebanon felt the veil worn by the bride in a wedding sequence should be placed on one side of her head, while another Lebanese actor, raised in Egypt, argued for the other side. The bride wore her veil in the middle. In other instances the Arabic cultures represented within

Community artist and musician George Haddad *(center)* in *Ghurba* (1993). Photo: Lynn Jeffries.

the cast, with participants from Palestine, Morocco, Lebanon, and Syria (in addition to a Lebanese Armenian and a Kuwaiti Greek), celebrated their distinctions with a variety of folk songs. The show also incorporated community-building tactics that underlined common immigrant experiences. Classical Arabic unified the cast while differentiating the group from non-Arab-speaking audience members. Kurup elaborates on the process: "We were interested in letting the 'Americans' feel the 'shut-out' that immigrants experience, asking them to assume certain assimilating properties like letting waves of laughter propel them towards their own osmosis-like enjoyment—a kind of forced integration."[12]

In working together to define performative compromises, the company created an authentic representative of their own diverse Arab community, not of *the* Arab American community. Thus, the performance process questioned the very idea of a bounded and unified Arab American community at the same time as it brought together several members of this group as performers and audience. Kurup complicates matters further: "The play was and was not about Arab culture in that it was about Arab and Arab-American culture as well as immigrant culture." Indeed, in classical Arabic, *Ghurba* means "the feeling of being away from home."

While grappling with these issues of cultural and community delineation, Cornerstone had to redefine its own membership. Previously, anyone who worked for Cornerstone had been considered a member, though some former company members expressed confusion about their sense of belonging. Ashby Semple explains: "In Long Creek [guest lighting designer] Loren [Brame] and I talked about the pronoun crisis. It was like we, they, us, them, you."[13] Once in Los Angeles, Cornerstone clarified distinct guidelines for membership in the ensemble, which administered the company, and for guest artists, who only worked on productions. But the politics of payment, volunteerism, and institutional diversity continued to challenge the company's restructuring.

As explicated in chapter 2, Cornerstone diversified its membership in 1993, noting at an ensemble meeting, "It is extremely problematic if both the people receiving the paychecks and making the decisions do not reflect the culture at large, and the people that we're collaborating with."[14] But diversification alone could not resolve issues of guest artist payment. In the urban environment of Los Angeles, living expenses were higher, per capita income was lower, and funding for arts organizations was more competitive than in most of the company's rural residencies. Deciding which participants were professional enough to receive compensation, and in what ways paid artists represented communities, enacted complex power dynamics in which Cornerstone could again be perceived as defining community boundaries.

The company had begun addressing these issues before moving to Los Angeles at a week-long planning session in Norcatur and at a 1994 ensemble meeting:

> The composition of the community and the existence of community-based artists cannot be ignored and not addressing these issues is a political act. . . . volunteerism is important, but it is problematic when all outsiders [to a community] are paid and all insiders are not.[15]

Debate continued and a proposal that "there be a paid person from the community in every project" remained unresolved as several members believed that this guideline would not fully address either economic issues or questions about community definition.[16]

Funding for Cornerstone projects was limited and decreasing. In order to survive as a full-time company, members felt that they had to prioritize their own reimbursement. In several discussions to which I was privy, the company debated the value of volunteerism. Several ensemble members emphasized the importance of training and experience, and that community shows were not meant to be economic enterprises. At the same time, they recognized the problematic nature of drawing boundaries between volunteer community "insiders" and paid professional "outside" artists.

Increasingly, the company has worked to dissolve boundaries of professionalism and payment within the community. Currently, when Cornerstone rehires community participants to run crew or act in a bridge or ensemble show, they pay these participants hourly wages. Grants supporting bridge shows between communities specifically provide for the payment of community participants. The company actively recruits experienced artists from within the community who are reimbursed on the same scale as guest artists. Observed Bill Rauch: "Quentin [Drew] is a man we've hired many times as a self-identified professional who lives in Watts. The lines between 'Cornerstone artists' and 'community members' have gotten blurred, I think in a good way."[17]

Community Revisions

INTERCOMMUNITY DIFFERENCE

While boundaries between Cornerstone and community artists had become less demarcated, defining the "community" identification of professional artists remained difficult. Quentin Drew and M. C. Earl, who have both participated in several Cornerstone productions, are African American artists living in Watts. Armando Molina and C. J. Jones, professional actors living outside of Watts who worked on several Watts/Cornerstone coproductions, are respectively of Latino and African American descent. They can be identified as artists of the community or excluded from the community, dependent upon definition. These definitions and distinctions grew increasingly murky within the Watts production process.

Intercommunity divisions emerged in part from a lack of clarity about the responsibilities and expectations of less theatrically experienced community participants. Ashby Semple, director of *The Love of the Nightingale* and *Breaking Plates,* advocated hiring M. C. Earl, who held a graduate degree in theater. Cornerstone also invited trained actor Daniele Gathier to participate in the *Nightingale* production when a community participant dropped out. Gathier and Earl had experience learning lines, had an understanding of stage vocabulary, and were also single and in their twenties, without family responsibilities or full-time jobs. In hearing praise of their "professionalism," other community participants felt that their own commitments were being undervalued. Outside responsibilities and a lack of training made learning lines and extra rehearsal time more difficult for these participants. Assumed theater values, such as being on time, putting the show first, understanding pace and storytelling, seemed at times an imposition. The idea of coming an hour early on opening night to speed through their lines did not, to say the least, appeal to these participants. As I recall one sixty-year-old chorus member with a memory problem putting it, "At 5:00 I'm going to be up to here in suds, soakin'." Another participant flatly stated that she had to cook dinner for her kids.

These reactions reinforce several internal boundaries of community within Watts and the *Nightingale* production team—generational, experiential, socioeconomic, and geographical. Three women, next-door neighbors in Watts, spoke frequently of Gathier as appearing "standoffish." Gathier, a trained actress who graduated from Northwestern University, had grown up outside of Watts. Though they are all of African American descent, the neighbors saw Gathier as outside of their more particularly bounded community. In *The Symbolic Construction of Community,* Anthony Cohen proposes that the smaller the boundaries and the narrower the differences between groups, the closer those boundaries are to an individual's identity. And the more important those differences seem, the more fiercely individuals defend their group boundaries.[18] When one actress overheard Semple refer to Gathier as being "best at her lines," she launched into a monologue about "some people having families that they are already making sacrifices to for this damn rehearsal, and some people can just go home and learn their lines, and some people better just kiss her black ass."

The tensions revealed in these exchanges underline a difference not only in "professional" attitudes but also in privilege of focus. "Work time" for professionals is "free time" for nonprofessionals. Class issues, who can and cannot afford the time to do theater, become another obstacle to negotiate in community-based performance. In addition to distinctions of class and theatrical training, boundaries of geography, education, and ethnicity also unfolded within the rehearsal process—boundaries so embedded they could not be redrawn by one play. I witnessed further divisions between those who studied acting and raised families, between participants who lived in a certain area of Watts and others who lived just far enough outside, and between a child who attended a charter school and kids in the regular public school system.

Intra-community Difference

While these divisions were perhaps more subtly indicated, those between African Americans and Latinos in Watts dominated much of the early rehearsal process. According to the 1990 United States Census Bureau, the percentage of Latinos in Watts increased to 43 percent in the previous twenty years, compared to a 54 percent African American population.[19] Though almost equal in numbers, Latinos maintain a lower profile in the community, as African Americans own more businesses and serve more prominently in local positions of leadership.

Cornerstone members were aware of this division prior to the residency, as one of the stated goals of the Watts project was to build bridges between these two communities. The National Endowment for the Arts had provided Cornerstone with a substantial grant to create theater that involved bridging boundaries between communities. Cornerstone's first sequence of residencies in Los Angeles between 1992 and 1993 had culminated in *L.A. Building,* bringing together the Arab American, Pacoima, and Angelus Plaza Senior Center communities. "In the second sequence of residencies," explains Bill Rauch, "we wanted to work with two communities that were geographically proximate but culturally distinct and potentially in conflict."[20]

This intra-community bridge-building goal at first seemed worthwhile to Cornerstone ensemble members and to board member Alejandro Nuño, a key proponent of the Watts residency. Nuño, who worked in Pacoima in the San Fernando Valley, had joined Cornerstone's board following *Rushing Waters* (1993). Nuño had also cofounded the Watts/Century Latino Organization (WCLO), which worked to bring together Latinos and African Americans in Watts. Already involved in bridging the two communities, Nuño led the drive to bring Cornerstone to Watts in order to further this goal. The expressed mission of bridge building had its problems however. As Rauch elucidates:

> As soon as we started working in Watts, a year in advance, putting together an advisory board and meeting with people, we began to realize how problematic it was to have the self-proclaimed goal of the project be to work [separately] with African Americans and with Latinos and then bring them together. To have any component of the project be about separation was problematic. But by the time we decided to address that issue we realized that structures of separation were already in place [in the community].[21]

Cornerstone members eventually recognized that their proclaimed goal in Watts implied a dubious power dynamic. By working separately with and then bringing together the two groups, Cornerstone might be ignoring other organizations and occasions in Watts that integrated Latinos and African Americans. Cornerstone could be perceived by these organizations as "looking for a fight," which they would mediate through the production process. As Rauch also pointed out, Latinos such as Nuño were passionate about focusing at least one of the projects in a Latino neighborhood. They felt that Latinos would otherwise get lost in the process due to African American political dominance in Watts. As it turned out, finding any kind of neutral space for the performances proved a challenge.

Though chosen through collaboration with an advisory board composed of both African American and Latino community leaders, Cornerstone members soon realized that audition and performance sites carried real and symbolic perceptions of ethnic association for Watts residents. While black and Latino children lived in the same neighborhoods and attended school together, several students and their parents claimed that they were afraid to enter territories they felt to be guarded by gang members from the other group—despite the fact that the city-run Watts Towers Arts Center hosted the "African American" performance and the "Latino" site was located in a church. By the time the company recognized this, the first shows had been cast. *The Love of the Nightingale* and *Breaking Plates* involved entirely African American performers. *Los Faustinos* had a mainly Latino cast, and the majority of guest artists, including the show's writer and director, were of Hispanic descent. The production was thus perceived as "Latino." This perception was reinforced when an African American member of the *Nightingale* cast joined and then quit *Los Faustinos,* citing her discomfort with the fact that "this was the Latino show."

This temporary cast member also believed that "the Latino show" had more resources, reflecting the fact that Cornerstone had decided to experiment in Watts with producing both larger epic and smaller chamber shows.

Cornerstone members felt that these smaller-scale shows could serve as a better model for seeding community theater. However, the company had not effectively communicated this distinction to the casts of either show. Thus, to many participants, it seemed as though Cornerstone favored the Latino community. This misperception initially increased rather than decreased tensions between the two shows, and the two groups.

At a September 1994 planning day, Cornerstone ensemble members discussed the perceptions and tensions that had arisen through lack of communication. The company tried to increase African American staffing on *Los Faustinos* but encountered difficulties because of the specific skills needed and the time involved. When the *Nightingale* actress quit *Los Faustinos,* ensemble members recognized the importance of more clearly defining their goals for the community. At a November ensemble meeting, the company resolved to reexamine site selection and the audition system for future shows in Watts. Remaining productions engaged a more mixed performance crew and audience. By the final bridge performance, the actress who had initially quit *Los Faustinos* confessed how much she had overcome her own prejudices through the *Chalk Circle* rehearsal.

COMMUNITIES AND GANGS

Relationships between guest artists and residents and Latinos and African Americans eventually improved. One final negotiation within Watts centered on a group that remained excluded from production development, raising questions about the limits of Cornerstone's inclusive ethics.

The Watts advisory board consisted mainly of civic leaders, some of whom had connected Cornerstone with Officer Robert Perez, a safety official who advised company members to avoid certain areas, watched over the San Miguel parking lot, generally sanctioned the production, and established a link with local police officials. The presence and warnings of Perez and other city officials raised concerns with *Los Faustinos* guest director Juliette Carillo, who had already cast a member of La Colonia, a Latino gang in the San Miguel area. She and others felt that the more official civic representatives might have been unnecessarily biased against local gang members. After talking further with community members, and after the gang member did not show up for rehearsals because he had been imprisoned for first-degree murder, Carillo became reluctantly convinced that including the gang member would have excluded those in the community who felt uncomfortable working with him.

Los Faustinos did eventually include gang members in the audience, leading to an intriguing exchange within the performance. Towards the end of

In *Los Faustinos* (1994), Christopher Liam Moore as Mephisto plotting to purchase the souls of the sleeping Faustino family, Watts residents José Luis Ortiz, Diana Flores *(center),* and Ava Chavez *(right).*

the second act, a gang bullet strikes and kills the college-bound Martín Faustino. The aesthetic of the show embraced the Mexican *Teatro* tradition and was thus narrated by La Muerte (death), a conventional *Teatro* character. In the show, La Muerte takes the bullet in his hand, traveling in silence to strike Martín's heart. The community cast then joins together over Martín's death in the Faustino rose garden. During a unifying cast song, children presented roses to front-row audience members. In several of the shows, these flowers were accepted by attending gang members.

Revising Urban Communities

The presence and exclusion of gang members reinforced certain myths about violence in Watts—myths propagated by the Watts Riots of late 1960s and embodied in films such as *Menace II Society* (1993). Much of the actual production and process in Watts entailed dispelling these myths. While *Los Faustinos* included violent moments, the show also worked to expand outsider perceptions of Watts. As one community participant in *Los Faustinos* commented in the show's evaluation: "[*Los Faustinos*] is about Watts because there is violence, but it lets us know that not everyone in Watts is gang-related. It dispels the myth even for the people in the community."

Cornerstone's collaborative re-presentation of Watts offers one method of revising these perceptions. For nonresidents, such as myself, physically entering the community was enough to dispel some misperceptions about the area. Ensemble member Benajah Cobb's entrance into the city echoes my own experience:

> The visual landscape of the city was so unfamiliar, in terms of the stereo-types I had. . . . if there's any sort of petty image I had of being afraid of the place, it was a thirty-story apartment complex. [When I got to Watts I thought] what is all this talk? These are like houses and yards and families. They all looked the same. It's so stupid, but instantly, [I had] no fear at all, from that moment, of going anywhere in that city. [The physical landscape of the city ended up] striking down that fear picture I had.[22]

Entering Watts rewrote the community for Cobb, me, and most Cornerstone members, even before the rehearsal process had begun. The landscape of the area made it less fearful, less stereotypically a "ghetto" or "inner city." This specific materiality replaced images and media myth with subjective experience, individually rewriting community identity for production participants. Further rehearsal transactions led to additional community revisions.

In conversing with retired state official Bill Nesbit, chess enthusiast Karen Ashe, theater graduate M. C. Earl, and honors student Chris Toler, all participants in *The Love of the Nightingale*, I realized that I had entered the process with biases about the socioeconomic and educational makeup of the community. The rehearsal process provided a context of commonality through which these misperceptions could be dispelled through conversation. At the same time, personal interactions exposed further complications of community boundaries and definitions.

One evening during dress rehearsal, Earl narrated a revealing story about himself, his lifestyle, and his involvement with community conflict and healing. Earl had been placed in a juvenile hall for driving with a suspended license "or something stupid like that." Sitting on his bunk bed, he felt the invading eyes of a young Korean upon him. "What are you waiting for, a proposal?" Earl challenged. The Korean explained that Earl simply looked familiar to him. After talking further, the two youths realized that they had worked together in an intra-community unification program following the 1992 Los Angeles riots.

Earl's narrative proposed how community belonging and exclusion could be read and rewritten. Within the context of the juvenile hall, Earl drew boundaries of ethnicity, illustrated by how he at first identified the other occupant as Korean. Individual transactions redrew this ethnic boundary of difference, reminding Earl and the other young man of a different commonality, one centered on crossing boundaries and uniting across ethnic difference.

Earl's narration of this event provoked further dialogue. Upon hearing the story, former juvenile officer and *Nightingale* participant Bill Nesbit asked in which hall Earl had stayed. The two proceeded to engage in a friendly, informed, and politically aware discussion about the juvenile justice system, including the cultural and socioeconomic causes of social rebellion and oppression. The context of the rehearsal process allowed for the enactment of common bonds between Earl and Nesbit. Though they could be perceived as divided by the roles of juvenile officer and delinquent, they crossed these boundaries through a shared understanding of the juvenile hall experience, within the unifying ritual of creating a play.

The rehearsal process provided numerous opportunities for participants to cross and redraw perceived cultural boundaries. *Los Faustinos* cast member Cynthia Bañuelo notes in her program biography, "This has been my first time I have worked with other people that are not from here." On the surface, Bañuelo's statement seems clear, reinforcing Cornerstone's mission of bringing people together and bridging communities. But Bañuelo's statement also provokes the question of where "here" is. Cornerstone explored this issue in a rehearsal game called "cultural mapping."

Cultural mapping, which Cornerstone borrowed from Molly Smith, formerly of the Perseverance Theater, illustrates how community boundaries can be continuously redrawn. Ensemble member Christopher Moore and guest director Juliette Carillo introduced *Los Faustinos* participants to this game on their second day of rehearsal. Participants, including residents, guest artists, and Cornerstone members, grouped themselves in response to a variety of associations, first dividing themselves onto a map of the world marking where they had been born. The group within the United States then divided into those born inside and outside California, Los Angeles, Watts, and finally San Miguel. The company replayed the exercise with varying divisions—according to age, number of languages spoken, and political affiliations. Within each division, groups had to pronounce one statement that described all of them. This last exercise underlined the difficulty of specifying the details of symbolic community construction that Anthony Cohen elucidates, as larger groups had greater difficulty coming up with a statement that unified them.

The way the game worked to include both "insiders" and "outsiders" to the Watts, Cornerstone, and professional theater communities additionally emphasized the relativeness of insider boundaries. The game implied that through the rehearsal process, preconceived boundaries could be redrawn on all sides. At a later Cornerstone planning day, Ashby Semple related a moment illustrating how the *Nightingale* production process allowed cultural stereotypes to be mutually dispelled: "One cast member was very aware how two white people [she and stage manager Nick Gilhool] lost their color during the process, in a good way."[23] This cast member had at first identified Semple and Gilhool primarily as "white people." Following rehearsal interactions, primary identification focused on their role in the rehearsal process and on their personas as individuals. As Semple further explained to me, these participants found that the rehearsal process allowed them to rewrite some of their preconceptions about whiteness, just as it allowed me to rewrite some of my preconceptions about Watts.

The rehearsal process made visible the complexity of negotiating internal and external boundaries of community. At times, structures within Watts, such as the absence of any "neutral" audition and performance sites, reinforced community divisions. For the most part, the rehearsal process enabled crossovers and the blurring of community boundaries. At the same time, as in many of its rural productions, the performance process reinforced mutuality while obscuring some complexities of community interaction.

COMMUNITAS CONUNDRUMS

Performance events framing the opening night of *Los Faustinos* underlined collaborative community involvement. Bilingual posters, publicity, and marketing, translated by playwright Bernardo Solano and guest artist David Barerra, with the help of cast members, ensured the inclusion of the Latino community. The program noted that Cornerstone was presenting the production "in association with the Watts/Century Latino Organization (WCLO) and San Miguel Catholic School." The program also included a description of other sponsoring organizations including the WCLO and the Watts Health Foundation. In the listing of thanks to funders, community organizations were prioritized above the names of individuals. Cornerstone additionally clarified earlier confusion about the purpose of production scale, explaining the difference between epic and chamber shows, and included an invitation for interested community members to work on the next Cornerstone coproduction in Watts.

The evening itself also emphasized community collaboration. The Watts advisory board hosted an opening night reception in the San Miguel School attended by Cornerstone board members, local police officers, and production, church, and school staff. Area children sold tickets and candy at the door and ushered the sold-out audience to bleacher seats. Watts residents, reception attendees, and actors from *The Love of the Nightingale* crowded along the sidelines and spilled onto the floor. Friends, relatives, and admirers of Cornerstone from Santa Monica, Hollywood, and outlying suburbs, most of whom had never before crossed the boundary into Watts, also waited in anticipation. As the lights darkened, the audience "shushed" each other in a comradely way.

Production semiotics reinforced this sense of camaraderie among audience members. Uniform bleachers and general admission ticketing disrupted the conventional hierarchy of audience seating. As the show progressed, the audience even began to blend with performers as children sitting on the floor in front of the bleachers crept into the performance space. Watching the play about Watts, taking place in Watts, performed by a group that included predominantly residents of Watts, among friends, family, and neighbors of the entire company, we the audience united in a moment of *communitas*.

This moment was both moving and temporary, overcoming and de-emphasizing the complexities of boundary negotiation during the production process. While a positive feeling about the show continued to inspire the cast and company, these negotiations also continued. The publication of laudatory reviews raised issues about the public perceptions of community collaboration. Though the highly positive reviews cited the performance of community participants as well as Cornerstone members, the reviews positioned Cornerstone as the sole producer of the show, and community leaders within the cast felt slighted. Many participants felt that the reviews erased the agency of community cosponsorship, and some blamed Cornerstone for this neglect.

This incident in Watts again points towards one of the many difficulties of producing theater within a diversified and dispersed urban environment. In this case, the urban cultural system, within which "professional" theater operates, amplified the difficulty of promoting unconventional artistic collaborations. Critics can endow a theater with professionalism via the conventions of a review. In the small-town environment of Cornerstone's early productions, public response tended towards feature articles and subjective, friendly reviews. Writers, sometimes participants in the production, highlighted the community sponsorship of the production. In the critical context of conventional professional theater, urban reviewers tended to establish the Cornerstone Theater Company as the sole producer of the artistic event.

In general, however, the moment of *communitas* experienced on opening night inspired a successful production run, infusing the cast, crew, and Cornerstone members with a feeling of unity and submerging many of the stressful aspects of the production process. In this atmosphere of camaraderie, I experienced difficulty communicating some of my own frustrations with the *Nightingale* rehearsal process; I too performed community, emphasizing the positive aspects of *communitas* and sublimating the problematic, exclusionary aspects of the production experience. Determining how to communicate those frustrations, which exist alongside many more positive moments, has led to ongoing conversations with Cornerstone members.

Reciprocal Reflections

I left Los Angeles before the evaluation of *Nightingale* occurred but did manage to speak about my experience with Bill Rauch. At the time, memories of *communitas* and camaraderie remained stronger than those of the dissonances experienced in the rehearsal process, more clearly reflected in my journal. I also held opinions about *Breaking Plates* that remained unexpressed to Semple, as I felt that it was not my place as a dramaturg and assistant to critique the process while working within it. Almost a decade later, I look back on these events as a scholar attempting to enunciate an engaged critical response to community-based performance—a scholar who has, moreover, chastised another colleague for withholding her opinion during the rehearsal process. I wonder, again, how I can reflect upon and most effectively communicate my critique *with* rather than against Cornerstone. This reflection weaves together my interpretations with responses from Cornerstone members and community participants.

My frustrations at the time of the production centered on Cornerstone's difficulties supporting relatively new directors within the company and on a lack of structure and follow-up with some community participants. Though Semple had been adamant about hiring M. C. Earl as a community actor, she was less able to supervise the additional responsibilities included in this hiring. Guest artists hired by Cornerstone to work on community projects were expected to work as mentors and assistants outside of their own rehearsal responsibilities. Thus, Cornerstone had hired Earl as both actor and assistant designer. Because of scheduling difficulties, however, designer Lynn Jeffries had to miss several weeks of the rehearsal process, so she was also unable to supervise Earl. No one else had the time to provide Earl with a structure within which to work, so he sometimes felt at a loss as to what he should be doing.

In addition to this frustration with process, I held a difference of opinion about the community's collaboration on *Breaking Plates,* an original piece about the Watts Towers presented as a prelude to *Nightingale.* Artists within Cornerstone have a variety of methods for engaging community collaboration, and Semple did include participating children's responses to the towers in the *Breaking Plates* text. I felt, however, that the script neglected to confront the perceived divisions between Watts and the county government of Los Angeles that oversaw the towers. M. C. Earl and Irma Ashe spoke strongly about these divisions on an excursion to the Watts Towers with the cast of *Breaking Plates.*

Ashe, who had lived in the area for over fifty years, rebelled at the admission price she was now expected to pay to enter the city-run facility: "[The city worker] wanted to charge us a dollar. I used to play in the Towers as a kid and now they want to charge us a dollar. I said, 'Nope.'" Earl discussed the political and social symbolism of the fence now surrounding the towers: "The fence reminds me of jail, or better yet, being locked out. The most colorful object in the city and they want to keep us away from it. Yes, we understand that the fence keeps out the vandals, but it also keeps us out."[24] I felt these statements to be essential in constructing a history of the towers from the perspective of the community participants. By not including the information, the production lost an important critical frame of reference, from my point of view.

Of course, I relate and support a subjective opinion about the show's politics, problematically stated long after the fact. In responding to these comments, Bill Rauch expressed disappointment with this lack of communication at the time, while acknowledging that Cornerstone tends not to seek out community exposés, trying to balance between celebrating and examining the challenges within a community. The question remains, who defines appropriate representational politics in collaborative productions: the community, Cornerstone artists, or some temporary critic/participant-observer? In this book's introduction, I discussed Sara Brady's response to *Steelbound,* which took Cornerstone and Touchstone Theaters to task for including Bethlehem Steel in their production. From Brady's point of view, this inclusion limited the show's potential for radicality. Even within Cornerstone, differences of opinion about the politics of this production emerged. After watching a CBS news show about the production (which he had not seen), Stephen Gutwillig expressed discomfort with the media's response. CBS lauded the show, asserting that positive responses from both Bethlehem Steel and former steelworkers evidenced the production's success. Gutwillig wondered: "Who wins and who loses around attempts to create so-called balance? Who loses, in my opinion, are the people who always lose. In the case of that community it's the workers who had already lost."[25] Playwright Alison Carey responded:

> The plant was long since closed, and *Steelbound* wasn't going to make it reopen no matter what its content. In the text and in the eventual production, the workers got to publicly establish their ownership of the mill and the role it played in building our country. I wonder what it was the workers lost.[26]

Others within the company proposed that bringing together management and workers enacts a different kind of politics, given a society in which "so many forces work to isolate members of different classes and communities."[27] This issue is not easily resolvable, and the company continues to wrestle with the representational politics that arise with efforts to cross various class boundaries. Intriguingly, internal controversy over *The Love of the Nightingale* focused less on the politics of representation than on the production's aesthetic choices.

AESTHETIC REVISIONS

During the company's first five years, Bill Rauch had directed all of Cornerstone's productions, Lynn Jeffries had designed, and members of the company had developed adaptations in concert with community partners. Consequently, rural shows tended to have an identifiable Cornerstone aesthetic. Along with the integration of local culture discussed in chapter 3, this aesthetic embraced dynamic staging, ensemble choreography, original songs, and choral commentary, with often surprising use of physical space. Norcatur residents still recall Christopher Liam Moore's entrance as Damis from the top of a basketball net. Adaptations often transformed lyrical verse passages into songs that reflected a particular local rhythm. The track team in Port Gibson grew so enchanted with teammate Edret Brinston's hip-hop soliloquies as Romeo that they incorporated parts of the show into their drills. Dancing gas pumps in *The Winter's Tale* typify some of the playful choral elements the company incorporated into productions, while also exemplifying the ongoing sense of motion in rural stagings. Bill Rauch excels at directing this kind of narrative-based production that unfolds in a generous, accessible manner.

Upon moving to Los Angeles, Cornerstone members expanded both the scope and nature of their productions. Guest artists and ensemble members contributed to the direction, design, and development of Cornerstone shows. New ensemble members and experienced theater artists Page Leong, Shishir Kurup, and Armando Molina radically expanded the aesthetic vision of the company, as did collaborations with playwright Lisa Loomer, director Juliette Carillo, and musicians David Markowitz and Joe Romano. Instead of relying on adaptation, the company experimented with developing original productions with communities. Kurup's training with Tadashi Suzuki, Leong's dance background, and Molina's experience with sketch comedy added more physical dimensions to the company's productions.

Some experiments with guest artists proved problematic. Armando Molina speaks for many Cornerstone members in expressing discomfort with Peter Sellars's tenure as a guest director in Boyle Heights in 1998: "Though he empathized with [the community's] 'oppression,' as he understood it, he never actually spent time there. Instead he affirmed his own misperceptions."[28] Bill Rauch acknowledges the disconnect between Sellars and the ensemble but feels that the company eventually learned a great deal from the collaboration. "As a renegade artist his instinct is to distrust and even destroy institutions," observes Rauch, noting both the pain and the positive results emerging from Sellars's challenge to the company. "He raised questions about the ensemble that led us to undergo a process of restructuring that made us stronger as a company."[29] "Peter thinks of himself as a trickster," adds Shishir Kurup. "The fact is his presence was disruptive and painful but ultimately powerful for the company, due less to him than to our own self-reflexivity."[30]

Outside artists can be effective irritants, rejuvenating the company's work. Following a difficult period developing *For Here or To Go,* an impressed artistic associate of the Mark Taper Forum related to the company, "We kept dumping cinders on your head and you just used them as fuel."[31] Artistic irritants overturn assumptions, while raising important questions about how much control Cornerstone should maintain over community-based productions. Questions about the company's contemporary, locally resonant, collaborative aesthetic were first raised by *The Love of the Nightingale* production but developed from changes in artistic direction after the company's move to Los Angeles.

According to Bill Rauch, early in their urban work, Cornerstone had begun "climbing out of the consensus model of artistic directing."[32] Company members grew less willing to subsume their individual artistic identity within the group. *The Toy Truck* (1992), coproduced with the Angelus

Plaza senior community, was the last show adapted by the group as a whole. When Shishir Kurup directed *Ghurba* in 1993, the company reached another milestone. Once the door had opened for individuals other than Rauch to direct Cornerstone productions, ensemble members such as Semple expressed interest in directing for the company. At the same time, Lynn Jeffries communicated her desire to try working with noncontemporary designs.

While the hunger for more artistic individuality grew, production scheduling at the commencement of the Watts residency complicated the company's ability to work with Semple and Jeffries. Cornerstone was experimenting with running one show, the ensemble production *Everyman at the Mall* (1994), while beginning rehearsals for three other shows—*Breaking Plates, The Love of the Nightingale,* and *Los Faustinos.* Because *Everyman* took place in a shopping mall, rehearsals either commenced under the stressful circumstances of competing with mall crowds or began after closing time at 9 P.M. Continuous technical problems and ongoing long-term planning responsibilities meant that Rauch had less time to supervise the Watts residency. Additionally, upon completion of *Everyman's* run, Rauch and Lynn Jeffries flew to Mexico for a Theater Communications Group–sponsored two-week artistic exchange program.

This constellation of events left Semple with strong ideas and little company guidance. She chose to direct an original play about the community, *Breaking Plates,* and a contemporary adaptation of a Greek myth, Timberlake Wertenbaker's *Love of the Nightingale.* Semple had intended to further adapt the text to resonate more directly with the Watts community, in concert with Cornerstone methodology. However, after an initial read through with the cast, at which they expressed their desire to work with an unadapted script, Semple determined to leave Wertenbaker's text as written. At the same time, Semple decided that she would like the costumes to reflect a Greek influence. Jeffries, who had been "getting kind of bored with the same old updating tricks," responded positively to this suggestion.[33] Thus the show reflected a more metaphorical and historical and less direct connection to the community.

The stress of *Everyman,* the greater needs of the larger *Los Faustinos* show, the necessity to commence long-term planning, the Mexico trip, cofounder Alison Carey's pregnancy, and Semple's desire for independence all conspired to keep Rauch and Carey from direct involvement in the *Nightingale* rehearsal process. It was not until they saw the show that they realized that it did not represent to them a "Cornerstone aesthetic." Indeed, the discomfort they felt raised the issue of whether the company needed to define and mandate an aesthetic. At a December 1994 planning day, some ensemble

Watts residents Bill Nesbitt *(left)* and Chris Toler *(right)* and guest artist
C. J. Jones *(standing)* in *The Love of the Nightingale* (1994). Photo:
Lynn Jeffries.

members noted that "setting [the production] in the past, with no adaptation, and connecting to the community in a metaphoric rather than literal
way, brings up questions about whether here-and-now shows are a part of
our artistic mandate."[34] Carey and then Managing Director Stephen Gutwillig felt that communication was at issue: "[The company] should have
artistic meetings about every show. We tell people that we do reflect community in a piece; if we're not going to we need to explain."[35]

The phrasing of these comments suggests a legitimate concern and potential remedy for regulating or explicating Cornerstone's aesthetic identity. The company had expressly told community cosponsors that all Cor-

nerstone shows would *directly* reflect the community. Semple's choice, made without reference to Cornerstone's statements to the community, thus seemed to some members to undermine Cornerstone's reliability. Semple responded that mandating aesthetic output for full-time ensemble members felt to her like a creative death sentence. Her choices were also grounded specifically in the mandate of community participants, who were vociferous at the first read through about their desire to keep the text as it was. I was present at this reading and grew excited by the possibilities present in the text as read at the time. Cast members vocally reacted to the events of the story with comments such as "you tell him" and "shut up" when the loquacious Philomele confronted her brother-in-law about her disgust for his desire. This reaction convinced Semple, Jeffries, the cast, and me that the community could react to the contemporary resonance of the story without further adaptation.[36] Yet, during the show itself, this vocal commentary was absent, suggesting to some Cornerstone members that text and costuming had prevented the audience from attending to the story's resonance.

Bill Rauch later wondered whether a design compromise might have better served the production and the community. Since the chorus in Wertenbaker's text often comments on the Philomele story as though it were a past event, perhaps costumes could have reflected a distinction between a contemporary chorus and historical characters.[37] While this particular choice may not have satisfied artists working on the production, the process of aesthetic contemplation bore fruit in the *Chalk Circle* production, which embraced a more fantastical design. *Chalk Circle* also benefited from greater experience with engaging the community in its own reflection, and, not insignificantly, from a larger budget and lengthier production process.

While *Los Faustinos* directly reflected the community of San Miguel through its localized setting and framing of community issues, the design, adaptation, and production process did not always operate with input from community participants. Designer Katherine Ferwerda's bedrooms, constructed in the style of altars, referred to Mexican American culture and *Teatro* forms[38] but did not directly involve the community in creation and decision making. To be fair to Ferwerda and others working on *Los Faustinos,* Cornerstone had not codified or communicated ideas about inclusive methodology. At the *Faustinos* evaluation in December 1994, Cornerstone members and guest artists recognized that lack of time, personnel, and inexperience with Cornerstone methodology had led to some miscommunication. Guest artists cited a lack of clarity in terms of their expectations and responsibilities. Ferwerda felt overwhelmed by the chaos and time constraints of the process. Some damage had been done, but Cornerstone members resolved to clarify and communicate methodology to future guest artists, emphasizing the importance of explaining and involving community members in their work.

Evaluations of *Sid Arthur* in July of 1995 and *The Central Ave. Chalk Circle* in November of 1995 suggest that participants and cosponsors felt more engaged in the creative process. *Sid Arthur* guest designer Nephelie Andonyadis led workshops that directly involved community participants in the show's design. A Cornerstone newsletter noted, "At 4-H Club Centers, the Senior Activity Center and the Watts Towers Arts Center, nearly 200 participants created birds, mandalas and 'mind mazes' which reflected the journeys of their lives and formed the basis of the play's scenery."[39] Neighborhood children presented an impromptu preshow skit at one performance. The experiences of the first residencies seemed to inform a greater and more mutual community participation in later Watts coproductions.

Coming Together with a Chalk Circle

The length of Cornerstone's fifteen-month residency in Watts, and ongoing projects with residents, allowed for increased aesthetic and social transactions among the various communities within the city, Cornerstone, and the professional theater community. Cornerstone's final coproduction, an adaptation of Bertolt Brecht's *Caucasian Chalk Circle,* brought together participants and associates from previous Watts productions as well as further bridging Cornerstone and Watts connections to the larger theater community. *Los Faustinos* playwright Bernardo Solano provided Spanish translations for *The Central Ave. Chalk Circle* adaptation scripted by Lynn Manning. Ed Haynes, a staff designer at the Mark Taper Forum, created the set for the production. Children who had acted in *Breaking Plates* ran crew for *Sid Arthur* and *Chalk Circle.* Benefit shows provided funding for Cornerstone's cosponsors and cemented Cornerstone's community involvement.

Within the adaptation and production process, Cornerstone worked to increasingly involve community members. Before putting together a production company the ensemble agreed on the inclusive priorities of the show at a 20 January 1995 ensemble meeting. The production would employ either a Latino or an African American writer or director, use a bilingual script, and include participants of all ages and cultural backgrounds from the four previous Watts and Cornerstone coproductions. The company eventually hired Los Angeles–based writer Lynn Manning, an African American artist raised in South Central Los Angeles, near Watts. The ensemble also expressed a desire that the production have a direct scripted and aesthetic connection to Watts, while exploring issues of cultural difference and the more fluid boundaries of community. The resultant production and adaptation engaged issues of aesthetics, community involvement, and cultural representation with a refreshing and somewhat controversial directness.

Lynn Manning's script confronted issues of racism, sexism, and class with and through Brecht's epic characters. Inspired by the earthiness of Brecht's writing, Manning endowed characters with language that at first offended and confused community participants. Manning set his adaptation in a near-future America in which California has recently seceded from the union. In one scene, an officer of the New Republic of California confronts Gertha Gibson, played by local African American actress Sándra Layne. Provoked by Gibson, the officers (ensemble member Christopher Liam Moore and then guest artist Armando Molina), wearing pig noses, inflict her with a stream of stereotyped invectives about her love for fried chicken, crack cocaine, and doggy-style sex. "As you can imagine," explained Bill Rauch in an interview following my viewing of the production, "there was a fair amount of controversy over the line. A lot people who recognized the parody were really into it and a lot of people found it offensive."[40] Rauch and I spoke about the line in terms of cultural representation as well as community involvement. While Manning, in this instance, remained firm about its inclusion, in other ways he respected community input and changed the language of the play to reflect this sensibility. Comments Rauch, "'Fucking' appeared in the play several times and Lynn eventually took it out after listening to the community's response."

Despite Manning's artistic convictions, in a number of ways the show reflected community input to a greater extent than previous Watts productions. Though the actual text was not set in the here and now, the show's prologue, reset as a town meeting, directly reflected community concerns, was directed by a community participant, and was written with input from Watts performers.

The show's embodiment both reflected and complicated assumptions about the Watts community. The actors, mostly African American or Latino/a, drew attention to the city's ethnic makeup. At the same time, the roles that participants played deconstructed gender and ethnicity, often framing their performative nature, and illustrating how ethnicity can cross class boundaries. Latino actor Armando Molina played the bigoted Officer Superior as well as a manipulative Latina mother. African Americans played the working-class hero and heroine, Derrick and Gertha, as well as the wealthy and corrupt Senator Charles. Racial epithets implied divisiveness, but multiracial choruses offered another view of community.

Americans tend to emphasize the importance of race and ethnicity over class. Lynn Manning worked against this perception, stating: "I stayed with [Brecht's class politics], definitely. Because I think the truth about what ails the society is more about class than race."[41] Manning also took care to portray characters reacting to and against their social circumstances. The fact that the main villainous characters were played by a Latino man and Asian woman and a scheming senator was played by a black man (Manning himself) is subordinate to the characters' wealth and greed.[42] Minor characters also reacted to the circumstances caused by the revolution. A black car jacker takes Gertha's vehicle and money to escape from Watts. A Latino store owner gouges prices on milk and cookies, explaining, "There's a state of emergency going on."[43] Gertha's rich black sister-in-law struggles to keep her from staying in the wine country, fearful of the costs the stay will entail.

In contrast to the show's inclusiveness and complex community embodiment, the production's nonrealistic aesthetics enacted a potential sea change in the manifestation of Cornerstone's "aesthetic identity." While Rauch had

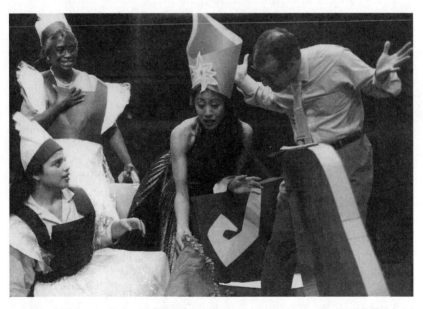

In act 1 of *The Central Ave. Chalk Circle* (1995), Watts residents Irma Ashe *(standing)* and Rocio Novoa as maids to Antoinette Montoya, played by Cornerstone ensemble member Page Leong. Guest artist (and later ensemble member) Armando Molina, as Press Secretary Buck Wild, gestures behind Leong. All wear paper and cardboard accessories. Photo: Jan Mabry.

been a vocal opponent of Semple's aesthetic choices in *Nightingale,* in many ways *The Central Ave. Chalk Circle* departed even further from the contemporary local realism the company had previously promoted as a "Cornerstone aesthetic."[44] Reasons for this departure mainly arose from Lynn Manning's adaptive take on the story of *Chalk Circle* itself. In Brecht's original, a contemporary prelude precedes the narration of an ancient tale that illuminates issues discussed in the prelude. Rauch and Manning felt that given the events of the play and their desire to maintain a contemporary prologue set in Watts, they had to establish a contrasting world for the remainder of the play:

> We felt we could not set it in 1995 because of the events that happened in the play. For a while Lynn and I tried to fit it in 1992 with the riots and it just didn't add up, because there needed to be a social conflict that went on for several years not just several days in order for the child to grow. We ended by setting the play in the very near future.

With the setting resolved, Jeffries encouraged Rauch to think about a nonrealistic design. She became excited by Lynn Manning's choice to divide Brecht's narrator into two characters and proposed that the design style change to reflect the style of the two narrators. At first Rauch resisted, feeling that this choice would be less accessible and interesting to an audience than contemporary realism, but given the somewhat fantastic narrative structure of the play, Rauch eventually agreed.

Jeffries designed the show in accordance with the narrative points of view of Azdak the artist and Gertha Gibson, a maintenance worker. In the first act, narrated by Azdak (Shishir Kurup), the production had a cartoony, expressionistic feel. Jeffries constructed the props and costume pieces from cardboard, paper, and chalk, the medium of Azdak's artwork (and a play on *Chalk Circle*). In the second act, narrated by Gibson, the aesthetic reflected a janitorial world, with duct tape handcuffs, crushed soda can police badges, and judge's robes made from plastic garbage bags.[45] In the final scene in which Gibson and Azdak appear together and neither narrates, the aesthetic reverts to realism. While the show as a whole did not entirely reflect the local setting of Watts, Jeffries's aesthetic choices achieved many of the same ends as earlier Cornerstone productions.[46]

When Rauch had directed another Brecht-based play, *The Good Person of Long Creek* (1988), in Oregon, he had discussed Cornerstone's adaptation of classic theatrical works to contemporary contexts in the Brechtian terms of defamiliarizing the familiar and of familiarizing the unfamiliar. That show, set in a cattle barn, framed the local space, culture, and community participants through performative representation. In *Chalk Circle,* the less

In act 2 of *The Central Ave. Chalk Circle* (1995), Cornerstone ensemble member Shishir Kurup as Azdak the judge, in garbage bag robe. He is flanked by Watts residents Aaron Meeks *(left)* and Marcie Ramirez *(right),* as Azdak's wards. Photo: Jan Mabry.

locally resonant production aesthetic had the effect of defamiliarizing the familiar symbols of a larger cultural reality. In the final, more "realistic" scene, symbols of authority—a police uniform, the judge's robe, the police badges—had a greater resonance because of their earlier juxtaposition to more playful representations: robes made from garbage bags and crushed soda can badges. The playfulness framed the realism in a way that addressed Brecht's notion of the alienation effect, defamiliarizing the familiar, and reawakening the audience into seeing what was not normally attended to, such as the symbols that transform an individual into a figure of authority.

While the text, production, and actors all emphasized class politics and their mobility, the economic context of production underlined the contradictions involved in producing a show critical of the extremes of capitalism. Minimal state support for artistic work in America dictates the need for either high ticket prices or institutional and individual funding. As Cornerstone strives to maintain accessibility to its productions, the company maintains a pay-what-you-can ticket policy for its community shows, necessitating outside funding. Much of this financial support, notes Rauch, was provided by corporate foundations and wealthy individuals, which the *Chalk Circle* production implicitly critiques. Rauch responds by asserting:

I know that's an old criticism loaded at Brecht, you know, people sipping champagne and eating caviar and going in to watch this indictment of the bourgeoisie and the class system. . . . I love the idea that Cornerstone could be supported in a 100% grassroots way and that every little child that we worked with sends in 50 cents of their allowance once a month and that that's how we pay for what we do, but the fact is that's not how we've been able to support ourselves.

Rauch suggests that the presence of wealthy individual Cornerstone supporters in the audience alongside Watts residents may actually have achieved a kind of social dynamic rarely felt within the audiences of more rigidly separatist regional and community theaters. By bringing together these individuals to experience the contradictions implied by the production, the show enacted a form of social interaction and potential change, similar to the collaboration of management and workers in *Steelbound*.

Cosponsorship of the production by the Watts Labor Community Action Committee (WLCAC) also complicates the fact of corporate and individual sponsorship. This group champions labor, in opposition to some corporate foundations supporting Cornerstone's work. Yet, WLCAC's philosophy points to the possibilities established by forging economic strength within the community. Rauch explains that founder Ted Watkins promoted the organization with the slogan "improve don't move": "The Watkins family urged people to do better economically and stay in the community, and to keep giving back to the community. WLCAC is a powerful entity in terms of empowering the community. That connects directly with our work."

The WLCAC warehouse setting for the production emphasized this tie to community sponsorship. Rauch staged the show to acknowledge rather than conceal this warehouse setting. At one point, background wall units opened up to reveal the entirety of the setting. The children reenacted an assassination far upstage, in the area of the prologue setting. Kidnappers drove onto this playing area in a working police car and van, opening the audience's point of view to take in the whole warehouse. The downstage action also emphasized the nature of the space, with a catwalk surrounding the main playing arena. The catwalk itself also completed the transactional exchange of space, sponsorship, and community support. At the end of the production run, it remained for the WLCAC's use. Community participants divided all other set pieces and props amongst themselves.

Through material and social exchange, process, adaptation, performance, audience, and setting, Cornerstone's *Chalk Circle* enacted a positive collaboration with the community of Watts. Yet, the fact of producing an adaptation, rather than original community storytelling, provoked controversy among some community artists and other individuals, persons mostly living outside of Watts. These individuals claimed that by not working directly with stories from collaborating communities, Cornerstone was in effect artistically colonizing these communities, or at least enacting a problematic power dynamic. Rauch elaborates:

> There are artists who have a problem with our representation. We interviewed different playwrights about working on this project. There was one playwright who I respect highly who was not interested because I wanted to direct *Chalk Circle*. He was hostile to the notion of an adaptation of a classic text for a community. He felt that communities need to tell their own stories. That's come up often for Cornerstone. I think it suggests that an adaptation of a German play, which is an adaptation of a Chinese play, is somehow not as good for a community because it's not as direct. I am troubled by those questions but also irritated by them. There are a lot of great stories that get passed around the world through human history.

LeRoi Jones (later Amiri Baraka) held a similar critique about classical texts. In a 1967 interview with Saul Gottlieb, Jones expressed disbelief that James Earl Jones would rather star in *Othello* than in his play *The Slave:* "Acting in stuff by Shakespeare and Molière is more important than a play about his own life."[47] Jones's critique remains valid, particularly within a more revolutionary social context. Yet, as I noted to Rauch at the time of our interview, I felt the attitude that adaptation is "not good for a community" implies that only intellectual middle-class European Americans should have access to world stories, even though those "European" stories are themselves rooted in other cultures. Herman Hesse based *Siddartha* on Hindu and Buddhist spiritual narratives. Brecht based *Chalk Circle* on an ancient Chinese story. Shakespeare adapted plots from Greek mythology, Roman playwrights, and his historical contemporaries. In each case, the authors translated one cultural epic to the context of their potential audience. Cornerstone's work proposes that when the residents of Watts claim and contextualize these stories, they enact social and political power. The rewriting of classic texts in the voice of the community prevents these texts from being selectively isolated for a middle-class audience or for university students. Involving community members directly in rewriting gives them a voice in the story's re-presentation. Resultant adaptations work against the idolization of the "original" text and notion that an audience needs to "rise to the level of the work" by learning the text's language.[48] "These classic plays," responds Rauch, "need to rise to the level of the community."

Cornerstone proposes a redefinition of the boundaries and context in which audiences receive and participate in writing "universal" stories. This community rewriting becomes political through the public act of representation. Theater is a representational medium and as such it has the power to provoke controversy about the content of representation. This controversy centers on issues of cultural authenticity, the nature of adaptation, community involvement in telling their stories, and the boundaries of community itself. Who decides what stories to tell? Who decides how to tell these stories? Who decides the limits and boundaries of community? The answers to these questions do not exist as authoritative truth. The debate that arises from addressing, framing, and asking the questions may itself provide insight into the validity and problematic aspects of the symbolic construction of community—a symbolism manifested in the representational aspects of theater.

Chalk Circle and the Watts residency as a whole ultimately worked towards larger concerns than expressing the community "in itself." *Chalk Circle* particularly worked to make audiences aware of how social forces impact individual and community behavior. Ironically, Cornerstone achieved this goal by moving away from either an idolization of Brecht's original text or an idolization of "the community." The collaboration among community participants, Cornerstone's cooperative methodology, and Brecht's text and ideology celebrated the community's participation while situating Watts within a larger social and historical context.

Ultimately, the production succeeded, in part because of the questions it provoked and as a result of this community collaboration. In her evaluation of the *Chalk Circle* experience, Assistant Stage Manager and Watts resident Janet Escobar provides evidence for the importance of Cornerstone's work with the Watts community. She cites Cornerstone's collaborative accessibility in drawing the community into the production, noting, "So few of the community would be able or willing to see a play elsewhere."[49] While much of Cornerstone's work succeeds in articulating the social forces that contribute to injustice, poverty, and racism, Escobar's comments point to the company's adherence to Brecht's caveat that a theater must above all engage. "A theatre which makes no contact with the public is nonsense," asserts Brecht.[50] Cornerstone's publicly accessible, thought-provoking, and aesthetically intriguing production of *Chalk Circle* was no-nonsense theater.

Chalk Circle succeeded on a critical level as well, as the production was nominated for an Ovation Award, Los Angeles's peer-judged version of the Tonys. *Chalk Circle* won the award for best production in a category including all 180 small-scale "professional" theater companies in Los Angeles. In accepting the award, Quentin Drew spoke quietly but firmly to the standing audience: "It's like a dream to stand here and represent Watts in something positive."

Cornerstone has continued to work with Watts participants throughout their tenure in Los Angeles. Drew has appeared in a number of productions. The LA bridge show *For Here or To Go* (2000) reunited Drew, the Escobars, M. C. Earl, and Theodora Hardie, among others. At a recent Festival of Faith ensemble production, I sat in the audience with Irma and Karen Ashe. The struggle to represent Watts, and expand the theater audience to include the wide variety of Los Angeles communities with whom Cornerstone has worked—Pacoima, library workers, police officers, those sharing a June 30th birthday, residents of Broadway and Hill Streets (Chinatown), Baldwin Hills, Boyle Heights, and Beverly Hills (the B. H. Cycle), immigrant Catholics and Buddhists (among many faith-based communities)—continues. Productions continue to confront the politics and dynamics of defining and redefining community and community artistry. Concurrent with these community collaborations in Los Angeles, the company has sought out other venues to develop their artistry and share their collaborative method, the very sites against which they had rebelled in 1986—regional theaters.

6

REGIONAL RETURNS: A TALE
OF TWO COLLABORATIONS

When Cornerstone is in its [community-based] environment there's
nothing else like it. You see people who would never have been in the
theater otherwise.
                        —Doug Wager, former artistic director, Arena Stage

Do I err on the side of excessive ambition when I say that if New Haven
can be captured onstage, we will have created a theatrical document which
may have much to say about the future of the American city?
                        —Doug Hughes, former artistic director, Long Wharf Theatre

Cornerstone's collaborations with Arena Stage in Washington, D.C., and
Long Wharf Theatre in New Haven, Connecticut, attempt in part to
stage each theater's urban community. But this chapter offers more than a
tale of two cities. "Regional Returns" relates the saga of two seemingly at-
odds theatrical practices, of two quite different collaborative processes, and,
not inconsequently, of two Dougs. Though narrative often suggests a lin-
ear progress through time, this tale centers on a series of returns: Cornerstone's return to the east coast regional theaters against which its founders
had initially rebelled, to a play that the company had already produced,
Brecht's *Good Woman of Setzuan*,[1] and to an often over-roasted holiday
chestnut, *A Christmas Carol*. This chapter also revisits assumptions about
the nature of and distinctions between community-based and regional theater, about the limits of inclusion, and about storytelling itself.

   The stance of the critic has been indirectly examined throughout *Staging America*. In previous chapters, I have looked at the relationship between
academic writing and community-based practice, investigated the nature
of performed ethnography, and adopted the role of a participant-observer.

"Regional Returns" builds on these various points of view. As I move among theories of urban geography and theatrical reception, materialist critiques and performance reviews, incorporating observations, interviews, and critical readings, as I shift between the tales of two collaborations, I alternate the more distanced stance of an analytic observer with the subjective involvement of a community-based practitioner. In doing so, I look at how two attempts to stage (parts of) America conjure distinct questions about representational ethics and artistry. While the landmark Arena coproduction broke ground on the nature of collaborative staging, New Haven's lengthier, more open-ended and flexible process, with multiple neighborhoods, forged stronger relationships among its collaborating partners. Yet, perhaps because of the difference between Dickens's familiar sentimentalism and Brecht's less customary cynicism, *A Community Carol* was generally better received by its subscriber audience. Determining which production was more "successful" demands, in the end, a reevaluation of the terms of theater making. In the meantime, this saga of institutions, ideals, and individuals calls for a number of perspectives to examine how the city and its surrounding community are staged and not staged in *A Community Carol* and *The Good Person of New Haven,* beginning with the institutional backdrop against which both collaborations played out.

Institutional Settings

Cornerstone did not seek out a relationship with either Arena Stage or Long Wharf, particularly as regional theater initially seemed anathema to the company's founders. "I think when we started there was kind of a 'burn down the house' mentality," elaborates ensemble member Christopher Liam Moore. "The company evolved because of a growing dissatisfaction we had with [professional] theater, being really upset by the audience. . . . it just didn't look like the world. It didn't even look like our classrooms at Harvard."[2] While important differences remain between the two practices, Cornerstone members have revised some of their assumptions about regional theater, understanding that the movement's initiating impulse also emerged from audience-based concerns.[3]

Zelda Fichandler founded Arena Stage in 1950 as part of a pioneering effort to decentralize professional theater, and to serve an audience outside of the economic, artistic, and geographic confines of Broadway. Over fifty years, Arena grew from a small experimental operation to a multi-theater institution employing a staff of over a hundred. Arena's mission in 1993 remained rooted in the liberal humanism Fichandler first enunciated, in "human centered stories" and "artistic excellence" derived through the "power of storytelling." Former Associate Artistic Director Laurence Maslon describes this as theater without a particular political agenda.[4] While Maslon's use of "political" refers here to the overt content of produced plays, Arena's defining structures—its decision-making, financial, and organizational compositions, even its professed humanism—embody a distinct contextual politics for producing theater.

Arena adopts a hierarchical decision-making structure that in the early 1990s strove to consider the artistic needs of the company's ever-decreasing (and eventually abolished) resident ensemble within the economic constraints of running a multimillion-dollar company.[5] While the arena stage that gives the theater its name embodies a self-conscious "democracy" in terms of audience seating, the Arena's administrative structure stages a necessarily limited access to power within the hierarchy.[6] Additionally, a white, middle-class audience base, 92 to 94 percent in 1993, according to then Artistic Director Doug Wager, challenges the company's rhetoric of inclusion and diversity.[7]

Long Wharf Theatre emerged from similar roots with related challenges. Jon Jory and Harlan Kleiman founded the company in 1965, with a distinctly regional mission. Long Wharf still defines itself as "cultivating audiences that reflect the state of Connecticut."[8] Yet, like many regional theaters such as Arena, Long Wharf depends upon a subscriber base that does not match this inclusive, diversified, and locally grounded description. According to the company's own statistics, 40 percent of Long Wharf's 11,000 member subscriber base resides outside of New Haven, and 20 percent live outside of the state.[9] Then Artistic Director Doug Hughes observed to me that in 1999 Long Wharf's 125,000 member seasonal audience included mainly older white suburban viewers.[10]

Arena Stage and Doug Wager

While similar in their institutional structures and audience base, each company's decision to collaborate with Cornerstone emerged from the discrete desires of their respective artistic directors, desires related to social and material concerns as well as aesthetic impulses. The Arena Stage collaboration arose initially from personal and artistic affinity between Bill Rauch and Doug Wager, and from a common funding sponsor. The two met and conversed at an AT&T dinner, following which Wager attended a production of *The Winter's Tale* on the Washington, D.C., mall in the early fall of 1991. Moved by the humanism and large-scale storytelling of the production, values important to both Cornerstone and Arena, Wager wondered whether he could somehow introduce his audience to Cornerstone's work. In a conversation with Rauch in early 1993, Wager invited Cornerstone to develop a community collaboration to be performed on Arena's main stage. According to Rauch, the potential to affect the way that Arena did business swayed Cornerstone ensemble members wary of working within regional theater's institutional context.[11]

An abundance of optimism about the project's potential benefits to both companies may have obscured a basic disjunction: Arena aspired to "mainstream Cornerstone's energy" while Cornerstone hoped to change the mainstream.[12] The financial considerations fueling each company's agenda also complicated their relationship. As the familiarity of Dickens's holiday show would almost certainly guarantee a large audience, Arena budgeted *A Community Carol* as the season's highest earning production. Staging the production within Arena's space rather than within the collaborating East of the Anacostia River community, however, made some Cornerstone members hesitant. In response, Arena agreed to provide enough pay-what-you-can tickets to assure that the same number of community residents would be able to see the show as in a conventional Cornerstone coproduction, and to set aside a percentage of box office income for future community productions. Committed to excellence in craft, Arena's major concession involved allowing nonprofessionals on its stage, a negotiation requiring permission from Equity and that Cornerstone's ensemble actors join the union. Further negotiations ensured the project's development, though Wager had to contend with ongoing resistance from some of Arena's board and staff.[13]

With initial compromises worked through, both Arena and Cornerstone foresaw increasing advantages to the project. Arena would be sharing a classic holiday story with its traditional audience base while the production would also serve the company's growing concern with diversity. Arena's resources and experience would allow Cornerstone members to invest more time in the community, produce a more fully realized production, reach a larger audience in the nation's capital, and expose this audience to a rethinking of regional theatrical conventions. Cornerstone members also felt that the project could lend a feeling of ownership to the collaborating community and open doors to what they may perceive to be a "cultural palace." The project thus proceeded with optimism, as well as some foundational tentativeness on the part of each company. The evolving process would fulfill senses of both apprehension and hope, as well as illuminate the difficulty of melding two distinct value systems and methods of producing theater.

Long Wharf Theatre and Doug Hughes

Benefiting from Cornerstone's collaboration with Arena, *The Good Person of New Haven* arose from a more expansive vision than interest in engaging storytelling. Doug Hughes arrived in New Haven in 1997 driven to discover his adopted city's "center of civic energy."[14] This energy seemed absent from a site whose diverse neighborhoods appeared disconnected from each other and from a cohesive sense of urban identity. Theater, he believed, could draw together the urban community and allow the city to look at itself. Yet, Hughes understood that the historical relationship between New Haven and its professional resident theaters had been as fraught and disconnected as the urban terrain seemed to be. Both the Yale Repertory and Long Wharf theatres focused their energies on producing classical texts and new works, unreflective of New Haven, and cast mainly with New York actors. In order to begin revising the relationship between the theater and the city, Hughes decided he needed to reflect New Haven not only by a representational narrative and semiotically resonant production but also by inviting the city onstage, casting local residents alongside professional actors. And he knew just the theater to work with.

While Hughes had no direct experience producing community-based theater, he had seen and admired a number of Cornerstone's rural shows, served as a Humanities scholar for *The Winter's Tale,* and heard of the Arena project. Based on these experiences, Hughes contacted cofounders Alison Carey and Bill Rauch. Intermittently between the summer of 1997 and June 2000, Long Wharf, Cornerstone, various civic organizations, neighborhoods, and residents of New Haven worked together to produce *The Good Person of New Haven.* This adaptation of Bertolt Brecht's *Good Woman of Setzuan,* set in New Haven and cast with local residents, manifested, celebrated, and critiqued the city.[15] Because the collaboration was, eventually, more widely supported by Long Wharf staff and because Cornerstone had by this time worked with several other regional institutions, the New Haven coproduction did not have to contend with as many foundational inquiries into the nature of regional/community collaborations. At the same time, the process raised provocative questions about what it means to bring together and stage the city. As in Watts, I encountered many of these questions personally, through visits to *The Good Person of New Haven* rehearsal process.

Urban Settings

New Haven Neighborhoods

My understanding of New Haven had been defined through memory and mediation before I arrived in March 2000 to observe the first read through of the newly revised *Good Person of New Haven* script. As a college student, I had traveled occasionally through the Yale campus and its perimeters, careful not to stray too far into what was reported to be a dangerous and poverty-stricken city. My experience of New Haven was thus restricted by my perceptions. Urban geographers Leslie King and Reginald Golledge propose that perceptions, or cognitive structures, directly influence the individual's understanding of the city.[16] A mental map of a place overlays its physical layout, so that we "see" a city through mediated accounts. I therefore saw New Haven from the point of view of the Yale campus as a vaguely undefined surrounding space of potential danger. But subjective reorientation to the urban terrain can alter perceptions, shift cognitive structures, and redraw the mental map.

Years after my initial encounter with the city, having worked with Cornerstone and written of how memory (re)constructs space,[17] I arrived at the New Haven train station and decided to walk to Long Wharf. I felt my way haptically, without a map, becoming a somewhat purposeful flâneur.[18] I got lost in the city. I wandered under a highway bridge, through a junkyard, past weathered convenience stores, newly built corporate structures, and an area post office before arriving finally at the theater, which was flanked by a vast parking lot and wedged between a meat-packing plant and an Italian take-out diner. This spatial isolation seemed to visibly challenge Hughes's hope for the theater as urban center. The geography of this urban landscape, so different from the Yale campus, from Hughes's vision, and from the terrain of my imaginings, began to reconstruct the city. One layer of New Haven unearths itself—the city as urban space.

Cultural geographers such as Henri LeFebvre and Edward Soja have argued that space is not neutral.[19] The city is a social space inscribed by individual relationships, determined by and determining the most basic unit of the urban panorama, the neighborhood—an area that maintains both a physical and psychological presence to its residents. Negotiation among neighborhoods and community organizations marked the Long Wharf/Cornerstone collaboration almost from its inception. Although initiated by Hughes's desire to stage the city and his contact with Cornerstone, the New Haven Project developed through a grant encouraging cooperation among arts and neighborhood social organizations.[20]

In 1997, Long Wharf's Development Director Pamela Tatge came across the Arts Partnership for Stronger Communities Program, established by the Connecticut Commission on the Arts. The New Haven Project or The City Comes Onstage (working project titles from 1997) evolved through the grant-writing process. An early grant narrative summarizes basic tenets of the proposed project and situates some of the challenges that would arise in attempting to spatially and psychically locate New Haven's civic center: "While New Haven can justifiably define itself as Connecticut's cultural capital, it has had great difficulty in defining itself as a community, one united in celebration of its history, its diversity and its considerable cultural treasures."[21]

Perhaps one of the reasons New Haven had such difficulties "defining itself as a community" might be the inherent difficulty of defining anything as a community. According to the grant narrative, a New Haven community established through the Arts Partnerships project would include both commonality (celebration of history and culture) and diversity. The conundrum of how to both celebrate commonality and pay homage to difference recurred throughout the process of planning, audition, adaptation, and performance of the New Haven/City Comes Onstage Project. Throughout the project's development, Long Wharf relied on Cornerstone's experience to balance inclusion and celebration with selection (and implicit erasure).

Thus, following initial conversations with Carey and Rauch, and spurred on by the Arts Partnerships grant, Long Wharf established relationships with various community organizations. Eventually renewed over the three years of the project's development, the grant included the Ethnic Heritage Center, LEAP (Leadership, Education and Athletics in Partnership), and Centro San Jose (later transferred to Pequeñas Ligas de New Haven when Executive Director Peter Noble left the first organization for the second). Community partners believed that the New Haven Project would further their various missions of cultural expression, dialogue, and opportunity. The selection of these partners also established an ethnically and somewhat geographically diverse representation of New Haven. Centro San Jose and Pequeñas focus their attention on New Haven's Hispanic population, LEAP works with urban high school students, and the Ethnic Heritage Center brings together African American, Italian, Jewish, Ukranian, Polish, and Irish residents.

Early in the process, the project moved from a mainly ethnic representation of the city's differences, marked by the collaborating partnerships, to a representation based in the more physical and psychologically grounded terrain of the neighborhood. During the summer of 1998, the participating partners determined that to be more inclusive, the workshops should be held in five sites, embracing a range of geographic, demographic, and ethnic differences. The sites chosen—The Hill, Newhallville, Westville/Beaver Hills, Wooster Square, and Fair Haven—did indeed represent a diverse cross section of New Haven. According to several media reports, and Long

Wharf and Cornerstone records, ongoing workshops at the five sites and sixteen additional "one-shot" workshops held in the fall of 1998 included New Haven residents embodying a range of ages, ethnic backgrounds, and residence locations within the city. That diversity, according to participants, was in itself exciting. Dana Fripp, who appeared in both the workshop and final productions of *The Good Person of New Haven* comments on her spring 1999 audition:

> I got a call from [site coordinator] Michelle Sepulveda, who was worried about getting enough auditioners to the school. Well, they had nothing to worry about. When I got there it looked like about 75 to 80 people at one junior high. There was such a buzz! All ages and races, fantastic![22]

The workshops resulted in a Fall 1998 presentation that focused on oral history and storytelling representing a wide variety of experiences in the city.

Yet, the foregrounding of diversity in age and race, and the assumption that a geographic cross section of the city's neighborhoods would result in an accurately embodied representation of the city, elides some of the complexities of urban representation, particularly when the project moved from oral history to adaptation. Fripp further illuminates some of these complications:

> It's interesting for me where I live in Westville, you're so close to the Hill [a lower income area], where it looks so different. When black people started moving in here, you got a different sense of the city just by crossing the street. That would have been a very interesting thing to address [in the play]. Just by waiting for the light to change you leave an area that was predominantly Jewish, that became a Jewish African American mix. . . . then right across the street you see boarded up buildings.

Fripp's commentary points towards the relationship between neighborhood and culture as more than a simple mapping of race and ethnicity onto space. Fluid borders and migration patterns impact the physical and psychological character of the neighborhood.

King and Golledge cite studies that conservatively estimate movement within a typical city at 15 to 20 percent of the population.[23] Migration factors often center on available housing and economic opportunity and are perceived differently dependent upon class and race. This perceptual difference became a point of contention in the adaptation process. In an early scene in *The Good Person of New Haven*, angels who have come to earth in search of a good person discover New Haven history books in the local library. They read from them throughout the first half of the play, providing a selective historical context for New Haven's present enunciation of itself in performance.

Angel 2: [reading from book] "Richard Lee, then mayor of our fair city, went into the tenements on Oak Street in the 1950's. He was so horrified by what he saw—no heat, no running water, no electricity—that he went outside, sat down on the curb and put his head in his hands. He promised himself then and there he'd do something about it, and thus was Urban Renewal born."

Angel 3: Except I met some lovely older ladies who lived here when he came. Those tenements were their homes. They scrubbed them spotless every Saturday. They loved their homes on Oak Street, and Dick Lee tore them down. It's been 30 years, and they still HATE him. They HATE him. (33–34)

The third angel's response complicates the mythology of urban renewal and migration patterns. Dialectic engagement between the angels illuminates how subjective perceptions impact interpretation of an event through its historical and experientially mediated context. Space is not neutral.

Varying perceptual understandings of migration patterns and living conditions were also expressed at the first read through of the revised *Good Person of New Haven* script, which I attended following my initial wanderings. In a discussion following the read through, Michael Gaetano, a fourteen-year-old from Hamden (a suburb adjoining New Haven), commented on the difference between his town and the depressed Newhallville neighborhood he passed each day on the way to school. A photo of Gaetano in front of his house in the *Hamden Journal* depicts a comfortable two-story Colonial structure with a manicured lawn.[24] "It's just down the hill," he explained about Newhallville, "but there's trash on the lawns, and nothing seems taken care of. How could they let life slip away like that?" At the read through, an older African American cast member, Horace Little, responded to Gaetano somewhat shortly: "People don't always *let* themselves slip away. A lot of times they started there." Little repeats the story, with a more conciliatory tone, in an article in the *New Haven Advocate:* "He hadn't lived there, so he didn't know."[25]

The performance-making process, with numerous opportunities for input from participants throughout script selection, adaptation, and performance, encouraged this kind of exchange—an exchange that enabled relationships across neighborhoods, ethnicity, and class, and expanded perceptions about the relationship between space and culture. At the same time, the process revealed complications that were not represented in performance—migration patterns in Westville and the Hill, and the more structural socioeconomic factors impacting the aesthetic differences between Hamden and Newhallville.

East of the Anacostia River

New Haven's complex conglomerations of class and ethnicity, perceptions and misperceptions, had some resonance with metropolitan D.C., though the capitol city's differences seem more easily reduced to black and white. While Arena Stage had less explicit interest in staging the city and examining these classifications, the company did hope to collaborate with the Anacostia Museum and the East of the Anacostia River (EOR) area of the city, a mostly black neighborhood suffering from actual and perceived urban poverty and violence. Wariness existed in both directions. Cornerstone and Arena had to address negative perceptions in the community of Arena Stage serving a mainly white audience in a predominately black city.[26] Early involvement with Anacostia underlined the difficulties of diversifying an audience base that had not felt part of the avowedly humanistic, inclusive mission of Arena Stage.

Unlike the more community-based Museum, which resident Diana Dale refers to as "our museum,"[27] according to Tamara Sibley, many EOR residents felt that Arena, which purports to serve the entire metropolitan D.C. area, "didn't speak to them."[28] Community residents had directly participated in the effort to build the museum, which, as Dale claims, houses "not just dusty stuff." In contrast, the city government had leveled a lot of low-income housing, driving former residents across the Anacostia River; Arena had later purchased a lot vacated by these residents in order to build a new theater complex. EOR residents felt no investment in Arena; they felt that the theater didn't speak to them and that they had reason to resent its very existence.

According to participant Toni White-Richardson, "Going to Arena Stage was like going to a foreign territory."[29] While White-Richardson cites the benefits of Arena's school outreach programs, conceding, "I don't want to take anything from them," she also definitively stated that prior to the *Community Carol* project, most Southeast Washington residents did not perceive of Arena as reaching out to or including the adults in the community.[30] White-Richardson elaborated that residents are imbued with skepticism about collaborative projects, having suffered from a number of aborted efforts to "help the community." She added however that "the proof was in the pudding." Once Arena and Cornerstone followed through with gathering an advisory board and setting up workshops and auditions, once the companies worked to *include* the community, EOR residents responded with great enthusiasm to the project.

From the perspective of EOR residents, the project offered a central stage to represent the area to metropolitan D.C. Residents had felt literally and figuratively disconnected from this national power base since Anacostia's incorporation. At the turn of the century, public services stopped at the predominantly black districts of D.C. Resident Ella B. Howard-Pearis explains, "Before they would run a line to [old Anacostia], the electric company told my grandfather he would have to buy 100 shares of [their] stock."[31] Physical access to central D.C. was also limited. Though subway lines snake far into the suburbs of Virginia and Maryland, only recently has the metropolitan line extended across the river to Anacostia, and then only for one or two stops into the area.[32] The Arena coproduction brought residents into the power base, for a limited time, while illuminating these issues of access to the power base.

Some Common Misperceptions

Long Wharf also had to overcome New Haven residents' perceptions of the theater, as well as subscribers' perceptions of New Haven. The theater understands the difficulty of serving its more local audience constituency in addition to its subscriber base. Former Development Director Pamela Tatge acknowledges: "The perception of Long Wharf was that it was a theater focused on New York. The prior administration [before Doug Hughes's tenure] didn't have a strong connection to the [New Haven] community."[33] Bronx-born Adelaida Nuñez affirms Tatge's assumptions, noting that she felt initially put off by Long Wharf, and theater in general:

> I was not raised to like the theatre. . . . It's kind of like the division of class. There's a certain kind of person who goes to the theatre. There's a certain kind of person who doesn't go to the theatre. Then there's a person who doesn't even know about the theatre. I was the one who didn't even know.[34]

Long Wharf is certainly not alone in reflecting perceptions that regional theaters serve mainly upper-middle-class audiences. Toni White-Richardson had expressed a similar vision of the Arena Stage prior to Cornerstone's collaboration. "The Arena is not some place [Anacostia residents] visit often," she explained, citing as reasons "cost and the nature of the place. . . . It's not universal enough. Sometimes the plays seem geared towards—uh, how can I say this—an audience that is not from Anacostia." Adelaida Nuñez is more direct in her response, proposing one possible reason for the improved relationship between Long Wharf and New Haven participants: "It's not just another show about a bunch of white people."[35]

White-Richardson and Nuñez both articulate the importance of perceptions—that regional theater is culturally elite—and imply that inclusion and involvement can at least temporarily redefine the relationship between a more local audience constituency and a regional theater. Arena project coordinator Tamara Sibley suggests that this representational inclusion became a deciding factor in shifting the relationship between the Arena and the Anacostia community:

> Everywhere people wanted to be involved, the response was overwhelming. People want an outlet. They were excited about the idea that they could perform things that they recognized, their own community, at the Arena. It was a coming together, a bridge to the community and people were willing to cross that bridge.

These conceptual bridges were strengthened by the development of an EOR community advisory board. The board helped to locate accessible community spaces in which to organize workshops and auditions and aided Arena and Cornerstone in developing pay-what-you-can group sales for the community to enter the Arena.[36] A three-week workshop period in the EOR area yielded 272 auditioners, a Cornerstone record at the time. Rauch cast ten adults of all ages, including Arena receptionist Donna Harris, and ten children, including two from a school for the deaf.[37] The rehearsal process continued to provide opportunities to rewrite misperceptions of Anacostia while contextualizing others, as well as to unite EOR participants through the common goals of the project.

Community Transactions

Social spaces, community gathering, and mutual support were clearly important to EOR residents, though the production brought them even closer together. "There were people in the show that lived like a block away from me that I never came in contact with outside of *A Community Carol*," notes Damion Teeko Parran. "It actually bridged the community. Because from that point on whenever I saw them, it wasn't a person, a face, it was a neighbor."[38] Rehearsal rituals sustained these relationships. During final weeks of late night and afternoon rehearsals, advisory board members prepared hot meals for community participants. This mealtime provided a chance to get together, support each other, and "put ourselves in check," explained Toni White-Richardson. "We pulled our own coattails. We felt responsible for each other. The meals and support got people to work towards a common goal."

As well as shoring up relationships within the EOR community, the process also built relationships across difference. Community liaison Tamara Sibley attests to positive interaction between deaf and hearing children and between Arena staff and EOR residents. Before the casting and rehearsal process began, resident Hank Brooks confided to Sibley that he didn't think Arena would want him in a show. However, in addition to being cast, Sibley professes that Brooks became a kind of spiritual center for all of the actors. In a transaction oddly reminiscent of Tiny Tim's revival in *A Christmas Carol*, Brooks, who had hip problems and walked with crutches, received assistance from an Alexander movement specialist working with Arena. The specialist helped Brooks to straighten up and walk with only one crutch. Other personal relationships within the rehearsal process again seemed to parallel the transformative morality tale central to Dickens's story. Both Sibley and Wager affirm that Arena actors voluntarily became "buddies" to community actors to the benefit of both. "At the first rehearsal I did a double take," explains Sibley. "'Wait a minute! Isn't that so-and-so, who never says anything to anyone, helping little kids read their scripts and get around the building?'"[39]

At Long Wharf, Doug Hughes also understood and acknowledged that inclusive storytelling and mutual involvement could improve the relationship between the theater and New Haven residents. In a letter to the Connecticut Arts Commission, Hughes refers to the diverse, local audience in attendance at the Fall 1998 neighborhood workshops presentation at Long Wharf: "New Haven citizens who would never have looked to Long Wharf as a community center were inside the building responding favorably to a project defined by the hopes and dreams, disappointments and defeats of their daily lives."[40]

The process of inviting the community to represent themselves, rather than to receive what many regional theaters term "outreach performances," allowed for increased engagement with the local constituency in both the Anacostia and New Haven areas. Yet, improved relationships also led to perceptual shifts at both regional theaters, particularly Long Wharf. While Doug Hughes initially hoped to make Long Wharf the city's civic center, two years later this notion changed. Rather than serving as the central agent of cultural engagement, Long Wharf began to refer to a mutual relationship with the community.[41] One key moment that shifted the relationship between New Haven Project participants and Long Wharf from suspicion to mediation to catalyzation occurred in October 1999 when the Community Foundation for Greater New Haven awarded one hundred thousand dollars to the project. At the press conference announcing this grant, Pamela Tatge stated: "The [New Haven] Project didn't belong to Long Wharf. It belonged to the community."

Who Is "the Community" in New Haven?

In his 1985 book *The Symbolic Construction of Community*, sociologist Anthony Cohen summarizes an understanding of the city as constituted by individuals whose differences become the foundation for urban integration and solidarity.[42] This understanding of a society brought together through difference manifests itself in accounts of the New Haven Project and in assumptions expressed by both Cornerstone and Long Wharf. In Cornerstone's specific articulation, theater can facilitate social mediation, offering a site where social roles can be reimagined and differences bridged, while individuals retain cultural distinctions. It is a delicate balancing act, at once echoed and troubled by an article in the *New Haven Register*.

The article, entitled "'A Little Melting Pot'" (based on a quote from cast member Adelaida Nuñez), begins by defining several community participants via their ethnic identity, age, and social roles:

> A 20-something African-American drama teacher who does his own one-man show. A 30-year old Puerto Rican mother of two who once did a Metropolitan Transit Authority commercial. An 82-year-old Italian American great-grandfather and GOP leader who has been Santa Claus for 55 Christmases.[43]

Like Cornerstone, the article celebrates distinctions among cast members, implying that the New Haven Project allows for interaction across difference. Yet, instead of maintaining these distinctions, the article later elides individual differences in an almost utopic narrative of community: "[The show's] cast members look and sound a lot like you and me. That's because they are our friends and relatives, our neighbors and teachers."[44] On their own, the statements only simplify the negotiation of difference and unity in the performance process. The statements are further complicated, however, by the fact that the writer had perceived a distinction that did not actually exist. Aaron Jafferis, the "African American drama teacher," looks and defines himself as white. While it is difficult to establish why the writer misperceived Jafferis's racial identity, one factor could be that Jafferis, a hip-hop poet, better fit the racial category of "black" rather than "white" in terms of the practice of his social role. The rehearsal process, in contrast, offered a site for a more subtle negotiation and reconceptions of individuals beyond their typed social roles.

As cited in Long Wharf's publicity literature—a format that does not generally invite complex critical discourse—comments from participants involved in the process can seem simple and selective. The History of the New Haven Project pamphlet quotes several cast members' responses to the project, including that of Michael Gaetano—"It's been a great opportunity to get to know other people in this area!"—and Gloria Richardson—"We've become a family." The process of theater making as a medium for individual exchange, and the renegotiation of social perceptions, is more complexly related by Dana Fripp. I quote at length her account of perceptual shifts in her relationship with two cast members, Michelle Masa and Adelaida Nuñez, to indicate the subtlety of social transactions that can arise through the rehearsal process.

> One of the most important things [about the process] was being up in the [dressing room] trailer with the other women. I remember the first time I saw Michele Masa, who played Mrs. Cash. I told her this week, "I looked at you and I said, that is a beautiful woman, she will never talk to me." I had all these preconceived notions about who people are, what they were going to be like to work with, and all of that just melted away. Michele and I got so close, I feel like it's just been orchestrated by God.
>
> I didn't know what to make of Addy [Adelaida Nuñez] the first time through. I blame myself in part—maybe you're not always meant to jive with everybody—but being in that trailer with her and watching her with her daughters and watching her work so hard on every line and everything, her level of commitment, how beautiful her daughters are, it's a credit to her, that she's here every single day, covering another role [Eddie's Mother]. Just sitting with her and hearing about her life and what she has been through, and in the midst of this she graduates with her GED. I cannot tell you the level of respect I have for this girl—this woman now.
>
> You know something, I could have missed this, I could have been left with this one-time assessment of her. . . . It's a small picture of what it should be like out there beyond the trailer, as far as the way we support one another in the city. We don't all grow up in the same way, but if you are a stranger with animosity trying to pick on one of us in this very diverse trailer, you'd be better off in an alley with junk yard dogs. It was just a—a lot of people describe it as spiritual. It became more than just a project.

Fripp's comments illustrate how the day-to-day interactions engaged in within the performance process remapped her initial perceptions of individuals. Her assessment of the situation illuminates both the potential for the performance-making process as a model for inclusive relationships in the city ("It's a small picture of what it should be like out there") and a suggestion of how new symbolic boundaries in fact depend upon exclusion ("if you are a stranger with animosity trying to pick on one of us . . . you'd be better off in an alley with junk yard dogs").

The negotiation of these many relationships within New Haven and D.C., between theatrical professionals and community participants, across a variety of racial, ethnic, class, and geographic boundaries, again relates only one part of a collaborative tale. One of the more difficult relationships across difference emerged between community-based and regional theater practices, particularly in the earlier Arena Stage collaboration.

Professional Practices

Cornerstone artists profited from Arena's extraordinarily skilled and supportive production staff. Working with a considerably larger budget and more resources, director Bill Rauch and designer Lynn Jeffries could manifest production design to the full extent of their imaginations. Jeffries attests:

> It was like dying and going to heaven. . . . I'd gone from having maybe, if I was lucky, one really great technical director and some community seamstresses, to having to just do the set and having a scene shop and a prop shop. There were fifteen extremely talented, dedicated, hard-working crafts people who were just there for me.[45]

Choreographer Sabrina Peck also felt blessed with the support Arena Stage offered, particularly noting the collaborative atmosphere: "It was kind of like paradise in terms of a working environment."[46] Cornerstone members go out of their way to praise the contributions of Arena costume designer Paul Tazewell, who designed over two hundred costumes for the show, and the collaborative energy of Michael Keck, who composed original music.[47] Lynn Jeffries additionally cites the contributes of Allen Lee Hughes: "Arena's fabulous resident lighting designer." She elaborates:

> Allen grew up east of the river himself, and began his career at Arena, so he had a substantial history on both sides. While I was in my research phase, he gave me a photo of a brick retaining wall beside the path leading to the door of his old doctor's office in Anacostia. For him it represented something typical about the look of the neighborhood. Allen Lee Hughes' doctor's retaining wall was incorporated into the set, going down one of the [stage exits].[48]

The company also praised the courageousness of Arena Stage for initiating the collaboration and allowing Cornerstone to, in some ways, temporarily reshape Arena's production process. But the benefits of Arena's professionalism intertwined with corresponding liabilities. These troubles had as much to do with the newness of process, and lack of knowledge about how to structure a complex coproduction, as with the inherent difference in organization and values of Cornerstone, Arena, and community participants. The collaboration also illuminates how professionalism gets manifested as a set of values and artistic principles that can on occasion resist innovations that seem to neglect the conventions of craft.

Professionalism cannot be easily dismissed as a calcified set of practices, as the term can refer to working standards (such as being on time and sober) as well as artistry. Still, excellence in craft, an oft-cited hallmark of professional artistry, remains difficult to pin down. Arena's mission, "to present and advance the art of theater," proposes an implicit understanding of the terms of artistry. When asked to define Arena's excellence and reputation, Laurence Maslon responded, "artistic craftsmanship, the quality of artists brought in to the Arena, the quality of the plays produced." While breaking down "excellence" into component parts, the response does not indicate how to measure craftsmanship and quality other than through agreement among practicing regional theater artists. Thus, professionalism can translate into the experience of working within the structures defined by regional theaters and the training institutions that serve them. But this somewhat facile categorization neglects the nuances of excellence; innovation may appear in unexpected places, recognized by those who work within regional institutions. Maslon relates the story of Lynn Jeffries's first design presentation, coincidentally preceded by that of a visiting design professional. The designer used all the resources of his craft to present detailed set models, drawings, and plans contrasting with Jeffries's foam core and magic-marker rendition. Despite this difference in presentation, Maslon affirms, "[Lynn's] intuition and naiveté were bolder and more endearing than the other highly sophisticated model we had seen earlier in the week."[49]

While Arena staff praised the artistry of some ensemble members and disparaged others, ultimately, Cornerstone's method of working with often-inexperienced community participants called for different techniques than those practiced by most regional theaters. Doug Wager seemed to understand the inherent differences between the two theaters, describing the *Community Carol* coproduction as in no way following "business as usual" at the Arena. But organizational structures and financial considerations constrained Wager's rhetoric.

Though the coproduction served as a first-time experiment for both Cornerstone and Arena, its budgeting as Arena's highest earning show pressured the production to fully engage Arena's audience base, to meet certain aesthetic standards in order to conform to Arena's definition of quality. This obliged both companies to achieve an "Arena product," defined through craft, via Cornerstone's methodology, defined through inclusion and community engagement.

Arena staff members felt caught between experimentation and the conventional working methods they believed were required to achieve a successful Arena product. This resulted, according to Wager, in a "lot of areas of resistance" and, according to Rauch, in "an aura of panic about the production." Wager at one point confided to Rauch that had this been a "normal production" he would have fired him and taken over the show's direction. Still anxious about the show's development, Wager canceled the first preview. Both events point towards the conflict between Arena's interest in a different kind of production experience, and reaction against a show that did not seem finished.[50]

According to Maslon, Wager's reactions exemplified a pervasive lack of trust about the Cornerstone venture among Arena's staff, resulting from Cornerstone's inexperience and some ensemble members' behavior. While benefiting enormously from Arena's resources, Cornerstone actors felt both the "luxury and sadness" of primarily focusing on acting work rather than community engagement.[51] There was some feeling among Arena staff that money set aside for Cornerstone members' salaries and accommodations could have been better spent on local professional actors. They felt that while community actors were authentic to their world, some Cornerstone actors provided ineffectual characterizations with poor diction. According to Maslon:

> As a professional theater in Washington DC, you would not have hired [some of] the Cornerstone actors in those spots if you could have hired other professional actors from the DC area. This put Cornerstone at a distinct disadvantage, as far as their creditability as performers were concerned. No one ever, to my knowledge, quarreled with their ability, as an ensemble, to recruit, train and enfranchise community members.[52]

Alison Carey contends that some tensions could have been better managed through improved communication. In some cases, however, gaps in methodology and foundational beliefs about what makes good theater may not have closed through conversation. Further tensions around contrasting theatrical values emerged in the process of textual adaptation.

Struggling to Adapt at the Arena

Four writers from various theatrical backgrounds contributed to adapting *A Christmas Carol*. Carey and Rauch had worked together adapting previous Cornerstone shows and operated under a trial and error system proven by experience working under considerably different conditions. Arena Associate Artistic Director Laurence Maslon approached the project with a background in professional dramaturgy and playwriting that sometimes clashed with Carey and Rauch's lack of a system and determination to include the voices of community participants; Maslon felt that this inclusion could work against the constraints of developing a cohesive, tightly written product. Short story writer Ed Jones had no theatrical background (other than a grade school role as Scrooge) but, according to Wager, would write dialogue "in the voice of the community." The cowriters eventually worked through a system of individually writing for specific scenes or characters. This process succeeded to a degree in the initial drafting stages, but tensions reappeared within the rehearsal process.

Speaking from within Cornerstone values and experience, Carey encouraged community members to add their voice to the adaptation at an early read through. Maslon felt that this invitation violated the rigors of theatrical writing by valuing individual input over the production as a whole. Rauch affirms that late in the process, he had to cut some scenes that had been added through community input, acknowledging that the scenes overburdened the structure of the play. But the lateness of the cuts and unfamiliarity with the production process led to resentment from some cast members. After a scene with a black soldier was cut from the Fezziwig party due to concerns about the show's length and the scene's relevancy to the overall production, the Arena actor playing the role commented, "I guess I'm just another dancing coon now."[53] The rewriting process magnified conflict between professionalism and inclusion. Maslon asserts that the script reflected "a little too much of a Christmas pudding. Every possible person, sexual preference and religion was on the stage." Maslon felt that over-inclusion diminished the strength of Dickens's dramatic narrative.[54] Alison Carey admits to reacting against these values and to her belief in Arena's blindness towards the nature of inclusion, exemplified by controversy over the name of a football team.

At the commencement of the *Community Carol* project, Rauch and Carey had proposed creating a number of choruses to replace the singular voice of Dickens's narrator. The choruses were intended to increase the opportunity for community actors' involvement, and to represent numerous voices in the metropolitan community—to enact a collectively told and sung "community carol." Choruses included construction workers, lawyers, fast-food workers, the homeless, joggers, kids in pajamas, and a football team, intended to represent the Washington Redskins. In thinking further about including this team, Carey felt that the writers would have to change the name or risk offending those, including herself, who felt troubled by the appropriation of Native Americans as sports mascots. Carey thus renamed the team the "Potatoskins." The renaming satisfied Cornerstone concerns but seemed to several Arena members as yet another example of Cornerstone's over-the-top political correctness, which neglected the overall artistry of the show. As Carey relates, "Doug Wager said, 'If you can find me one subscriber to Arena Stage who's offended by Redskins I'll give you the theater!'"[55] To Carey, this comment only affirmed the rationale for changing the name: "It would never occur to Arena that Redskins may be offensive to some audience members."[56]

Lynn Jeffries's *Community Carol* (1993) set, blending a realistic depiction of Martin Luther King Street in Anacostia with more fantastical elements, such as Christmas presents transforming into furniture. The renaming of the Washington Potato Skins chorus seemed overindulgent to some Arena staff members. Photo: Lynn Jeffries.

While inclusiveness and artistry remained points of tension throughout the production process, collaborative writing also raised issues of cultural authenticity. According to Rauch, some Arena staff felt that the writing was "not street enough," while community members reacted that people from EOR "wouldn't behave like that."[57] Arena perceptions about what sounded like an urban voice clashed with some participants' desires to offer positive images of their community. As Cornerstone found in producing *Ghurba* with Arab Americans, theatrical framing can lead to essentialism, as representation within a narrative format often allows for only one interpretation of a rite, individual, or group. Consequently, that one interpretation can be read as representing the whole. Community members thus felt that they had one opportunity, one stage to represent an image of a black family, and they made great efforts to create positive images through their characterization. Bill Rauch describes a conversation with Toni White-Richardson about Penny Cratchit's line, stated upon entering work late on the morning following Christmas. White-Richardson worried that the line "I had a rather large holiday dinner" might reinforce stereotypes about the eating habits of African American women. She felt that as the Arena Stage offered limited representations of contemporary black women, she bore a responsibility to positively represent these women as much as the individual character of Penny Cratchit. Arena staff members who were not invested in the representation of the EOR community felt that these discussions detracted from the artistry of the performance by focusing on political issues of representation rather than pace, character, and timing.

In addition to these troubling issues of authentic representation, *A Community Carol* also had to contend with how to write the EOR community, to present a positive image of the area without neglecting the presence of poverty and violence. The writing and staging made efforts to contextualize rather than merely present images of urban blight. A deaf white girl and a young black boy carrying an Uzi represented ignorance and want respectively, suggesting that ignorance can result from a loss of access to knowledge, and that violence can arise from want in a materialist society. Jennifer Nelson of the Living Stage also discussed the possibility of presenting TT (Tiny Tim) as a young drug runner. Both she and Rauch felt that this presentation would de-sentimentalize the character, making the characterization less patronizing, as well as commenting on the culture within which TT lives. Jones, Carey, and Maslon vetoed the idea, feeling that the characterization would be misread as reinscribing the community's drug culture, and also wasn't "true to Dickens." The play did include at least one reference to drug economy in the community. During a party scene, Penny Cratchit referred to a particular child's father as serving time for drug dealing. This comment raised issues with several community actors about the cultural erasure of the white drug problem. At one point, the script included a reference to an upper-middle-class business associate, "Jack," who was "coked up as usual"; however, the lines seemed, even to community artists, too gratuitous to include. All of which points to the difficulty of presenting complex images and dialectics onstage in service of a particular story line.[58]

Value clashes between art and inclusion surfaced due to a Cornerstone casting decision. Rauch had cast teenager Michael Anderson, whom Christopher Liam Moore admits was "unskilled" as an actor but talented as a cellist.[59] Because of Musician's Union rules, however, Anderson had to play his cello as part of an acting role. Rauch faults himself and the process for the fact that a synthesizer eventually took over Anderson's part as a cellist, and he appeared onstage only as a hard-to-understand performer. Yet, Cornerstone had made the decision to cast Anderson for reasons other than his acting talent. "He was a good kid from a bad situation who needed an outlet," defends Moore, "and two minutes of painful acting was worth it." Within Cornerstone's purpose, "there is room for Anderson," contends Moore, and there is room for community input, ongoing revision, and the

Washington Potatoskins. Within Arena's purpose and mission there was not, as these inclusions were perceived to detract from the overall artistic product. For Cornerstone members, these tensions illustrated the limitations of their inclusive values within the regional theater realm, while also underlining the complications and exclusions inherent in "inclusion."

Further Adaptations in New Haven

Cornerstone and Arena Stage tried to adapt to each other's methodology, with mixed results. Seven years and several regional collaborations later, Alison Carey rewrote Brecht's *Good Woman of Setzuan* on her own, with community input staggered throughout a lengthy development process. The issues at stake in New Haven arose from within the text itself rather than through the process of its adaptation. The challenges of adapting Brecht's dialectical engagement forms yet another terrain to investigate the complexities of regional representation.

As with most phases of the New Haven Project, community participants were invited to contribute their input in choosing the source text to be adapted for eventual production on Long Wharf's main stage. In August 1998, Cornerstone and Long Wharf, working with Arts Partners, Centro San Jose, Project LEAP, and the Ethnic Heritage Center, brought together a group of 150 community respondents. The participants heard summaries of five plays and read aloud lengthy excerpts. They commented on whether the concerns of the plays seemed to reflect for them the concerns of the city, assuming that a production would be adapted and set in contemporary New Haven. According to Carey, the results of the reading were clear: "I've never had the experience where people from all over the city, from all walks of life, felt so overwhelmingly connected to a play."[60] Participants responded to the difficulty of negotiating goodness, to the resemblance of the central characters' concerns with their own, and to the tensions between idealism and materialism expressed in Brecht's story. They felt that these concerns and tensions could be easily adapted to resonate within a specifically New Haven context, particularly with ongoing representation and commentary from residents.

The goal of the New Haven Project's initial workshop phase was to give theatrical voice to New Haven's daily lives and to allow the experiences of the workshop participants to shape the final results. In the fall of 1998, aided by New Haven Project Coordinator Shana Waterman, Carey, Rauch, and community artist Gracy Brown conducted a series of workshops in the five neighborhood communities selected for the project. The workshops, culminating in a November presentation at Long Wharf, provided Carey with direct input that she mediated through the adapted text.

Over the following winter, Carey drafted a script that became the basis for a June 1999 workshop presentation, part of New Haven's International Festival of Arts and Ideas. The eventual goal would be to "greet the millennium with a celebration of New Haven, its people, and its history."[61] But this focus on celebration and inclusion challenged the representational process at the levels of both textual adaptation and casting. Many responses did affirm the goals of the project; for example, one audience member stated, "I like the diversity of the cast; it reflects the city."[62] Yet, other responses suggested gaps in the representational strategies at work. Bill Rauch explained that some white audience members felt underrepresented. "I think they imagined that the play would be a more historical focus on the 'city proper.' I remember one asking 'Where are the Italians?'"[63] Cornerstone actor Christopher Liam Moore recalls a few audience members stating emphatically, "That's not my New Haven; it's not about us."[64]

According to Rauch, the cast itself was split between reflecting the city's diversity and reflecting Brecht's story, set in a poor neighborhood that would be mostly black and Latino.[65] Rauch and Carey also struggled with the depiction of the Angels who come to earth in search of a good person. In the initial workshop, Rauch had cast the three angels to reflect the multicultural diversity of New Haven, with Latino, deaf African American, and Italian American actors. For Rauch, this casting seemed vital to the project of placing "the city onstage." But in discussions with Doug Hughes, Rauch and Carey realized that the casting did not effectively help to tell the story, which depended finally on the angels as "clueless white tourists, which better represented the somewhat exaggerated version of divine patriarchal control in the adaptation."[66]

The difficulty of resituating Brecht's story, adequately representing the concerns of New Haven Project participants, and including symbolic aspects of New Haven that would locally ground the text and the production proved challenging to say the least. In addition to representing New Haven in a respectful, provocative way, Carey also needed to address the complexities of Brecht's text. Doug Hughes had spoken of Brecht's play as "realistically harsh and hopeful, both serious and funny," and had referred to its potential to represent the "specific hopes and concerns of New Haven."[67] Carey's adaptation grappled with all of these representational challenges, offering numerous specific references to the hopes and concerns of New Haven as well as to its architecture, history, folklore, and political structure.

In Brecht's original play, a water seller narrates the tale of three gods who visit Setzuan in search of a good person. The prostitute Shen Te harbors the gods, and in return, they offer her money, which she uses to purchase a tobacco shop. Shen Te soon discovers that the city's residents, including the former owner of the shop and a Family of Nine, take advantage of her goodness and endanger her ownership of the shop. So Shen Te invents a cousin, Shui Ta, a hard-nosed businessman who maintains the shop through his lack of generosity. Meanwhile, Shen Te meets a would-be pilot, Sun, who seduces and impregnates her. Worried that Sun will reject her if he knows of the baby, and hoping to gain financial stability for the safety of the child, Shen Te takes on the character of Shui Ta, who increases the profitability of the shop through exploitative labor practices. With growing suspicion at Shen Te's absence, Sun accuses Shui Ta of doing away with Shen Te. The play ends with Shen Te's revelation of her necessary deception implying the ambiguities and tensions of balancing goodness with social survival.

In the New Haven adaptation, a homeless can collector, Quinn (played by Moore), narrates the tale. Shen Te becomes Tyesha Shore, portrayed by the African American actor Patrice Johnson, who purchases a mini-mart with her gift from the angels. The Family of Nine transforms into an ever-growing multicultural mix of in-laws, portrayed by various New Haven community participants. The aspiring train engineer Eddie replaces Sun, and Tyesha's invented cousin becomes Taiwo Highwater, a businessman from Greenwich who transforms the mini-mart into a factory producing "New Haven Goods" driven by the slogan "New Haven's Good!" Other characters include a slightly sleazy but good-natured urban black minister, the Korean former mini-mart owner, and a couple who owns a furniture store (with one member of the couple, Pat, played on alternate nights as male or female by New Haven performers William Graustein and Edi Jackson).

The adaptation and production resounded with New Haven participants on a number of levels. "The homeless people, the prostitution, and people constantly struggling," explains Gracy Brown, "that hit home with a lot of people in the New Haven area."[68] The text also referred to the problems of single motherhood, lack of job opportunities, and working conditions for the urban poor. "It has little bits of . . . no it has *everything* of New Haven!" exclaimed sixteen-year-old cast member Leididiana Castro.[69] Like most Cornerstone productions, *The Good Person of New Haven* also included original songs and choreography, additionally resonating with its New Haven locality. Aaron Jafferis notes enthusiastically, "The more the play has developed the more it's become like New Haven, particularly in the music."[70]

Yet, for all its inclusions, adaptations, and references, the play could not embrace or fully represent the city. "New Haven is hard to catch in two hours and thirty minutes," explains Dana Fripp.

The cast of *The Good Person of New Haven* (2000). Photo: T. Charles Erickson.

> I think we may have missed some of the things we struggled with. At the workshop I thought, "I'm missing my city, where's my city?" It's more than about a mention of organizations and local landmarks, you know, there's so much more that we're dealing with. It's never going to get it so balanced that everybody's satisfied, it's just not possible.

The inherent lack of balance in the city's representation actually enlivened rehearsals, particularly in the read through I attended in late March 2000. Bill Rauch asked the cast to comment on the textual revisions added in response to audience feedback from the 1999 workshop production. Stephen Papa, an eighty-three-year-old who represented some more conservative aspects of the city, said he was worried about how the adaptation erased "the true New Haven." Rauch asked whether he could identify specific concerns, and Papa immediately responded, "pages 8, 14, 20, 24, and 25." Papa found particularly offensive negative references to Mayor Dick Lee (quoted above). The cast exchanged a variety of opinions about the mayor, his intentions, and the results of those intentions. Cast member William Graustein reflects positively on the experience: "What I heard was not only the connection between the town and the play but also people from all different parts of New Haven talking about politics in a way that was really respectful of one another."[71]

The staging of this dissent would seem to reflect some of the Brechtian dialectical strategies of the play, as well as the community's expressed interest in a text that was both "realistically harsh and hopeful," or "kind of deep and ugly as well as entertaining."[72] However, the difficulty in representing dissent lay in the tendency to view and represent this dissent as even handed. At a symposium in May, featuring Henry Fernandez of the Livable City Initiative, Fernandez praised the production for its "balance." He summed up the message of the play: "There are so many good people and they come in all shapes and sizes."[73]

Brecht's play and Carey's textual adaptation both suggest more complexity. Towards the end of the adaptation, a Godlike Woman In White character, played by Dana Fripp, appears. The advice she offers to the young prostitute Tyesha seems knowingly problematic: "You'll manage. Just be good and everything will turn out all right!" (69). Yet, the notion of "goodness" is foundationally at stake in *The Good Person of New Haven*. As in Brecht's original, the main character, a prostitute, must divide herself by inventing a harsh male cousin who is better at surviving in the context of capitalism. At the end of the play, after receiving the troubling advice of the Woman in White, Tyesha reprimands the angels:

> Your order to me
> To be good and to live
> Tore me into two halves.
> I couldn't be good at the same time
> To others and to myself
> It was too hard.
>
> (69)

In an earlier segment of the play, the homeless can collector, Quinn, tries to explain to the naïve angels the challenge of progressing towards goodness. He had been reminiscing with the angels about his youth on the Yale green, attending a Black Panther rally with his mother. One angel responds enthusiastically:

> *Angel 2:* Yale and Black Panthers (to the other ANGELS) See? Not just good people, but good *groups* of people working together to make the world a better place. . . . When's the next rally for Yale and the Black Panthers? I want to be there!

Baffled, Quinn tries to explain, "They don't . . . Well, they never really . . . It was such a time, all of it. Sometimes good intentions don't work out the way you want them to. . . . Things aren't always that simple" (47–48). While the text thus tries to establish the complexity of goodness, and the tension between ethics and capitalism, Carey also foregrounds the organizations that are striving to do good in New Haven, in response to audience feedback.

As outsiders to the city, Cornerstone members felt a particular responsibility to create a responsive representation of New Haven.[74] The high point of the show for local audience members arrived with Quinn's monologue, which named over fifty New Haven organizations working to improve the city, including, of course, Long Wharf's Arts Partners. In local reception to this piece, the adaptation became less of a dialectic about the nature of goodness and more of a reflective recognition, again complicated by the disparities between onstage and offstage manifestations of the city.

The play's epilogue evokes this tension between the representative and the real, and of conceptions of goodness complicated in the play:

> Our New Haven, as we hope you understand
> In which one can't survive and still be good,
> Was just a play, and it will disappear.
> But something else remains extremely clear:
> The real New Haven, the one outside that exit,
> Might be too much like this one that reflects it.
> Dear audience, if you care about this town,
> Make sure it's changed before it gets you down.
> Earth has no happiness that can compare
> With freedom to do good while you are there.
>
> (71)

Spoken by Moore, who resides in Los Angeles, the "Our" in the opening phrase slips into the "our" of the ensemble that had created the play, including but not exclusive to the residents of New Haven. The epilogue additionally evokes the staged New Haven city "in which one can't survive and still be good" in relation to the "real," a space of potential freedom to do good. The realm of the utopic is rhetorically reversed, from the staged city to its external counterpart. At the same time, the notion of "goodness," complicated throughout the play, and the rehearsal process, becomes potentially simplified in the play's final line as something knowable that requires only effort.

The potential collapse of the Brechtian dialectic in the play's final line, and expressed friction between the representational and the real, is situated in relation to the embodied representations of New Haven. Twenty-four New Haven residents acted in the production with ten Equity actors. Participant Aaron Jafferis comments: "I think the most special thing about the play is the people who are in it. The individuals who are in the play bring New Haven with them."[75] The "realness" of these actors' presence seems to defy the more distanced character quotations Brecht advocated by provoking intellectual rather than seductive emotional engagement. Defamiliarizing the familiar became less essential in this production than familiarizing the unfamiliar. Small moments of conscious estrangement—Mrs. Shin, the former shop owner, drops her Asian accent to underline a point about putting on an act to achieve various ends, and Moore removes his homeless character wig before speaking the epilogue—pale next to the familiarized presence of the amateur actors onstage. Yet, Brecht himself suggests that this presence may in fact contribute to a more politically aware rendering of events.

In "One or Two Points About Proletarian Actors," Brecht proposes that nonprofessional actors tend to play "from a specific outlook and a specific context . . . shed[ding] a surprising light on the complex and baffling relationships between the people of our time."[76] By remaining simple in their performance, by not trying too hard to *not* be themselves, community actors draw attention to their specific concerns, to the context of contemporary New Haven. The bodies of the actors, a mix of African American, Latino/a, European American, and Asian American, also draw attention to the ethnic makeup of the New Haven community. Yet, this very presence, along with strategies of depicting New Haven's "hopes and concerns," the aesthetic enactment of "joyful" musical theater that Cornerstone strives to engage, and the fact that this production was, as Adelaida Nuñez put it, "not just another show about a bunch of white people," did not quite reach a number of Long Wharf's nonlocal subscribers.

Reception and Marketing

> For a theater whose older, white and suburban audience is accustomed to seeing its own lives reflected onstage, [*The Good Person of New Haven*] is a serious, and quite conscious, deviation from business as usual.
> —Laura Collins-Hughes, "Idealism in Action"

RESPONSES TO *THE GOOD PERSON OF NEW HAVEN*

Preproduction coverage of the New Haven Project in local newspapers maintained a high profile for the event, contextualizing the process, and creating what reception theorist Hans Robert Jauss terms a "horizon of expectations."[77] These expectations, presented through media coverage, program notes, and advertising, oriented audience members with reading strategies for performance. Media coverage from initial city workshops through final performance provided a reading of the project as staging the city.[78] Program notes emphasized "the creation of the elusive and desirable phenomenon of 'community'"[79] and offered a vividly illustrated history of the project over its three years of development. Program biographies emphasized the personal concerns of New Haven performers. In interviews, Doug Hughes framed the hoped for critical reception to the production: "I would ask those [who question the aesthetic standards of the work] to remember that there are times when aesthetic standards are not the only standards—that there are other standards, standards of citizenship, standards of hospitality."[80] But Long Wharf's subscriber audience, 40 percent of whom were not local to New Haven and were therefore unlikely to have read these media accounts, carried with them their own horizon of expectations, determined in part by their subscription to Long Wharf.[81]

Long Wharf's subscriber brochure for the 2001 season emphasizes aesthetic standards and the comfortable context of theatrical experience rather than standards of what Doug Hughes had termed "citizenship or hospitality." Quotes from the *New York Times,* the *New Haven Register,* and the *Hartford Courant* praise the "mastery," "daringness," and "entertainment" values of Long Wharf productions, while also signaling by their selection the targeted suburban subscriber audience base. Doug Hughes's note to subscribers stresses the "rediscovery of timeless classics" and new works. The brochure also touts the benefits of free parking, flexible ticket exchange policies, ticket access *prior* (brochure's emphasis) to public sale, and restaurant discounts. The subscriber is thus figured as a commuter, out for a night of relaxed entertainment supplemented by a fine dining experience, and an individual privileged over the rest of the public.

Like many audience members for *The Good Person of New Haven,* I drove to the performance from New York City on Highway 95. In low traffic, the drive takes just over two hours. About 20 percent of Long Wharf's subscriber audience enters the theatrical space along this route from New York. With an exit located only a few hundred yards from the theater, one could have attended *The Good Person of New Haven* without every passing through the city of New Haven. "Before Doug Hughes arrived," remarked Alison Carey in an interview:

> Long Wharf didn't take its identity from New Haven. The Theatre took its identity from being two hours from New York. But the subscriber base doesn't change that quickly, and they were not fully prepared for the show. They came in with a set of expectations more appropriate for [Long Wharf's second stage production of] *Hedda Gabler.*[82]

As Carey elucidates, while Long Wharf's collaboration on the New Haven Project changed "business as usual," the subscribers were not necessarily prepared for this shift. "I could assess the audience by the first minute of the play," comments Dana Fripp, "depending on whether they got the New Haven-esque jokes. If they laughed when [model] churches [on the Green] came down, then we've got them, if they didn't, they're from out of town." "Most of the response was positive," observes Long Wharf General Manager Deb Clapp,

> but a few people didn't feel represented. Some of the more middle-class audience members saw only black people on stage [despite the fact that numerous key characters were played by white, Asian, and Latino/a actors], and found the prostitute's story uninteresting.[83]

Bill Rauch adds:

> [A] lot of people felt like "It's not about us. We can't relate to this." I overheard one woman on opening night say, "My Grandmother struggled like that, but not me. And everyone knows socialism doesn't work." Some audience members were also offended by a show about people of color, and saw this as a personal affront. They disliked the cartoonish aesthetics and what they termed the "pageantry" of the show.[84]

Dana Fripp builds on Rauch's statement, critiquing this kind of audience response:

> One lady said it was a "pageant," which I don't quite understand how she makes the distinction of what is theater. But she had her little cheering section saying, "Yeah, we want to see theater for theater's sake." I heard a lot of the subscribers say that. I thought, "I hope you don't like opera because Mozart never wrote something just to write something, because the *Marriage of Figaro* ticked people off." It's as though, "Because I lay my dollars down, I can say what's theater and what's not."

Fripp's comments imply ideological expectations maintained by some audience members, and promoted in part by Long Wharf's subscriber brochure. This "art for art's sake" mentality resists Doug Hughes's call for standards of citizenship as opposed to aesthetics. But subscriber audiences cannot be homogenized. While some subscribers resisted the production, others responded with standing ovations. "It's easy to talk about the subscription base, but I think that's too pat," critiques Moore.[85] Still, local pay-what-you-can audiences tended to be more receptive to the production. "They make house management crazy, but those audiences are our best nights," remarks Stage Manager Allison Lee. "I used to think they were too difficult, they don't behave the way an audience should. Now they're our favorites."[86] While many audience members were not prepared to transform their expectations and aesthetic standards, Lee's comments illustrate a transformation of expectations *about* audiences. Her standards of appropriate audience behavior and response shifted in part due to the contrast between well-behaved but less-receptive audiences.

The audience difference can feel palpable. On 21 May 2000, I returned for a second showing of *The Good Person of New Haven*. I planned to see the evening performance but arrived early for a symposium following that day's matinee. I stood at the door before the audience let out and heard tepid applause before a more traditional-seeming older, white theater audience began streaming out to the lobby. About fifty audience members remained for the symposium. Before beginning the discussion, Henry Fernandez asked how many resided in New Haven. Three people raised their hands. He opened up the question to include the surrounding suburbs. One additional person added her hand. Ninety percent of the remaining audience members resided in other counties, many in New York. Fernandez and Connecticut State Senator Martin Loomis proceeded to urge suburban residents to "look beyond their narrow self-interest and embrace the city." At this, many of the audience members around me noisily departed, with barely concealed murmurs of "this is awful."

Despite Hughes's urging, it was not so easy to change some audience members' expectations and standards. Future community-based collaborations with regional theaters may need to think further about orienting audience members to the experience. Long Wharf staff initially had a difficult time as well, with early resistance to the project's size and perceived "invasion" by community participants. Over time, however, and with attention, this pattern was disrupted. "Cornerstone doesn't do theater the way that many regional professional theaters do. And maybe we need to rethink our assumptions about professionalism," proposes Allison Lee. "This production reminded me what theater is supposed to be about. I've done a lot of big commercial stuff, now I'm not sure whether I can go back." "We are stronger as an institution," adds Long Wharf Production Manager Jean Routt. "We have learned to do theater better—in many senses of the word."[87]

Miscommunications at Arena

Long Wharf staff's enthusiastic support of Cornerstone's methodology and resultant belief that professionals could learn to "do theater better" and even "rethink assumptions about professionalism" indirectly benefited from the collaborative struggles enacted on and off the earlier Arena production's stage. While the *Community Carol* production writers grappled with appropriate ways to develop a well-crafted, community-inclusive script, Arena's communications department faced the challenge of marketing a show that fell outside the conventional parameters of seasonal planning. Arena generally produces a season that includes a number of classical and contemporary hits, performed with a multiracial cast, and one or two shows featuring a playwright, cast, and/or director of color, often explicitly targeted to an audience of color.[88] Within the conventional seasonal structure, *A Community Carol* resisted easy categorization. As a classical, humanistic, multiracial holiday production, the show could be marketed as "Dickens' timeless parable of joy and redemption."[89] According to Cornerstone members, Arena had a harder time promoting the production's community-based aspects, eliding collaboration with an African American community within the more elusive terms of "modern day D.C."

Cornerstone members suggest that the marketing department attempted to conceal the community-based nature of the production in order not to confuse their predominantly white audience. Emphasizing the African American aspects might suggest that this was Arena's targeted "multicultural" production rather than one of their larger audience and income-generating "universal humanist" shows. An episode centering on a poster image for *A Community Carol* affirmed this suspicion for several Cornerstone members.

The poster image featured a Santa figure riding a combination Metro car/sleigh over metropolitan D.C., indicated by the predominance of a snow-tipped Washington Monument. Out of Santa's toy-stuffed sack can be glimpsed a dolly, a sailboat, a hard-to-identify sheaf of corn, and a menorah. A ghostly creature rattles his chains behind Santa, and a pajama-clad man clings to the back of the Metro/sleigh. "A Community Carol" is scrawled above Santa in green-wired Christmas lights. The poster highlights several elements of the show featured in publicity releases: its holiday aspects, its metropolitan D.C. setting, its classical storytelling, and seasonal inclusiveness (menorah for Hanukkah and corn for Kwanzaa). Controversy focused on the perceived race of Santa and on the lack of emphasis on the Anacostia community. The first image that the marketing department created had a white Santa Claus. Bill Rauch explains:

> Basically their fear was that if Santa Claus were black, it would drive away their white audiences. And this was a show being done with a community that was entirely African American . . . and it would have been absurd and very rude to have only a white image, white person on the image. And then they agreed that it would be a black person; and then they printed the 500,000 brochures.[90]

Rauch contends that though Arena and Cornerstone had agreed on Santa's race, the communications department darkened the image (and added a white Marley figure next to the darker Santa). Still, the poster image seemed problematic.

Adapted from
A Christmas Carol
by Alison Carey,
Edward P. Jones,
Laurence Maslon,
and Bill Rauch

The controversial Santa Claus on the Arena Stage program for *A Community Carol,* following revisions by the marketing staff. Photo: Arena Stage.

Alison [Carey] and I asked people at Pizza Hut, waiters and waitresses, "Is this a white person or a black person?" And everyone said it was a white person. Maybe a white person with a tan, but definitely a white person. So then we went and had another meeting saying it has to be a blacker person, actually—black. They reprinted it for the program cover and some posters, but the main damage was done because the main damage was the mailing to Arena's subscriber base.[91]

Again differences in values lie at the root of these marketing difficulties. From Rauch and Cornerstone's point of view, "damage" resulted from not highlighting the specifically African American community-based nature of the show. "The whole episode was sort of sad and stupid," adds Lynn Jeffries,

> because it wasn't a particularly apt poster for the production, anyway. There's no reason to put Santa Claus on a poster for *any* version of *A Christmas Carol,* and it would have been so easy to come up with an image with lots of faces on it, which could have reflected better both the story and the diversity of the cast. And why show the Mall if the story mostly takes place in Anacostia?[92]

The marketing department in turn felt charged with the responsibility to draw Arena's largely white, middle-class audience base through an emphasis on the inclusive holiday aspects of the show. The perceptual blackness of the Santa figure became open to interpretation. A random survey of Pizza Hut customers cannot completely define the relative blackness or whiteness of the figure, but this response does suggest a racial ambiguity in the advertisements for the show.[93]

Controversy about professionalism in marketing, rehearsal, and adaptation again underlines value differences between Arena and Cornerstone, corresponding to each theater's audience relationship. While both theaters ultimately desire to attract audiences, their desired makeup and involvement differs. Because community members participate in all aspects of production, Cornerstone generally attracts an involved and informed audience for whom ticket prices are not at issue, given the company's pay-what-you-can policy. Artistry and excellence are important but considered to relate directly to the degree of community collaboration. In contrast, Arena attracts its audience base and strives to diversify its membership in a less directly inclusive manner. Audiences do not participate in producing the theater's shows, and while the company does target some of its multicultural or ethnically specific shows, Arena depends financially on season subscribers. As the theater readily admits, this subscriber base encompasses an educated, white middle class that can afford a twenty-plus dollar ticket price. It was to them that the show had to be sold. The eventual audience makeup and reception to *A Community Carol* curiously affirmed both theaters' stances.

From Cornerstone's point of view, the production succeeded in drawing not only a large and receptive audience but a diverse community-based one as well. In the context of general appreciation for the biracial draw of the show, however, Bill Rauch professes some disappointment that as the show became a critical success, audiences "got whiter and whiter."[94] Despite group sales to the EOR community, the Arena remained a perceptually white theater in the larger metropolitan D.C. area. Positive reviews drew a greater percentage of those predisposed to attend Arena. For Cornerstone members, this factor reinforced their dedication to collaborations within the community as a way to increase involvement and diverse attendance.

From Arena's point of view, the show's mostly full houses attested to appreciation from their member base. Laurence Maslon refers to the positive feedback that Arena received from its subscribers, exemplified by a letter stating: "My family and I were deeply moved by last night's stunning performance."[95] On the other hand, the limited pay-what-you-can ticket policy, essential from Cornerstone's perspective to the inclusion of EOR residents and the resultant diversity of the audience, made the show less of a financial success for Arena. Doug Wager noted that even with full houses the show generated the income of a production with half- to three-quarter-full houses.[96] As financial stability remains an important concern for Arena, this measure of the production contributed to Arena's ambivalence about future community-based collaborations.[97]

Critical reception to the show's artistry and inclusiveness also referred to each collaborative partner's concerns. The EOR community's response, as articulated by Toni White-Richardson, emphasized the importance of personal connection in affecting and amplifying the show's success. Referring to the "hundreds of friends and relatives" she had personally enticed to the show, she emphasized, "[N]obody said that they did not enjoy it." While White-Richardson's comments in part affirm Arena's concerns with humanistic connection; they also accentuate the fact that most EOR audience members attended because of their connections to cast members.

Arena staff members contend that the positive aspects of audience and critical reception had more to do with the show's artistry than with community inclusiveness. The theater's emphasis on the artistic excellence of the production, refined by Wager's intervention, seemed vindicated by critical reception. While generally positive, a few reviewers tended to reflect overt skepticism or distaste for the show's contemporary updating and inclusiveness. "It's wise to be leery of works that attempt to update the classics, make them 'relevant' to a modern audience," warns Susan Berlin.[98] One student reviewer thought the show "translated poorly" and recommended that audiences interested in Dickens's original attend the more traditional *Carol* showing at the Ford's Theater.[99]

Opinions varied as to the successful integration of community inclusion and the show's resultant artistry. Many reviewers evidenced biases against amateur participants. Lloyd Rose of the *Washington Post* cautioned, "This is the part of *A Community Carol* that holds the most risk of embarrassment."[100] Writing for the *American Weekly*, Gary Tischler echoed Rose's misgivings:

> While the project seems a worthy one on paper, it's also the kind of thing that seems unlikely to be a success in execution. . . . The mixing of amateurs and professionals, including children, always makes critics cringe a little with foreboding because often the mix tends to act like an anchor on both parties.[101]

While initially skeptical, both Rose and Tischler acknowledged the successful outcome of the collaboration. "The amateurs . . . acquit themselves well," admits Rose. Tischler concludes his report by suggesting that the potential pitfalls of the project become "one of [its] principal virtues," affirming that the show's contemporary setting and community-based nature resulted in the fact that "the tale of Scrooge became our story."

While these critics responded positively to the collaborative nature of the show and its worthwhile accessibility, others expressed unwillingness to overlook what they viewed as overt political correctness. *Time Magazine* reviewer William Henry III refers somewhat benignly to the production's "worn-on-the-sleeve liberalism."[102] The *Baltimore Sun* is more harsh in its review headlined "*A Community Carol:* Dickens of a Story, Updated and Unrelentingly PC."[103] The review berates the production for its inclusion of AIDS ribbons, Kwanzaa, Hanukkah, and nursing home patients. "It tries too hard—and succeeds too well—at being achingly politically correct." Critical responses suggest both the values and potential detractions of community inclusiveness in relation to the perceived success of *A Community Carol* as a show. From the viewpoints of the show's coproducers, the long-term impacts of the production and its process must also be considered in measuring its success.

Some Remains

ARENA AND ANACOSTIA

The long-term impact of *A Community Carol* can be assessed in part by the project's initially articulated goals. In preliminary notes to the EOR advisory board, Cornerstone and Arena outlined their intentions: to support community-based theater in the EOR area, to develop a relationship between Arena Stage and southeast Washington that would allow the two to share resources, audiences, and artists, and to recapture the spirit of *A Christmas Carol* within a contemporary local context.

Commentary from project participants and critical reception affirmed, for the most part, the production's success as a contemporary, local adaptation. As for supporting community-based theater in the EOR area, a portion of box office receipts helped to establish the East of the River Arts Coalition, which, while it did not establish a new community-based theater, did support existing arts organizations. In terms of sharing resources, Arena invited younger *Community Carol* participants to audition for season productions and provided advisory board members and community participants with complimentary tickets to Arena previews. More expansive audience transactions, however, remain limited to the *Community Carol* production. Toni White-Richardson attests that the hundreds of audience members she invited to the show through her relationships with community organizations, friends, relatives, and her national sorority only ventured into the Arena because of her involvement in this particular project. Asked whether these audience members might return to the Arena, Richardson thought briefly and answered no.

White-Richardson's response implies the failure of the process to provide any long-term changes in Arena's audience base—a response complicated by the fact that Doug Wager did not initiate the project with this goal in mind. Wager had hoped primarily to introduce Arena's established subscription membership to Cornerstone's work. Audience expansion developed as a potential, though not necessary, benefit in Wager's eyes. Though the project "shook up the culture of the institution" in a healthy way, according to Wager, the institution did not change. Laurence Maslon accords that the structural preservation of the two different organizations remains beneficial for both, as Cornerstone and Arena serve different needs in a larger theatrical context.

In a more immediate realm, relationships between Southeast Washington and Arena Stage improved in individual ways. Wager cites the importance of greetings on the Washington mall, letters of recommendation, and mutual invitations to artistic events in increasing communication. White-Richardson commends Arena for the "impact and change made in people's lives." Both assert the success of the project in contrast to most outreach programs. "I think the concept of wanting to 'reach out' is becoming obsolete," explains White-Richardson. "Sometimes a reach-out can be perceived as a handout. [It's more beneficial to] tell somebody, 'I need your help, I need your collaborative effort, I need your brainpower to help me with this.'"[104]

While Arena and the EQR community were in some agreement about the results of their collaboration, Arena and Cornerstone diverged, not surprisingly, around key differences in defining and prioritizing aspects of professionalism. Wager cites as one benefit of the production to Cornerstone the fact that "Bill [Rauch] and Lynn [Jeffries] proved to me and to others within the professional theater world that they are artists of the highest caliber and not just practitioners of community theater." Laurence

Maslon valued the experience as "the most gratifying thing I worked on in seven years." Yet, Maslon's critiques of the project center on Rauch's artistic priorities.[105] "The Arena staff was asked to take on a project of enormous, unprecedented complexity with a new director. The stress came from the size of the show. Ironically, it was the fact that Bill's vision is so large that overwhelmed us."[106] The Arena never intended to adopt Cornerstone's methods or purpose; it intended to create an engaging, possibly edifying production; unlike staff at Long Wharf (a smaller theater with a different agenda), the process did little to change Arena's way of working.[107]

The project in turn affirmed to Cornerstone members the value of their own inclusive theater making and collective administration. Additionally, the residency offered a template for rethinking certain production strategies, such as allowing more time for season planning and for navigating future institutional collaborations. While neither company drastically altered its foundational beliefs about how to produce good theater, the Arena collaboration became only the first of many more cooperative institutional partnerships for Cornerstone. The New Haven Project enacted a more balanced relationship between regional and community-based practices on the whole, but the production raises different kinds of questions about how to measure collaborative success, good theater, and the staging of community.

OTHER REMNANTS

Speaking to a local reporter during *The Good Person of New Haven* rehearsal process, New Haven resident Stephen Papa waxed enthusiastic about the project's potential for wide-scale social change: "If we can only do this city-wide, statewide, nationwide—this is the way you get rid of the racial tension, with things like this. We have black and white and Spanish-speaking people and they're all friends and we get along wonderfully."[108] Papa's optimistic proposal suggests that changes in the tense racial landscape of America can commence at an individual level, with people simply getting along. Ongoing assessment of Cornerstone's work begs the question of whether this interaction eliminates or simply elides tensions that emerge from structural economic differences and deep-seated historical circumstances. Can the New Haven project's success be measured only in terms of individual and communal relationships? What else remains from the New Haven Project's three-year effort to stage the city? How should the engaged critic appraise the project, particularly in relation to Arena's staging? I contend that an evaluative paradigm must encompass not only community involvement, audience response, and critical review but also institutional imagination.

In contrast to Arena's reversion to its professional standards and principles, Long Wharf staff began to re-envision what it meant to do "good" theater. Issues of access were understood as a combination of cultural and material factors; Long Wharf recognized that New Haven residents needed to feel welcomed into the theatrical space, while often requiring transportation to get there.[109] Additionally, the theatre reexamined its assumed position as the "center of civic culture," reimagining a relationship with its urban community as an ongoing, mutually engaged process. The Legacy of New Haven Project, established after the close of *The Good Person of New Haven,* provides a site for these engagements between the theater and its local constituency to continue.[110]

Yet, other aspects of the project suggest that some civic structures and theatrical strategies remain more difficult to alter. Economic and racial factors contributing to the maintenance of ghettoized neighborhoods in New Haven require transformation at a deeper socio-structural level than the New Haven Project is able to offer. At the same time, Long Wharf's ongoing commitment to produce "vigorous classics" may be perceived as more shows "about a bunch of white people" by its local constituency. A mentality among some subscribers that community-based theater is not for them or about them and represents a kind of social service pageantry that is destroying the experience of "theater for theater's sake" also complicates the relationship between Long Wharf and its expanding audience constituency. In trying to do "good," Long Wharf may find itself constrained by its own theatrical culture, much like Shen Te/Tyesha in Brecht's parable.[111]

Cornerstone did not definitively "change the mainstream." It may have been naïve for the company to think that they could, given the structural and material constraints that limit the changes any theater can effect, and the vast ideological difference between regional and community-based theaters. Still, too many instances of exchange and insight occurred to dismiss either project as failed, self-deceiving, or simply opportunistic. It may seem appropriate then to give up on making any definitive statements about either collaboration's success, to say that on the whole each project succeeded and failed in different ways, or to suggest that evaluation seems beside the point. But it is not. For if the nature of "goodness" and "community" is never addressed, we all stagnate as artists and citizens. The standards of regional theater, valued by Arena Stage in 1993, cannot be the only terms by which theatrical achievement is measured; this excludes too many ideas, potential audience members, and ways of thinking about representational strategies. There is a courageous hubris implicit in Long Wharf's dare to stage the future of the American city. There is bold audacity in Arena Stage's desire to try something different, even once. Simply diversifying who is on the stage and in the audience will not shift how we think about theater, nor will merely refining craft and artistry. Reimagining what is performed, where, with whom, and for what reasons will. This ongoing rethinking, rather than any particular methodology—either community-based or regional—ultimately creates good theater. Determining how to assess the accomplishments and meanings of such a theater will take up *Staging America*'s concluding chapter. As Dana Fripp notes in speaking about the profound difficulty of the work in general, "There's gonna be some labor pains. I know that."

7

CONCLUSION: CURTAIN CALLS

> You know what my favorite part of the play was? Curtain call. And you
> know why? Because that's when we all came together: Cornerstone, the
> local actors, and the crew—all out there as a team. It was always a
> wonderful feeling.
> —Suzanne Pollastrini, actor in *Three Sisters from West Virginia*

In a theatrical production, the final onstage moment, the curtain call, enacts a threshold space of unity, a moment on the edge of the stage for
mutual acknowledgment of performers and audience. At the same time, the
bow recognizes the individual, as actor and character, as self and performer.
The curtain call concedes, even foregrounds, the role playing of the individual while bringing together various groups. These elements of communal association, individual achievement, and the role playing that can characterize both, weave together intertwining strands of community-based
theater and myths of American citizenry.[1] *Staging America,* as an idea and
a text, must confront the tension between these interwoven strands, while
keeping an eye on the place of the critic in this weaving. This closing chapter
revisits ideas introduced throughout *Staging America* of the importance of
community-based theater in addressing how we negotiate social identity,
enact culture, and play out various reciprocal relationships between theater
and community, representation and America, critic and performance. This
final chapter also grapples with the problem of closure, an occasion that
can sometimes sweep aside questions raised during a process.

The moment Suzanne Pollastrini refers to as "a wonderful feeling," when
everything comes together, hangs fleetingly on the border of the stage, is a
potentially intense moment of *communitas.* Then, cast and crew break apart,
divisions between audience and performers break down, the crowd mills,

fluidly reforming into various groups. Performers and audience members return to the social roles that they play off the stage, the production possibly influencing those roles as the impact of performance continues. The curtain call provides a sense of closure while reopening another terrain of questions about the very nature of conclusion, of ending and certitude. After ten years of practicing and writing about community-based theater, what I have written and thought remains open for reevaluation. This concluding chapter offers a space to ponder the performance of the previous six, to review and regroup the ideas generated, and to try not to forget the more complex questions. In reaching towards closure, I focus on two essential queries: How does Cornerstone and, more broadly, community-based theater stage America? And what is the role of the scholar in framing this and other questions about the work?

STAGING AMERICAN THEATER

> To my mind, Cornerstone is on the forefront of cultural democracy. We always hear from artists telling us what America is about, but we've seldom seen artists such as these who go out and meet America. They just go out and do it.
>
> —Peter Sellars

Peter Sellars proposes that contemporary stagings of America can embrace at least two distinct possibilities, representation (what America is about) and inclusion (cultural democracy). As elaborated upon in earlier chapters, including discussion of the production Sellars directed for Cornerstone, each of these notions is fraught with its own chain of questions and complexities. Who represents what for whom? How and where does this representation take place? In what ways does inclusion imply exclusion? What are the limitations of inclusion as a mode of administration as well as production? Grappling with questions of authenticity and agency in each of these realms requires focus on how theater negotiates social identity, a focus intimately linked with the terms of its artistry and geography.

Manifestations of American theater in the early-twentieth century often followed divergent paths, trying to either centralize or decentralize performance. Broadway theaters and playwrights of the 1920s and 1930s established a principal site for American-made drama. In 1930s New York, the Group Theater sought to redefine an American, as opposed to European, dramatic repertoire and engage a specifically American acting style. In direct opposition to these movements, Little Theaters in the early 1900s, grassroots and regional theaters in the 1950s, each strove to decentralize American theater, to locate and play for an audience based around the country.

Yet, despite geographic decentralization, a unifying force persisted in regional theater. Dominated by notions of cultural humanism and established rites of professionalism, most of these theaters developed an audience firmly rooted in the educated, white middle class. Regional theaters often claim to reflect common concerns, but due to factors such as perception, location, marketing, and ticket prices, and despite outreach programming and efforts to embrace diverse theatrical representations, these theaters continue to primarily serve a narrow audience constituency. Thus, American theater also encompasses movements that do not attempt to claim a central or unifying representational space. These theaters, including the Workers Theater Movement of the 1930s, the Chicano theaters founded in the 1960s, and the women's theaters initiated in the 1970s, suggest that identity can be decentralized, foregrounding more particular aspects of American identity rooted in class, ethnicity, and gender.

This fragmentation of cultural identity cannot adequately convey its complexity and multiplicity, or the occasional need to build coalitions across difference. Community-based theater, in its current forms and links to past practices, offers another way to think about staging America, and some of the more problematic aspects of establishing and performing a common cultural identity. Efforts to engage a progressive, Americanizing practice through civic theater walked a fine line between inclusion and control, while tapping into the potential for theater to awaken a sense of common purpose. Grassroots and folk theater resisted trends towards unifying nationalism and instead sought to unearth a more popular voice, a tactic veering into romanticizing practices that ventriloquized or muffled the sounds of those voices. More fragmented movements grounded in socialism and identity politics proved essential in resisting oppressive normalizing forces, though less focused on bridging differences between resistant groups. Each tactic served and continues to serve its particular sociohistorical moment.

Emerging in the 1980s, largely ignorant of other community-based performance, Cornerstone represents neither the ideal form of these practices nor of American theater. But as a company continuously grappling with tactics of inclusion, decentralization, bridge building, and artistic engagement, Cornerstone offers a rich site to probe the limitations and possibilities of staging America through community-based practices.

RESTAGING CORNERSTONE AS AMERICAN THEATER

Over the course of its sixteen-year history, Cornerstone conspicuously staged and restaged itself as an American theater. Tropes of travel and geography defined the company's early years, a time when founding members felt literally driven to discover what Americans wanted through theater. Nothing symbolized this drive so well as the company van, emblazoned on the cover of Cornerstone's first newsletter. Emblematic of the group's early nomadic existence, the van invoked the creation of community through travel and mutual activity. The van also exemplified an understanding of America defined by place, a concept reinforced by logos featuring maps of the United States.

Cornerstone's rural years also focused on the embodiment of America through a matrix of diverse locations and individuals, brought together through *The Winter's Tale.* This production strove to stage America through representation of the urban and rural, iconically signified in its adaptation and stage settings, as well as through travel across the country, and a process emphasizing participation. The act of bringing together people, places, and process ironically foregrounded the impossibilities of fully realizing such a task; some areas of dissent could not be accommodated within the desire for inclusion.

Cornerstone restaged itself once again upon the company's move to a more permanent base in Los Angeles. This sprawling urban terrain reinforced the impossibility of "covering" America through theatrical representation. Christopher Liam Moore elaborates: "The feeling that I had driving around LA, my head was literally spinning. It was unbelievable. People suggested hundreds of communities. We saw hundreds of communities. It seemed to me like LA had more communities than the United States."[2] So the company burrowed into the very notion of community, uncoupling the term from its geographic connotations. Ensemble members also became energized about rethinking the company's and the city's identities. At a meeting prior to the move, Stephen Gutwillig exclaimed, "What excites me about being in one place for longer is that Cornerstone gets to work on its identity and the identity of the city over and over again."[3] This act of ongoing reconfiguration found expression in the company's bridge shows, which brought together individuals from different residencies. One of these more recent productions, *Broken Hearts* (1999), illuminates the process of redefining the city's identity.

Broken Hearts, written by Lisa Loomer, brought together participants from Boyle Heights, Baldwin Hills, Beverly Hills, and Broadway and Hill streets of Chinatown (Cornerstone's B. H. Cycle). Loomer's neo-noir mystery journeyed across seventy years of Los Angeles history through four ethnically distinct neighborhoods. Structured as a search for a missing ring, the play embraced both a celebration of ethnic specificity and the possibility of border crossing. Interracial relationships and friendships played out next to shootings, injuries, and forced migrations, while casting choices implied a possible play of identity against the body's visual markings. Nine-year-old Emily Hong took on the role of an elderly Chinese waiter, blind actor Lynn Manning played a (sighted) deaf character, and a Latina actress represented the younger version of a white character.

The various celebrations and subversions in the production offered a utopian vision of Los Angeles—a "no place" that became a site of possibility in its stage representation. In a city striated into neighborhoods that rarely commingle, Cornerstone's bridge show enacted literal and figurative boundary crossings. As the various plot lines of *Broken Hearts* came together, so too did the various communities and individuals onstage, including professional actors, a school teacher, a trial lawyer, a former gang member, and Miss Chinatown 1998. *Broken Hearts* did not pretend to resolve racial differences in Los Angeles, nor did it grapple with all of the material and historical relations that can construct difference in the city. The production instead offered an imaginative construction in which the bodies of the various performers remained center stage. In this enactment, the possibility of boundary crossing and community bridge building seemed at least momentarily actualized.

Broken Hearts, Ghurba, and *The Central Ave. Chalk Circle* each restaged questions about how groups perform and reform cultural difference. These productions, and others in Los Angeles, enact aspects of negotiating social identity in one particularly diverse urban landscape in the United States. But does the work here, alongside regional coproductions around the country, fully stage America? Prior to moving to Los Angeles, the company felt it would remain a national theater. "I will just say," affirmed Bill Rauch at a 1991 company meeting, "that I definitely see LA as one local project that's part of our national program."[4] Over ten years in Los Angeles, the company's self-definition shifted. When asked in 2001 whether Cornerstone continues to function as a national theater, former Managing Director Leslie Tamaribuchi responded: "That hubris doesn't sit well with me. I value too well the diversity and complexity of America to pretend to represent it. Maybe a better question is, 'Do our values have resonance with principles that hold our nation together?'"[5] This articulation of the company's work in relation to principles rather than representational practices proposes perhaps a way of un-staging America. Cornerstone no longer claims to be an American theater, or to fully represent America, but rather explores through performance the constituent values that compose the aggregate entity "America."

Over sixteen years, Cornerstone's conception of America transformed from a collage of geographically bounded areas to a matrix of diverse cultures, to a rethinking of how community and identity could be defined and bridged. That rethinking removes the necessity to proclaim the company as an American theater at the same time as it perhaps more accurately reflects the difficulties of defining American identity. Cornerstone's early conceptions of America moved beyond commonality and plurality to an understanding of the nation as a matrix of continuously refigured difference. This rethinking parallels ongoing sociopolitical debate about nation, culture, and identity. In *National Culture and the New Global System,* Frederick Buell describes a paradigm shift in the view of American identity, "from the notion of a pluralist society—a society composed of a mosaic of separate cultures—to a view of America as a complex but common social system."[6]

While no longer claiming primary identity as an American Theater, Cornerstone enacts a fundamental understanding of the complexities of negotiating social identity. The company's process, itself always *in* process, reflects a sensibility about the paradoxical essentialness, elusiveness, and multiplicity of identity. In his article on new communitarianism, Richard Ford elaborates, "It is not the idea of politics based on identity but a wrongheaded definition of identity, the insistence on a singular 'authentic' or essential identity, that proves problematic."[7] Problematic or not, for many individuals, identity remains emotionally essential, and a belief in fluidity must take into account what bell hooks terms "the authority of experience."[8] Cornerstone's community-based productions allow for recognition of essential (that is, important) categories of social and individual identity as well as for recognition of their nonessentiality, their negotiability, and thus their potential for coalition.

But here the company must struggle with some divergent ideological principles as they maneuver between radical democratic and liberal inclusive practices. Cornerstone recognizes the complexity and play of identity and the need to build coalitions that don't erase difference while also attempting to affect and shape more conventional theatrical practices within the regional theater system. The company remakes classical stories (and creates new ones) but maintains a model of authoritative expertise, in which professional artists write, direct, and design productions (with input from participants). Here too, perhaps, Cornerstone plays out the American nation-building dilemma contrasting democratic inclusion and representational expertise.

Cornerstone's community-based work contributes to a rethinking of community, additionally confronting the idea that society can, as Ford puts it, "actually live with difference rather than either flatten and assimilate it or reflexively fret about or celebrate its irreducibility."[9] Cornerstone's community-based projects thus participate, in Buell's terms, "in an ongoing anxious debate about American cultural identity, rather than the resolution of that debate."[10] This debate, he proposes, has been what makes one an American.

CRITICAL ENDINGS

But is this play of social and national identity all we "want to know," in Clifford Geertz's phrasing, or "seek to understand," following Elaine Lawless?[11] How does this interpretation, focusing on community-based theater and identity, forward other conversations about aesthetics and critical ethics? Staging, after all, implies artistry as well as role play, and practitioners of community-based theater and its affiliates have emphasized this no less than their critics. "We must be no more tolerant of bad art, than of bad civics," asserted Percy Mackaye in 1917.[12] Of course, adopting standards of measurement that distinguish good art from bad remains embedded in cultural politics, as elaborated upon in previous chapters. Still, laying bare those standards can clarify the framework within which interpretation and critique occurs.

I seek complexity, surprise, and imagination both on the stage and in the performance field, and responsiveness to and from the audience. In outlining these criteria, I recognize once again their interrelationship with methodology. Because of a participatory ethics, the makeup of the community-based theater audiences differs radically from more "professional" productions. Cornerstone's artistry remains embedded in a philosophy of locality and inclusion. "Everything [in our productions] has been about developing an American aesthetic through the specificity of where we are," notes former ensemble member Benajah Cobb.[13] That specificity has additionally relied upon the surprise derived from cultural collisions between more classic texts and contemporary adaptations. At their best, these productions tell old stories in new ways that often take into account the specificity of place. A bus drives away to reveal a different rural landscape each night of *The Winter's Tale*. Everyman's hypocritical kin approach him with seeming love, walking down an up escalator in the Santa Monica Mall. A young girl plays God to Faust in a parish hall cafeteria. Police officers and a former felon sing and dance together on the stage of LA's self-described cultural center.

Surprise also derives from the makeup of an audience. A Buddhist nun sits next to a Jewish businessman at a festival of faith event. Future director Christopher Liam Moore speaks enthusiastically of how community collaborators from Watts, Boyle Heights, and Chinatown will come to the gay and lesbian center to see a new Cornerstone play.[14] Yet, this delight can shift back into the actuality of difference. A talented African American woman drops out of the "Latino" *Faustinos*. The nuns depart from a faith-based production when conflict erupts. Inclusion runs the risk of flattening out difference or of transforming it into "a little too much of the Christmas pudding."[15]

Artistic inclusion can also risk ignoring institutional politics and the complexities of engaging progressive social change, if that is at all feasible or desirable.[16] In a recent article in *Theatre Journal,* Jill Dolan argues for the utopian potential of theater "as a participatory forum in which ideas and possibilities for social equity and justice are shared."[17] Dolan locates part of our desire to attend theater in the search for new ideas about how to be with each other, believing that "theatre and performance can articulate a common future, one that's more just and equitable, one in which we can all participate equally."[18] But this vision of utopia presumes the possibility of a common future and shared ideas of justice and equity. Though I too have argued for the imaginative potentials enacted within community-based work, I wonder how this attitude can grapple with deeply held differences about "better futures." Someone who believes in avoiding conflict cannot literally remain in the room with those committed to the expression of dissent.

Perhaps what is required is yet another in-between position, shifting between utopian thinking and practical cynicism. Critical challenges can sometimes lead to insights that progressive assumptions might not recognize. "Maybe we did have rose-tinted glasses," admits Christopher Liam Moore, "Thinking 'everybody is part of this piece.' [The critical writing] made us realize that, 'no you're not.' You're picking and choosing in every single decision you make and there's another story you're not choosing to tell."[19]

I have chosen to tell a tale of Cornerstone, community-based theater, and America. In the course of its narration, I have been challenged as well as challenging. The story fragments, breaks apart, turns back on itself. A set of sub-stories breaks out in narrative endnotes. The terms of this book's premise remain both more detailed and more in question at the tale's end. Would it be better if one were able to define conclusively "community, Cornerstone, America"? Definition remains a snapshot of where we are at a moment, not where we are going or how we are changing. "If everything is dangerous, then we always have something to do," proposes Michel Foucault, explaining his wariness of seeking solutions rather than exploring problems, an exploration he claims leads not to apathy but to activism.[20] We are always in the midst. There is always more to do and question. And that is a joyful possibility.

APPENDIX

NOTES

WORKS CITED

INDEX

Appendix: Cornerstone Production History, 1986–2001

All community-based and ensemble productions through 1991 were directed by Bill Rauch with music by David Reiffel. All ensemble shows through 1990 were choreographed by Sabrina Peck.

Rural Community-Based Productions, 1986–1991

Newport News, Virginia, 1986
  Our Town. By Thornton Wilder. Produced with residents of Newport News.
Marmarth, North Dakota, 1986
  The Marmarth Hamlet. Adapted by the company and people of Marmarth from *Hamlet* by William Shakespeare.
Prince George County, Virginia, 1986
  The Snow Queen. Adapted by the company from *The Snow Queen* by Hans Christian Anderson. Produced with students from Prince George County.
Marfa, Texas, 1987
  That Marfa Fever. Adapted by the company and people of Marfa from *Hay Fever* by Noel Coward.
Dinwiddie County, Virginia, 1987
  The Pretty Much True Story of Dinwiddie County. By Douglas Petrie. Produced with residents of Dinwiddie.
Miami Beach, Florida, 1987
  The Dog Beneath the Skin: An Epidemic Epic. Adapted by the company and members of the Miami AIDS community from W. H. Auden and Christopher Isherwood.
Norcatur, Kansas, 1987
  Tartoof (Or, An Imposter in Norcatur—and at Christmas!). Adapted by the company and people of Norcatur from *Tartuffe* by Molière.
Long Creek, Oregon, 1988
  The Good Person of Long Creek. Adapted by the company and people of Long Creek from *The Good Woman of Setzuan* by Bertolt Brecht.
Schurz, Nevada, 1988
  The House on Walker River. Adapted by the company and people of the Walker River Paiute Tribe and Schurz from *The Oresteia* by Aeschylus. Choreography by Sabrina Peck.

Port Gibson, Mississippi, 1989
> *Romeo & Juliet.* Adapted by the company and people of Claiborne County from *Romeo and Juliet* by William Shakespeare.

Montgomery, West Virginia, 1989
> *Three Sisters from West Virginia.* Adapted by the company and people of the Kanawha Valley from *Three Sisters* by Anton Chekhov.

Eastport, Maine, 1990
> *Pier Gynt.* Adapted by the company, people of Eastport and Perry, and the Pleasant Point Passamaquoddy Reservation from *Peer Gynt* by Henrik Ibsen.

National Tour, 1991
> *The Winter's Tale: An Interstate Adventure.* Adapted by the company from *The Winter's Tale* by William Shakespeare. Choreography by Sabrina Peck. Produced with participants from prior Cornerstone residencies.

Productions in Los Angeles and Environs, 1992–2001

THREE DEFINITIONS OF COMMUNITY, 1992–1994

The Toy Truck. Adapted by the company and Peter Sagal from *The Clay Cart* by King Sudraka as translated by J. A. B. Van Buitenen. Music by Nathan Wang. Directed by Bill Rauch. Produced with residents of the Angelus Plaza Senior Center, 1992.

Rushing Waters. By Migdalia Cruz. Music by Danny Vicente, Darren Brady and La Rue Marshall. Directed by Bill Rauch. Produced with residents of Pacoima, 1993.

Ghurba. Written, composed, and directed by Shishir Kurup. Produced with Los Angeles Arab Americans, 1993.

L.A. Building. Adapted by Alison Carey from Hsia Yen as translated by George Hayden. Music by David Markowitz. Directed by Bill Rauch. A bridge show produced with participants from Cornerstone's first three Los Angeles residencies, Angelus Plaza, Pacoima, and Arab Americans citywide, 1994.

WATTS, 1994–1995

Breaking Plates. Written and directed by Ashby Semple with participants from Watts. Watts Towers Arts Center, 1994.

The Love of the Nightingale. By Timberlake Wertenbaker. Music by Jan Mabry. Directed by Ashby Semple. Produced with residents of Watts. Watts Towers Arts Center, 1994.

Los Faustinos. By Bernardo Solano. Music by Robert Ceja. Directed by Juliette Carillo. Produced with residents of Watts. San Miguel Parish Hall, 1994.

Sid Arthur. Written and composed by Shishir Kurup. Inspired by Herman Hesse. Directed by Page Leong. Produced with residents of Watts. St. John's United Methodist Church, 1995.

The Central Ave. Chalk Circle. By Bertolt Brecht, adapted by Eric Bentley and Lynn Manning with Spanish translations by Bernardo Solano. Music by Shishir Kurup. Directed by Bill Rauch. A bridge show produced with residents of Watts. Watts Labor Community Action Committee, 1995.

BIRTHDAY AND WORKPLACES, 1996–1997

The Birthday of the Century. Written and composed by Shishir Kurup. Directed by Bill Rauch. Produced with Angelenos born on 30 June. California Plaza, 1996.
Work/Place. A collaboration with downtown workers featuring oral history-based stories from the Central Public Library and the Los Angeles Police Department's Parker Center, 1997.
Candude, or The Optimistic Civil Servant. Adapted from Voltaire by Tracy Young. Music by Joe Romano, Shishir Kurup, Laurence O'Keefe, and Kyle Glass. David Markowitz, music director. Directed by Shishir Kurup. Produced with Los Angeles Police Department, Metropolitan Transportation Authority, Los Angeles Public Library, and U.S. Postal Service employees. Los Angeles Central Library, 1997.

B.H. CYCLE, 1997–1999

Los Vecinos: A Play for Neighbors. Adapted by Luis Alfaro and Diane Rodriguez with residents of Boyle Heights from the Mexican shepherds' play *La Pastorela.* Music by Shishir Kurup. Directed by Diane Rodriguez. Performed in the Community Service Organization Building, Boyle Heights, 1997.
Los Biombos/The Screens. Adapted by Gloria Alvarez from Jean Genet with the collaboration of Pete Galindo, Lynn Jeffries, and Peter Sellars. Music by Blues Experiment. Directed by Peter Sellars. Produced with Boyle Heights residents. East Los Angeles Skills Center, 1997.
A Beautiful Country. Written and directed by Chay Yew. Produced with Chinatown residents at Castelar Elementary School in Chinatown, 1998.
Magic Tricks. Adapted by Rickerby Hinds from *Esu and the Vagabond Minstrels* by Femi Osofisan. Music by Shishir Kurup and David Markowitz. Directed by Armando Molina. Produced with residents of Baldwin Hills. Baldwin Hills Crenshaw Plaza, 1998.
A.K.A.: A Beverly Hills Musical Morality Play. Adapted by Shem Bitterman from *The Marquis of Keith* by Frank Wedekind. Music by Shishir Kurup. Directed by Bill Rauch. Produced with residents of Beverly Hills at Beverly Hills High School, 1999.
Broken Hearts: A BH Mystery. By Lisa Loomer. Music by Michael Abels. Directed by Bill Rauch. A bridge show produced in collaboration with participants from four B.H.–initialed neighborhoods, including Boyle Heights, Baldwin Hills, Beverly Hills, and Broadway/Hill (Chinatown). Los Angeles Theatre Center, 1999.

LOS ANGELES COMMUNITY-BASED
PRODUCTIONS AND FESTIVALS, 1997–2001

bUS plays. A festival of nine short plays with past collaborators at the Los Angeles
Museum of Contemporary Art.
Each play was staged on a city bus parked in the museum. Cornerstone's ensemble
contribution was *Token, Alien* (see ensemble productions), 1997.
Mall Plays. A festival of nine original works by past community collaborators per-
forming in three Southern California malls. Cornerstone's ensemble contribu-
tion was *Foot/Falls* (see ensemble productions). Performed at Santa Monica Place
Shopping Center, Montclair Plaza, and Fashion Square Oakdale, 1999.
For Here or To Go? By Alison Carey. Inspired by Francis Beaumont and John
Fletcher, *The Knight of the Burning Pestle.* Directed by Bill Rauch. Music by
Michael Abels and Shishir Kurup. A bridge show produced with participants
from all previous Cornerstone projects in Los Angeles. Mark Taper Forum, Los
Angeles, 2000.
Growing Home. By Bernardo Solano. Directed by Mark Valdez. Produced with resi-
dents of Fresno and California State University students. Fresno, California, 2001.
The Festival of Faith. A series of collaborative community performances presented
at five places of worship throughout Los Angeles, 2001.

Regional Coproductions, 1993–2000

A Community Carol. Adapted from Charles Dickens by Alison Carey, Edward P.
Jones, Laurence Maslon, and Bill Rauch. Music by Michael Keck. Directed by
Bill Rauch. Choreography by Sabrina Peck. Produced at Arena Stage with resi-
dents of Anacostia. Washington, D.C., 1993.
The Too Noble Brothers. Adapted by Alison Carey and hundreds of members of the
Seward Park High School community from *Two Noble Kinsmen* by William
Shakespeare and John Fletcher. Directed by Bill Rauch. Choreographed by
Sabrina Peck. Produced in association with the New York Shakespeare Festi-
val/Public Theater at Seward Park High School. New York, 1997.
Steelbound. Adapted by Alison Carey. Inspired by *Prometheus Bound* by Aeschylus.
Music by Ysaye M. Barnwell. Directed by Bill Rauch. Movement Director
Jennie Gilrain. Produced with Touchstone Theater Company and residents of
Bethlehem. Bethlehem Steel Plant, Bethlehem, Pennsylvania, 1999.
The Good Person of New Haven. Adapted by Alison Carey from *The Good Woman
of Setzuan* by Bertolt Brecht as translated by Ralph Manheim. Music by Shishir
Kurup. Directed by Bill Rauch. Choreographed by Sabrina Peck. Produced in
collaboration with Long Wharf Theatre and New Haven residents. Long Wharf
Theatre, New Haven, Connecticut, 2000.
Peter Pan. Adapted by Alison Carey from J. M. Barrie. Music by Paul James. Di-
rected by Bill Rauch. Choreographed by Ken Roht. Produced at Great Lakes
Theater Festival with residents of Cleveland, Ohio, 2000.

Ensemble Productions, 1986–2001

I Can't Pay the Rent. Adapted from familiar melodrama by the company. Premiered 1986.

The Maske Family Musical. Adapted by the company from Carl Sternheim. Directed by Bill Rauch. Choreographed by Sabrina Peck. Premiered in Front Royal, Virginia, 1986.

A Midsummer Night's Dream. Adapted by the company from William Shakespeare. Directed by Bill Rauch. Premiered in Radford, Virginia, 1988.

Slides of Our Trip. A revue of Cornerstone songs by David Reiffel. Codirected by Sabrina Peck and Bill Rauch. Premiered in San Francisco, 1988.

The Video Store Owner's Significant Other. Adapted by the company from *The Shoemaker's Prodigious Wife* by Frederico Garcia Lorca. Directed by Bill Rauch. Choreographed by Sabrina Peck. Premiered at the American Place Theater, Washington D.C., 1990, as part of Cornerstone's February Festival, in which former collaborating communities each adapted versions of Lorca's script and performed their adaptations in the same month.

Twelfth Night or As You Were. Adapted by Alison Carey from Shakespeare. Directed by Bill Rauch. Los Angeles Theatre Center, 1994.

Everyman at the Mall. Adapted by Shishir Kurup and Bill Rauch from Anonymous. Directed by Bill Rauch and Shishir Kurup. Premiered at Santa Monica Mall, Santa Monica, 1994.

California Seagull. Adapted by Alison Carey from *The Seagull* by Anton Chekhov as translated by Maria Ashot. Directed by Bill Rauch. Premiered at Santa Monica Mall, Santa Monica, 1995.

Mallière. Adapted by Alison Carey from Molière as translated from the French by Albert Bermel. Directed by Bill Rauch. Santa Monica Place Mall, Santa Monica, 1996.

Token, Alien. By Christopher Liam Moore. Directed by Bill Rauch. Premiered at the Museum of Contemporary Art, Los Angeles, 1997.

Medea/Macbeth/Cinderella. Euripides, Shakespeare, and Rodgers and Hammerstein performed on one stage simultaneously. Directed by Bill Rauch and Tracey Young. Choreographed by Sabrina Peck. Produced in collaboration with the Actors' Gang at The Actors' Gang Theater, Hollywood, 1998.

Foot/Mouth. Including Samuel Beckett's *Footfalls* and Alison Carey's adaptation of Luigi Pirandello's *The Man with the Flower in His Mouth.* Directed by Christopher Liam Moore. Premiered in Montclair, California, 1999.

An Antigone Story. Adapted and directed by Shishir Kurup from *Antigone* by Sophocles. Subway Terminal Building, Los Angeles, 2000.

Zones. By Peter Howard. Directed by Bill Rauch. Produced in multiple religiously affiliated locations in Los Angeles, 2001.

NOTES

Preface

1. Benedict Anderson, *Imagined Communities: Reflections on the Origins and Spread of Nationalism* (London: Verso, 1983).

2. Michael Kimmelman, "In a Square, A Sense of Unity," *New York Times* (19 September 2001): E1, 5.

3. Bill Rauch, e-mail to the author, 5 September 2001. Christopher Liam Moore adds, "Sometimes in reading a critical response, having not been trained in that, I think, 'I just don't understand what's going on here, and they're writing about me'" (interview with the author, Los Angeles, 29 October 2001).

1. Introduction: Surveying the Terrain

1. Peter Brook, "The Deadly Theater," in *The Empty Space* (New York: Athaneum, 1968). Brook discusses four types of theater in *The Empty Space:* holy, immediate, rough, and deadly. He characterizes deadly theater as "depressingly active" (40), replicating conventional form without thought, succeeding because of its very dullness, as audiences can associate culture with duty. That a theater is community-based and in tension with high culture is no guarantee of its liveness but of a different kind of potential for immediacy. Community-based theater that relies on replicating conventions faces similar threats of deadliness. For this reason among others, critical questioning as well as celebration characterizes this book's attitude towards the form.

2. The use of "America" to designate the people and entity of the United States is problematic, as the term encompasses North, South, and Central America. I use "America" strategically, as an accepted popular reference, and as a way of exploring how the term functions culturally and symbolically.

3. Cornerstone also develops ensemble touring shows such as *California Seagull* (1995) adapted by Alison Carey from *The Seagull* by Anton Chekhov, *Everyman at the Mall* (1994) a restaging of *Everyman,* and *An Antigone Story* (2000) adapted by Shishir Kurup from Sophocles' *Antigone.* Like their community-based productions, these shows often feature adaptations of classical texts and environmental stagings. The company believes that ensemble shows foster craft, which benefits community performances, and vice versa. In recent years, there has been some overlap, as community participants such as Quentin Drew and Omar Gomez have acted in ensemble productions. Cornerstone also hires stage crew members from a pool of

community youth. As *Staging America* focuses on community-based performance, I emphasize this aspect of Cornerstone's work rather than their ensemble shows.

4. Elaine J. Lawless, "'I was afraid someone like you . . . an outsider . . . would misunderstand': Negotiating Interpretive Differences Between Ethnographers and Subjects," *Journal of American Folklore* 105 (1992): 302–14. Lawless strives to move beyond the self-conscious "reflexive ethnography" of sociologists such as Geertz, James Clifford, and Pierre Bourdieu into a more dialogic relationship with the ethnographic subject. I would like to thank my research assistant John Fletcher for leading me to this article.

5. Lawless, 302.

6. Bertolt Brecht, "Emphasis on Sport," in *Brecht on Theatre,* trans. and ed. John Willett (New York: Hill and Wang, 1964), 7.

7. Baz Kershaw, *The Radical in Performance: Between Brecht and Baudrillard* (New York: Routledge, 1999).

8. Kershaw, *The Radical in Performance,* 8.

9. Augusto Boal, *Theatre of the Oppressed,* trans. Charles A. McBride and Maria-Odilia Leal McBride (New York: Theatre Communications Group, 1985). Boal developed his interactive theatrical form with "spect-actors" (rather than spectators) to combat oppressive class structures in Brazil. He has since adapted Theatre of the Oppressed to a Western context, grappling with internal as well as external oppressive forces. He describes these internal forces as "cops-in-the-head." See also *Rainbow of Desire,* trans. Adrian Jackson (New York: Routledge, 1995).

10. Robert Coe, "Verona, Mississippi: Cornerstone Reinvents 'Community Theatre' in America," *American Theater* 6.5 (May 1989): 14–21, 52–57.

11. Cornerstone articles include "Staging the City with the Good People of New Haven," *Theater Journal* 53.2 (2001): 197–222; a performance review of *Broken Hearts: A BH Mystery, Theater Journal* 52.3 (2000): 397–99; "Cornerstone's Community Chalk Circle," *The Brecht Yearbook* 22 (1997): 239–51; "Beyond Brecht: An Interview with Bill Rauch," *Theater InSight* 16 (1996): 35–41; and "A Cornerstone for Rethinking Community Theater," *Theater Topics* 6.1 (1996): 91–104. Articles featuring community-based work in the Balkans include "The Art of Bridge Building in Mostar," in *Performing Democracy,* ed. Tobin Nelhaus and Susan Haedicke (Ann Arbor: University of Michigan Press, 2001), 58–66; "Fighting Fences: Theatrical Rule-Breaking in the Serbian Republic of Bosnia," *Slavic and Eastern European Performance* 19.2 (1999): 50–57, "Playing with the Borders: Dramaturging Ethnicity in Bosnia," *Journal of Dramatic Theory and Criticism* 13.1 (1998): 143–56; "Ghost Town: Cultural Hauntologie in Mostar, Bosnia-Herzegovina," *Text and Performance Quarterly* 18.2 (1998): 81–95; and *"Odakle Ste? (Where Are You From?)* Active Learning and Community Based Theater in Former Yugoslavia and the US," *Theatre Topics* 7.2 (1997): 171–86.

12. Victor Turner, *From Ritual to Theatre: The Human Seriousness of Play* (New York: Performing Arts Journal, 1982), 45–46.

13. In a definition of community related to use, Anthony Cohen focuses on boundary as a distinguishing concept that requires both similarities and difference.

The Symbolic Construction of Community (New York: Youngstock, 1985), 12. Cultural theorist Paul Gilroy observes in his study of British blacks that "community is as much about difference as it is about similarity and identity" (*"There Ain't No Black in the Union Jack": The Cultural Politics of Race and Nation* [London: Hutchinson, 1987], 235). Iris Marion Young suggests that the ideal of community may repress difference by encouraging an assumption of unity (*Justice and the Politics of Difference* [Princeton: Princeton UP, 1990], 230).

14. Frederick Buell, "Theorizing Ethnicity in America," in *National Culture and the New Global System* (Baltimore: Johns Hopkins University Press, 1994), 147–76.

15. Clifford Geertz, "Blurred Genres: The Refiguration of Social Thoughts," in *Local Knowledge: Further Essays in Interpretive Anthropology* (New York: Basic Books, 1983), 35.

16. Richard Schechner, *Performance Theory* (New York: Routledge, 1988), 72.

17. Raymond Williams, *Keywords: A Vocabulary of Culture and Society,* rev. ed. (New York: Oxford University Press, 1985), 75–76.

18. Colin Bell and Howard Newby, *Community Studies: An Introduction to the Sociology of the Local Community,* 3rd ed. (London: Allen, 1978), 27.

19. Cohen, 21.

20. Williams, 87–93.

21. Larry Neal, "The Black Arts Movement," *Drama Review* 12.4 (1968): 36.

22. The company has also commissioned several original scripts such as *The Pretty Much True Story of Dinwiddie County, Ghurba,* and *Growing Home* (2001) by Bernardo Solano.

23. James Clifford, *The Predicament of Culture: Twentieth-Century Ethnography, Literature, and Art* (Cambridge: Harvard University Press, 1988), 35. Clifford summarizes William Dilthey's 1914 argument in "The Construction of the Historical World in the Human Sciences," in *W. Dilthey: Selected Writings,* ed. H. P. Rickman (Cambridge: Cambridge University Press, 1976), 168–245.

24. Bronislaw Malinowski, *A Diary in the Strict Sense of the Term* (New York: Harcourt, Brace, and World, 1967).

25. In a footnote to his chapter "On Ethnographic Authority," Clifford specifies his assumptions that "ethnography is a process of interpretation, not of explanation" (22).

26. *From the Ground Up: Grassroots Theater in Historical and Contemporary Perspective,* ed. Dudley Cocke, Harry Newman, and Janet Salmons-Rue (Ithaca: Cornell University Press, 1993).

27. John Aguilar, "Insider Research: An Ethnography of a Debate," in *Anthropologists at Home in North America: Methods and Issues in the Study of One's Own Society,* ed. Donald A. Messerschmidt (New York: Cambridge University Press, 1981), 15–26.

28. Anne Elizabeth Armstrong, "Paradoxes in Community-Based Pedagogy: Decentering Students Through Oral History Performance," *Theatre Topics* 10.2 (2000): 125.

29. Richard Owen Geer, "Out of Control in Colquitt: Swamp Gravy Makes Stone Soup," *Drama Review* 40.2 (1996): 103–30.

30. José Luis Valenzuela, telephone interview with author, 6 June 2001.

31. Aguilar, 25.

32. Homi Bhabha, *The Location of Culture* (New York: Routledge, 1994), 2.

33. Angela McRobbie, "Strategies of Vigilance: An Interview with Gayatri Chakravorti Spivak," *Block* 10 (1985): 5–9. I am indebted to Harry Elam for this reference.

34. Geertz, "Blurred Genres," 27.

35. Victor Turner, *The Ritual Process: Structure and Anti-Structure* (Chicago: Aldine, 1969), 13–14.

36. Bruce McConachie, "Approaching the 'Structure of Feeling' in Grassroots Theater," *Theatre Topics* 8.1 (1998): 33–53.

37. Alison Carey, Letter to the Editor, *The Drama Review* 45.3 (Fall 2001): 22. The journal includes several responses to Sara Brady's article, "Welded to the Ladle: Non-Radicality in Community-Based Theater," *Drama Review* 44.3 (2000): 51–74, as well as further comments from Brady.

In a later e-mail to me, 29 December 2001, Carey clarifies that her comments referred specifically to Brady's critique rather than to critics in general. She adds:

> If the play had been written while the plant was open, it would have been so different. There is no party line on when to challenge/go against any set of participants' thoughts on what we produce and when we don't, or how to do it when we do or don't. It's all part of the mutual seduction, and you simply go on instinct and the filter of your experience.

38. Linda Frye Burnham, "Factors for Success," a report for the Irvine Foundation's Telling and Listening in Public: Organizers and Artists Building Civic Partnerships, March 2000.

39. Mat Schwarzman, qtd. in Jan Cohen-Cruz, "A Hyphenated Field: Community-Based Theater in the USA," *New Theatre Quarterly* 16.4 (2000): 373, from a conversation on critical writing about community arts, convened by Cohen-Cruz at *National Gathering with an Attitude,* University of Berkeley, California, May 2000.

40. Richard Schechner, *Between Theater and Anthropology* (Philadelphia: University of Pennsylvania Press, 1985), 25–26.

41. Brady critiques Cornerstone and Touchstone Theaters' coproduction of *Steelbound* after participating in the project.

42. Suzanne Lacy, "Cultural Pilgrimages and Metaphoric Journeys," *Mapping the Terrain: New Genre Public Art* (Washington: Bay Press, 1996), 20–21.

43. Arlene Croce, "Discussing the Undiscussable," *New Yorker* (26 December 1994/2 January 1995): 54–60.

44. The Community Arts Network is designed and managed by a partnership of Art in the Public Interest, a national nonprofit organization, and the Virginia Tech Department of Theatre Arts Consortium for the Study of Theatre and Com-

munity. Virginia Tech personnel include Bob Leonard, Ann Kilkelly, and Len Hatfield. Steve Durland and Linda Frye Burnham are the cofounders and codirectors of Art in the Public Interest.

45. Robert Gard, qtd. in Burnham, "Factors for Success," 14.

46. Ann Bogart, untitled public lecture, University of Minnesota, 17 January 1999.

47. Lacy, "Cultural Pilgrimages and Metaphoric Journeys," 44.

48. Lucy Lippard, *The Lure of the Local: Senses of Place in a Multicentered Society* (New York: New Press, 1997), 286–87.

49. Gilles Sandier, qtd. in Josette Féral, "'The Artwork Judges Them': The Theatre Critic in a Changing Landscape," *New Theatre Quarterly* 16.4 (2000): 314.

50. In a personal e-mail, 29 December 2001, Alison Carey adds:

> I absolutely cop to the dangers of being an outsider and know I am guilty of many moments of paternalism, etc., although I don't think they are necessarily always ethnically/culturally based. Artists, as we all know, can feel quite outside their own ethnic and cultural group—and even feel contempt for what is familiar to them, which frequently fires their art—and paternalism can happen within cultures as well as from outsiders.

Carey complicates the dynamics of insider/outsider artistry, echoing John Aguilar's writing about insider ethnography (see note 27).

51. For further critical reading on community-based theater, see Bruce McConachie, "Approaching the 'Structure of Feeling' in Grassroots Theatre"; Ann Elizabeth Armstrong, "Paradoxes"; Doug Paterson, "To For With: Some Observations on Community-Based Theater," in *ReImaging America: The Arts of Social Change*, ed. Mark O'Brien and Craig Little (Santa Cruz: New Society Publishers, 1990), 237–43; and Jan Cohen-Cruz, "A Hyphenated Field."

52. Jan Cohen-Cruz, "When the Gown Goes to Town: The Reciprocal Rewards of Fieldwork for Artists," *Theatre Topics* 11.1 (2001): 55–62; and "A Hyphenated Field."

53. David Román, "Visa Denied," in *Queer Frontiers: Millennial Geographies, Genders, and Generations*, ed. Joseph A. Boone (Madison: University of Wisconsin Press, 2000), 350–61. Román's essay examines the relationship between queerness and diaspora in Chay Yew's *A Beautiful Country*, a collaboration with Cornerstone and the Los Angeles Chinatown community.

54. All subsequent references to this article will be indicated parenthetically within the body of the text.

55. While Brady does not explicitly define "radicality," the article expresses concerns about the influence of the corporate institution on the production narrative, positing that "community-based companies and big-budget projects of late have operated less by the principles of the company and more by the demands of governmental funding agendas" (52).

56. In an e-mail to me, 15 January 2001, Brady expressed feeling that she and others in the process were not treated as major players and therefore not given the

opportunity to voice concerns, despite rhetorical encouragement to do so. Others who have worked with Cornerstone have felt what they describe as an "invisible hierarchy." I address this issue further in chapter 2.

57. Christopher Liam Moore appreciates Brady's frustration, and how it clarifies the difference between her view of radicality and Cornerstone's mode of production and storytelling: "We would not have done the project unless [Bethlehem Steel] had been involved. They are as much a part of the story—management is—as the people who work there" (interview with the author, Los Angeles, 29 October 2001). See Stephen Gutwillig's critique of this position in chapter 5.

58. Brian Olivieri, qtd. in Laura Collins-Hughes, "Idealism in Action," *New Haven Register* (7 May 2000): F7.

2. Identity Traces: Historiographic Perspectives on Cornerstone and Community-Based Theater

1. It is difficult to determine the source of the term *community-based theater,* and perhaps not entirely necessary in a historiographic approach less concerned with origins. However, the term's affiliations with activism shed light on the social focus of most community-based performance practices. Scholars and practitioners concur that the phrase was likely adopted from activist terminology and popularized sometime in the early 1980s. Road Company Artistic Director Bob Leonard, who has developed a data base on social change performance, explains, "I have my own memory of the emergence of the term, sometime in the mid-eighties, as the NEA and other agencies began recognizing the serious work being done by arts organizations in neighborhoods, rural areas, amongst tribal peoples etc." (e-mail to the author, 27 July 2001). *From the Ground Up* documents a weekend long symposium held at Cornell University in 1992. The report settles on the term *grassroots* as opposed to *community-based,* emphasizing this kind of theater's connection to progressive politics. Much of Cornerstone's work, and other twentieth-century projects and movements that I detail in this book, are not necessarily grounded in progressive politics, nor in expressing "the values of those without privilege," terminology used to define grassroots theater in *From the Ground Up* (13). I adopt "community-based" in part to question assumptions of the work's radicality.

2. John Anderson, *The American Theatre* (New York: Dial Press, 1938), 73.

3. Terry Eagleton, *The Ideology of the Aesthetic: From Polis to Postmodernism* (Oxford: Basil Blackwell, 1990); Pierre Bourdieu, *Distinction: A Social Critique of the Judgment of Taste,* trans. Richard Nice (Cambridge: Harvard University Press, 1984).

4. John Malpede, Transcript from Los Angeles Focus Group, 18 November 1999, *Connecting Californians: Finding the Art of Community Change.* Community Arts Network Reading Room (www.communityarts.net), 28.

5. In *The Radical in Performance,* Baz Kershaw eloquently explicates the dilemma of writing history in a postmodern moment: "Historians cannot presume to create a continuous story out of the traces of the past without violating the nature of those

traces, which is characterised primarily by discontinuities, gaps, lacunae, ambiguities and uncertainties" (161). While Kershaw strives to balance modern and postmodern theories, with this statement he emphasizes a poststructural critical attitude, referring to the loss of stable truth foundations in knowledge construction.

6. I would like to thank my research assistant John Fletcher for proposing the missionary/mercenary distinction.

7. Michel Foucault, "Nietzsche, Genealogy, History," in *The Foucault Reader*, ed. Paul Rabinow (New York: Pantheon, 1984), 76.

8. J. Anderson, 6.

9. See especially Bernard Hewitt, *Theatre USA 1665–1957* (New York: McGraw-Hill, 1959). While Hewitt's range and grasp is extensive, he too heads a chapter on O'Neill, "Fulfillment," and generally focuses on professional theater in the United States. Glen Hughes, *A History of the American Theatre, 1700–1950* (New York: Samuel French, 1951), offers headings on Percy Mackaye, the Little Theater Movement, College and Community Theaters, and Nonprofessional Theaters. However, these are relegated to the chapter endings as marginalia to the dominative narrative of professional theater. Neither the *Concise Oxford Companion to American Theater*, ed. Gerald Bordman (New York: Oxford University Press, 1987), nor *The American Theatre: A Sum of Its Parts: A Collection of the Distinguished Addresses Presented Expressly for the Symposium "The American Theatre—A Cultural Process," at the First American College Theatre Festival, Washington D.C., 1968* (New York: Samuel French, 1971), refers to community or community-based theater.

10. Oscar G. Brockett, *The History of the Theater*, 8th ed. (Boston: Allyn and Bacon, 1999).

11. Brockett made this claim of ideological neutrality at a 2001 Association of Theatre in Higher Education panel on "Theater and the New Student," in which I participated (Chicago, 5 August 2001).

12. Brockett, *History*, 489–90.

13. Brockett is well aware of the difficulties confronting historiographic production. In an introduction to *The American Stage: Social and Economic Issues from the Colonial Period to the Present*, ed. Ron Engle and Tice L. Miller (Cambridge: Cambridge University Press, 1993), 1–5, he offers a concise account of historiographic trends and cultural forces impacting the production of American theater histories. Still, neither *The History of the Theater* nor *The American Stage* refer to community-based theater as such.

14. *Cambridge Guide to American Theatre*, ed. Don B. Wilmeth with Tice Miller (New York: Cambridge University Press, 1996). Volume 3 of *Cambridge History of American Theatre*, ed. Don B. Wilmeth and Christopher Bigsby (New York: Cambridge University Press, 2000), offers a more extensive rendition of American theater. An excellent introduction includes the Little Theater Movement, Federal Theater Project, and radical workers theaters. However, a timeline of events focuses mainly on professional theater, and while the index to the issue includes community theater, there is no mention of community-based theater or some of its antecedents.

15. *The History of North American Theater from Pre-Columbian Times to the Present,* ed. Felicia Hardison Londré and Daniel J. Watermeier (New York: Continuum, 1998), 8.

16. See in particular *Theater for Working Class Audiences,* ed. Bruce McConachie and Daniel Friedman (Westport, CT: Greenwood Press, 1985); Theodore Shank, *American Alternative Theater* (New York: Grove Press, 1982); Karen Malpede Taylor, *People's Theater in Amerika* (New York: Drama Book Specialists, 1972); Arthur Sainer, *The Radical Theater Notebook* (New York: Avon, 1975); and Jay Williams, *Stage Left* (New York: Scribners, 1974).

17. Loren Kruger, *The National Stage: Theatre and Cultural Legitimation in England, France, and America* (Chicago: University of Chicago Press, 1992); and *Performing America: Cultural Nationalism in American Theater,* ed. Jeffrey Mason and J. Ellen Gainor (Ann Arbor: University of Michigan Press, 1999). Charlotte Canning's "'The Most American Thing in America': Producing National Identities in Chautauqua, 1904–1932," 91–105, and Ann Larabee's "'The Drama of Transformation': Settlement House Idealism and the Neighborhood Playhouse," 123–35, both in *Performing America,* offer particularly astute examples of scholarship examining the relationship between performance and American identity in the early-twentieth century. See also Shannon Jackson, "Civic Play-housekeeping: Gender, Theater, and American Reform," *Theater Journal* 48.3 (1996): 337–61.

18. A recent anthology of urban community-based performance practices, *Performing Democracy,* ed. Tobin Nelhaus and Susan Haedicke (Ann Arbor: University of Michigan Press, 2001), contributes to a growing, though still marginalized discourse on community-based performance. Scholars and practitioners such as Dudley Cocke of Roadside Theater, Bob Leonard, Jan Cohen-Cruz, Lucy Winner, and Linda Frye Burnham have expanded documentation of current community-based practices mainly through oral histories, surveys, and transcribed conversations as well as through journal articles and essays. See especially contributions to the Community Arts Network (www.communityarts.net).

19. Constance d'Arcy Mackay, *Patriotic Drama in Your Town* (New York: Henry Holt and Company, 1918), 115–22.

20. Mackay, 119.

21. Percy Mackaye uses both the terms *civic theatre* and *community drama* in his lectures and publications, switching to the latter following publication of Louise Burleigh's *Community Theatre in Theory and Practice* (Boston: Little, Brown, 1917). I refer to both terms in this section, preferring "civic theater" to distinguish this particular emergence from later grassroots community theaters. Mackaye refers to "constructive leisure" in *The Civic Theatre in Relation to the Redemption of Leisure* (New York: Mitchell Kennerley, 1912), 21.

22. Mackaye, *Civic Theatre,* 15.

23. Mackaye, *Community Drama: Its Motive and Method of Neighborliness* (Boston: Houghton Mifflin, 1917), ix.

24. John Anderson summarizes one strain of critical praise regarding Mackaye's lack of influence on American theater claiming that Mackaye,

with much of his father [Steel]'s insurgence about him, and an equal in-
heritance of visionary daring, attempted the establishment of spectacles and
pageantry with a certain attempt to link such an idea of the theatre with
civic and sociological purposes. Very little came of that. (66)

Ann Larabee's contemporary critiques prove more thoughtful and probing. In her
insightful article, "The Drama of Transformation," Larabee challenges the construction of community through theater as an "overt ideological mission of erasing people's differences, complexities, conflicts, shifting aggregations, and fluid
identities" (125). Hiroko Tsuchiya critiques coercive elements of Industrial Drama
in "'Let Them Be Amused': The Industrial Drama Movement, 1910–1929," in
Theatre for Working Class Audiences, 97–110.

25. Burleigh proposes that theater is the ideal art form for democracy, as it allows for inclusion and opportunity (105). Charlotte Dumbold, too, views drama
as a way to embody democracy through direct participation ("Proceedings of
the Conference of Cities Held in Connection with the Pageant and Masque of
St. Louis, May 29–31, 1914" [St. Louis: St. Louis Pageant Drama Association,
1914], 27).

26. Mary Russell, *How to Produce Plays and Pageants* (New York: George H.
Doran, 1923), 169.

27. Mackaye, *Community Drama*, 11.

28. Mackaye, *Community Drama*, 10.

29. Tsuchiya, 99.

30. Mackaye, *Civic Theatre*, 43.

31. Mackaye, *Community Drama*, xii.

32. Mackaye, *Community Drama*, 75.

33. In *A Handbook of American Pageantry* (Taunton, MA: Davol, 1914), Ralph
Davol refers to pageantry's usefulness in celebrating community anniversaries,
heading one of his chapters "Pageant as Nursery of Patriotism." Numerous practitioners refer to both purposes in advocating for pageantry on holidays. Mary
Russell encourages production of "the Patriotic Pageant which embraces in its
committees the representative persons of the community," opposing this practice
to "anti-social Fourth of July noise" (14).

34. Davol, 40.

35. Russell, 172–84; Mackaye, *The New Citizenship: A Civic Ritual Devised for
Place of Public Meeting in America* (New York: Macmillan, 1915).

36. Russell, 168–69.

37. Russell, 177–78.

38. Russell, 177.

39. Mackaye, *The New Citizenship*, 83.

40. In a footnote to the "Second Group Movement" in *The New Citizenship*,
Mackaye notes, "The essential object is, of course, to represent, through symbols
of eye and ear, the distinctive national cultures contributed to our country" (34).

41. Mackaye, *The New Citizenship*, 14.

42. Robert Gard, *Community Theater: Ideal and Achievement* (New York: Duell, Sloan and Pearce, 1959), 10.

43. Paul Green, "The American Theatre Today," *Pioneering a People's Theatre,* ed. Archibald Henderson (Chapel Hill: University of North Carolina Press, 1945), 62.

44. Alexander Drummond, undated notes, Department of University Archives and Manuscripts, Cornell University Libraries, in "Alexander Drummond and New York Stories," *Storytelling Theater: Culture, Communication, and Community.* The Community-Based Arts Project Final Report, Janet Salmons-Rue, project director (Cornell Center for Theatre Arts and Roadside Theater, 1993), 16.

45. Frederick H. Koch, *The Carolina Playmakers* (New York: Henry Holt, 1941), vi.

46. Koch, *American Folk Plays* (New York: D. Appleton-Century Company, 1939), xiii.

47. Koch, *American Folk Plays,* xv.

48. Koch, *American Folk Plays,* xiii.

49. Fred Eastman, *The American Saint of Democracy,* in *Plays of Democracy,* ed. Margaret Mayorga (New York: Dodd, Mead, 1944), 41.

50. Crafton, qtd. in Robert Gard and Gertrude S. Burley, *Community Theatre: Idea and Achievement* (New York: Duell, Sloan and Pearce, 1959), 32.

51. Crafton, qtd. in Gard and Burley, 32.

52. Joseph Wesley Zeigler, *Regional Theatre: The Revolutionary Stage* (Minneapolis: University of Minnesota Press, 1973), 8–9.

53. J. Anderson, 74–75.

54. Cofounder Harold Clurman spoke of producing "good new American plays that reflected the temper of the American moment" and about creating "'true theater' based on 'life values' in America" (qtd. in Foster Hirsch, *A Method to Their Madness: The History of the Actors Studio* [New York: Norton, 1984], 67 and in Helen Krich Chinoy, "Reunion: A Self-Portrait of the Group Theatre," *Educational Theatre Journal* 28:4 [1976]: 472).

55. Cheryl Crawford, interviewed by Helen Krich Chinoy, in "Reunion," 494.

56. Feminist revisions adopt the term Chicano/a as more inclusive. I use Chicano strategically to indicate a certain historically rooted discrimination.

57. Yvonne Broyles-Gonzalez, *El Teatro Campesino: Theater in the Chicano Movement* (Austin: University of Texas Press, 1994), specifically resists a "great man/text-centered/chronological-linear approach" to history (xiii).

58. Jorge Huerta, *Chicano Theater: Themes and Forms* (Ypsilanti, MI: Bilingual Press, 1982).

59. Unlike Yiddish and German terms existent prior to individual immigration to the United States, "Chicano/a" was created in the 1960s. This marker of identity signals a new hybrid and specifically unassimilated group, neither Mexican nor American nor Mexican American.

60. Amiri Baraka, *The Autobiography of LeRoi Jones* (New York: Freundlich, 1984), 323.

61. LeRoi Jones, qtd. in Larry Neal, 31.

62. *Free Southern Theater by the Free Southern Theater,* ed. Thomas C. Dent, Richard Schechner, and Gilbert Moses (New York: Bobbs-Merrill, 1969), 3.

63. Larry Neal, qtd. in James Flannery, "Southern Theater and the Paradox of Progress," *Southern Exposure* 14.3–4(1986): 16.

64. Jackson Hill, "A Farewell Without Mourning: A Jazz Funeral for Free Southern Theater," *Southern Exposure:* 14.3–4 (1986): 76.

65. John O'Neal, qtd. in Hill, 73.

66. bell hooks, *Yearning* (Boston: South End Press, 1990), 27.

67. O'Neal, qtd. in Flannery, 16.

68. hooks, 27.

69. American Festival project brochure.

70. Pat Bryant, qtd. in Mat Schwarzman, "Drawing the Line at Place: The Environmental Justice Project," *High Performance* 72 (Summer 1996): 11.

71. O'Neal, qtd. in Schwarzman, 10–11.

72. Martin Platt, qtd. in Flannery, 14.

73. Dudley Cocke et al., 66.

74. Founding members tossed about a number of ideas before settling on "Cornerstone," including "Honest Bill's Traveling Theater: New and Used Plays" and "Stepping Stone," which sounded crass to many member, as though on their way to something else. According to members, "Cornerstone" connotes not only building and foundation but also something useful in an everyday, accessible way, like a corner store. Durfee Oral Retreat, Los Angeles, tape 2, transcript page 4. Additional citations will list only tape and transcript numbers.

75. "I think a lot us at Cornerstone really had no concept of [community-based theater] whatsoever," explains Christopher Liam Moore.

> What was a huge influence on Cornerstone was the Wooster Group, because we saw them and just had our minds blown aesthetically. Also, the model of working together forever on a project as a group directly influenced the Kronauer Group, the precursor to Cornerstone. . . . But we really didn't have any idea about Roadside Theater or the San Francisco Mime Troupe who were doing community specific work. (Interview with the author, Los Angeles, 29 October 2001)

76. In a personal e-mail, 5 March 1995, Payette discusses her frustrations, framing her comments by stating how much she generally enjoyed working with the company.

> In West Virginia, I became upset (and I still get teased about this) because my desk in the community office was constantly being used and abused by others. After I left in the early evening, other company members would come in and eat at my desk, mess up papers, take pens, leave food wrappers there, and it drove me crazy. In the "share everything—community feeling" of Cornerstone, I wanted my desk to be the one place that would not get trashed. . . . it was the lack of respect that I was protesting, and I don't know if that ever really got through to them!!

77. Stephen Gutwillig, Durfee 14:21.

78. Misha Berson, "Keeping Company," *American Theatre* 7.4 (April 1990): 16–23.

79. Sociologist Cecilia Ridgeway proposes

> open decentralized communication is best if the group task is ambiguous, technically complex, or requires innovation. . . . Groups faced with a technically or socially complex task, then, would do better if they organized themselves democratically with a relatively flat status hierarchy. (*The Dynamics of Small Groups* [New York: St. Martin's Press, 1983], 295, in Mark Weinberg, *Challenging the Hierarchy: Collective Theater in the United States* [Westport, CT: Greenwood, 1992], 15)

80. Steven Gooch, *All Together Now: An Alternative View of Theatre and the Community* (London: Methuen, 1984), 49.

81. David Reiffel, Durfee 8:24.

82. Bill Rauch, telephone interview with the author, 13 March 1996.

83. Reiffel also referred to these boundaries of inclusion and exclusion at the Durfee retreat: "Cornerstone's like a circle, you know. There's inside and there's outside. And it's very delineated, very clearly delineated" (Durfee 3:15).

84. Amy Brenneman, Durfee 9:23–24.

85. Rauch, telephone interview with the author, 13 March 1996.

86. Rauch, telephone interview, 13 March 1996.

87. Alison Carey, Cornerstone Newsletter 2.2 (1988): 2.

88. In a personal conversation (15 November 2001), Alison Carey explained to me that the company had contacted a number of theater departments and companies that had connections to communities of color, with no result. She wondered whether potential candidates may have been afraid of the racism they might encounter in rural areas, a particular concern of ensemble member Page Leong.

89. In *From Ritual to Theater*, Victor Turner proposes that mandated *communitas* may try to codify what is in essence a temporary state of being, asserting that "it cannot be legislated or normalized since it is the exception not the law" (49).

90. In a personal e-mail, 29 December 2001, Alison Carey clarifies:

> We never had "life-time tenure." What we had was a system that required someone to bring up getting rid of someone; review of membership was not automatic outside of the regular self-evaluation process. Bill felt that, gutless slugs that we are, no one would be emotionally capable of bringing up removing anyone. But we absolutely could at any time, whether people wanted to think about that or not.

91. Carey, Durfee 2:16.

92. Douglas Petrie, Durfee 2:19.

93. Petrie, Durfee 2:19.

94. Lynn Jeffries, Durfee 2:20.

95. Alison Carey expands on the difficulties of initiating this residency, and her fears that failure to connect with Perry would lead to Cornerstone's dissolution: "We were afraid that if we didn't come up with something, the company would dissolve." Failing to receive an answer from city hall, she called the police department:

> So I called and a woman answered the phone, and I said, "Hi, is this the police department?" And she said, "No, he's out huntin." And I thought, "I have to go to this town." And so I said who I was and she said, "Oh yeah, Patty's at a goat convention in Wyoming but she'll be back tomorrow." And so Patty got back from the convention and she agreed that we could come— for just no apparent reason that I could figure out. Two weeks later the company pulled in. And the reason that city hall didn't answer was because it was just a phone in the fire house. (Interview with the author, Los Angeles, 30 October 2001)

96. Christopher Liam Moore, Durfee 3:5–6.

97. Wanda McHatton, "Roping Nets $1,200 For Theater Group," *Blue Mountain Eagle* (Long Creek, OR) (11 August 1988): 6.

98. Valenzuela, interview.

99. Dyann Simile, Letter to Cornerstone, 4 December 1989.

100. Bill Earney, Jessica Carrasco, Bruce Aguilar, qtd. in Mary K. Earney, "Marfa Residents Catch Stage 'Fever,'" *San Angelo Standard Times* (San Angelo, TX) (30 January 1987): 2.

101. Rod Prichard, letter to Cornerstone, June 1987.

102. Ramona Dewey, letter to Cornerstone, June 1988.

103. *Cornerstone,* a documentary produced by Michael Kantor and Steve Ives, 1999.

104. Mayor Anita Collins, qtd. in Peter Sagal, "Playing America's Backroads," *Los Angeles Times Calendar* (18 August 1991): 78.

105. Cornerstone Newsletter 1.1 (1987): 3.

106. Anne Cavalier, qtd. in William Shebar, "'Three Sisters' in West Virginia," *Theater Week* (18–24 June 1990): 25.

107. As with much of Cornerstone's methodology, this transaction resulted from a residency experience. In Marmarth, North Dakota, Cornerstone members had been trying to work out payment of utilities in the theater. The company suggested that instead of merely covering the cost of utilities, they could leave behind a portion of the box office receipts, enough to cover utilities and a little extra to allow for the possibility of Marmarth residents mounting their own production

108. Fadwa El Guindi, qtd. in Richard Stayton, "Never More Than a Stranger," *Los Angeles Times Calendar* (5 September, 1993): 9.

109. Brian Brophy, "Perspectives on Urban Community-Based Theater: Peter Sellars in East Los Angeles: The Postcolonial Dilemma of Artistic Occupation," Masters Thesis, California State University, Los Angeles, 1999: 5.

110. Alison Carey suggests that having community board members represent Cornerstone in Watts may have contributed to tension in one production. One

of the participants in *Los Faustinos* believed that profits from the show were being pocketed by board members. Interview with the author, Los Angeles, 3 April 1996.

111. Karen Lordi, "Santa Claus in the Video Store: An Interview with Bill Rauch," *Yale Theater* (September 1990): 16.

112. Rauch, interview with the author, Los Angeles, 30 June 1995. Lynn Jeffries adds:

> Actually we were going to set it in a gynecologist's office until Bill heard that the folks in West Virginia were setting the play in a video store. He liked that idea so much better, he called and asked whoever it was if she would mind if he borrowed it. I had already started designing a gynecologist's office when the switch was made. (E-mail to the author, 4 January 2002)

113. Moore, Durfee 11:2–3. Cornerstone did increasingly introduce homosexual relationships in both urban community and ensemble shows. The large-scale Los Angeles bridge show, *For Here or To Go,* featured a gay character whose monologue, written and performed by Peter Howard, reflected on the complexities of homosexuality, trust, and fear in a community-based context.

> If we put a gay character in a community play, then we'd have to be willing to talk about it, and we'd have to talk about how some of us are gay, and that's scary. . . . for 15 years we've asked people in communities to share their dreams and their families and every spare minute of their time. . . . But way too often we don't trust them enough to return the favor. (Alison Carey, *For Here or To Go,* inspired by Francis Beaumont and John Fletcher, *The Knight of the Burning Pestle,* 60–61)

114. Noel Gillespie, "An Insignificant Video Store," rev. of *The Video Store Owner's Significant Other, Washington Blade* (9 February 1990): 25.

115. Armando Molina, interview with the author, Los Angeles, 11 March 2001.

116. Joan Shigehawa, qtd. in Rauch, interview with the author, Los Angeles, 30 June 1995.

117. Carey, interview with the author, Los Angeles, 30 October 2001.

118. Rauch, interview with author, Los Angeles, 10 October 1994. This comment is not as facetious as it may at first seem. Amiri Baraka (LeRoi Jones) advocated a theater on every corner, like a grocery store (qtd. in Saul Gottlieb, "They Think You're an Airplane and You're Really a Bird," interview with LeRoi Jones, *Evergreen Review* [December 1967]: 51).

119. Vorhees, Casement, and Temple, qtd. in Sagal, "Playing," 79.

120. Alison Carey expresses less surety about the need for Rauch to remain in order to sustain Cornerstone's operations:

> What's going to happen to the company when he leaves, I don't know. It could go under. I think it probably wouldn't. Either way it would be fine. If there are people who don't want to do the work, then we should say goodbye. As co-founders, and even with Bill as Artistic Director, it's been

heavy lifting, but he's not carrying the thing on his back, and I'm certainly not. I'm not even carrying it in my purse. But if it stops being a great thing, I hope Cornerstone dies a quick and appropriate death. (Interview with the author, Los Angeles, 30 October 2001)

3. Perfor(m)ations: Cornerstone and Transactions of Community

1. Williams, *Keywords*.

2. Geertz, "Thick Description: Toward an Interpretive Theory of Culture," *The Interpretation of Cultures* (London: Hutchinson, 1975), 5.

3. David Reiffel, Durfee 2:10–11.

4. Alison Carey, qtd. in Nina Lelyved, "In Cornerstone's Shakespeare, Romeo Raps," rev. of *Romeo & Juliet* by Cornerstone Theater Company adapted from *Romeo and Juliet* by William Shakespeare, *New York Times* (7 May 1989): E6.

5. Alison Carey, qtd. in Lelyved.

6. Salam Al-Marayati, qtd. in Cornerstone's Animating Democracy Initiative Grant proposal narrative, 3.

7. Peter Howard, Durfee 3:7.

8. Lucinda Benjamin, letter to Cornerstone, June 1988.

9. Saul Alinsky, *Reveille for Radicals,* 1946 (New York: Vintage Books Edition, 1969).

10. Cohen illustrates this point through an occurrence in Scotland's islands. A debate arose in the local *Shetland Times* between the Shetland Women's Group, a body of women from outside the islands, and residents. The women's group opposed plans to bring a stripper to perform for local construction workers. Letters to the editor of the *Times* focused as much on the perceived interference of this outside group as on the striptease. Notes one irate Shetlander:

> I am not at all sure why they call themselves the Shetland Women's Group, while admitting they are *soothmoothers* (outsiders). Furthermore, whatever gave them the idea that Shetland womanhood was about to be exploited, and that they were qualified to prevent such an unlikely event taking place? (25 August 1978, in Cohen, 45–46)

11. Brady contends that leadership extends to the entire casting project, influencing the stories told and not told. "Connection with community entities inevitably means connection with dominant voices . . . who will agree to audition for a play if not the outgoing leader types?" ("Welded to the Ladle," 70–71).

12. In a personal e-mail, 30 December 2001, Lynn Jeffries offers a more detailed version of events:

> It was really the city council, under the leadership of Mayor Bill Nelson, and it was mostly Bee and Bill Nelson and their closest friends, Bob and Imogene Sawdon and Lee Eckhart, who furnished the schoolhouse with beds, repaired the furnace, and stocked the refrigerator with groceries prior

to our arrival. Lee painted the famous "Welcome, Cornerstone" sign that stood on Main Street at the turnoff to the schoolhouse, and that reappeared from storage every time the company returned to Norcatur.

13. Dorothy Kelley, *Tartoof* Program Notes, 4.

14. Bruce McConachie, "Historicizing the Relations of Theatrical Production," *Critical Theory and Performance,* ed. Janelle G. Reinelt and Joseph R. Roach (Ann Arbor: University of Michigan Press, 1992), 168–78.

15. Cornerstone Newsletter 1.2 (October 1987): 4.

16. Toni White-Richardson, telephone interview with the author, 31 January 1996.

17. Carey, *For Here or To Go,* 1.6.

18. Christopher Arnott, "Streets on Stage," *New Haven Advocate* (11 May 2000): 2–3. In a later review of *The Good Person of New Haven,* Arnott retreats from his prior skepticism: "Does New Haven need a Cornerstone Theater Co.? OK, I'll shut up now. I wasn't alone in being apprehensive about this project. . . . Well, I was wrong" ("The People Triumph," *New Haven Advocate* [18 May 2000]: 5–6).

19. Durfee 6:10.

20. Bill Rauch, qtd. in "Cornerstone Theater Play Set Depicting Dinwiddie 'History,'" *Times-Dispatch/Good Neighbors* (Dinwiddie, VA) (17 May 1987): 4

21. Beth Chrichlow, "Ibsen in Eastport," *Down East* (Eastport, ME) (10 August 1990): 10.

22. A betrayal of the attitude that performers and more experienced theater practitioners have separate though equally important skills can lead to a disruption of the community building process. Richard Owen Geer, who works with community members in Colquitt, Georgia, developing a flexible performative oral history of the community in *Swamp Gravy,* describes a moment in rehearsal when he became angered by the performers' unprofessional lateness to rehearsal. After his harangue, several cast members walked out offended by his language and attitude. Geer later recognized that "he had betrayed a fundamentally hierarchical attitude" in his treatment of the cast that had led to this temporary revolt (qtd. in Linda Frye Burnham, "The Cutting Edge is Enormous," *High Performance* [Summer 1994]: 13).

23. Durfee 5:32.

24. Dorothy Kelley, Letter to Cornerstone, June 1987.

25. Cornerstone Newsletter (October 1987): 6. Cornerstone's early experiences with rural and urban residencies resonate with turn-of-the-century theories describing organizational evolution. Ferdinand Tönnies distinguished between the close social ties in a community *(gemeinschaft)* and the impersonal, work-centered relationships of a larger urban association *(gessellschaft).* According to Tönnies, community is not a part of the city. Contemporary scholars refute the simplicity of these divisions; Iris Marion Young goes so far as to suggest that the city provides the ideal site for communities of difference (Young, "City Life and Difference," *Justice,* 226–56).

26. In a personal e-mail, 30 December 2001, Lynn Jeffries adds intriguing details about the interaction with the Passamaquoddy tribe:

> When we arrived at the "Welcome, Cornerstone" dinner in what was then Eastport's nicest restaurant, Bill [Rauch] and I were greeted at the door by two women from the reservation, Deanna Francis (who later played Pier Gynt's mom), and Mary Bassett (Paula Altvater's mother). They sat us down at a table and said they had read about us in the *New Yorker*, I think it was, which said we were coming to Eastport next, so they had been waiting for us. They then lay out, in a friendly but almost businesslike way, a plan for what activities they wanted us to do on the reservation. Besides holding auditions there, they wanted us to conduct theater workshops in the elementary school, and they had specific grades and classrooms in mind. It was an amazing conversation, very different from anything we experienced before or since. They knew what we did, and they were so clear and specific about what they wanted.

27. Lynn Jeffries clarifies that this distinction reduces an even more subtle distinction in the town. Long Creek included a small population of conservative Christians who attended the same church. This group eventually founded a separate café, one that did not have a bar in back (but did sell liquor by the bottle). The three women who played angels in the play, two of whom attended the church, and one who had stopped going due to a painful, personal conflict with the other two, set aside their grievances for the length of the production, singing in close harmony (Interview with the author, Los Angeles, 14 December 2001). Like many Cornerstone production anecdotes, this story can be read as both a parable of community coming together across difference, and as an example of performance obscuring difference.

28. Rauch, Durfee 3:10. Alison Carey adds, "The women didn't want the men to know [about the language women used]" (e-mail to the author, 29 December 2001).

29. Rauch, Cornerstone Newsletter 2.1.1 (November 1992): 3.

30. Durfee, 8:25.

31. With only one or two exceptions, all of the town's white children attended a private academy, and all the black children attended the public school across the street.

32. Coe, 57.

33. Leslie R. Myers, "Racially Mixed Production Prospers in Port Gibson," *Clarion-Ledger* (Clarion, MS) (19 March 1989): 1.

34. Animating Democracy Grant Narrative, 7.

35. Personal conversation, Los Angeles, CA, 15 November 1994.

36. Cornerstone Newsletter 1.1 (January 1987): 2.

37. Cornerstone Newsletter 1.1 (January 1987): 2.

38. Rauch, Durfee 3:8.

39. Reiffel, Durfee 3:7. The issue of sacred and profane continued to impact the production. A minister at a local church banned his congregation from attending

the production, due to its blasphemous references (both Shakespeare's and Cornerstone's). At the same time, a cast member, a local Sunday school teacher who had been offended by the play's references and had at one point wanted to quit the show, later sat with director Bill Rauch at a rehearsal. Watching Hamlet confront Gertrude in her bedroom, he commented, "This play is about really important things, isn't it?"

40. Carey, telephone interview with the author, 3 April 1996.

41. Durfee 3:10.

42. Cornerstone Newsletter 1.1 (January 1987): 1.

43. Wanda Daniels, qtd. in Shebar, 29.

44. Cornerstone Newsletter 4.2 (August 1990): 3.

45. Patty Payette, personal journal, 5 October 1989.

46. Cheryl Keenan, "From the Balcony," *Montgomery Herald* (Montgomery, WV) (November 1989): 1.

47. Otis K. Rice, *Three Sisters from West Virginia* Program Notes.

48. Coe, 52.

49. Rauch, *The Good Person of Long Creek* Program Notes, 3.

50. Mel Brown, letter to Cornerstone, June 1990.

51. It is significant that Cornerstone members did not impose this phrase. It was decided upon by the consensus of the racially mixed cast. Thus it can be said that the community cast maintained a sense of ownership of the word choice.

52. In England, where community theater evokes alternative and political as well as nonprofessional theater, community theater producer Ann Jellicoe notes, "If a community theater performs in a village hall, say, the community is inevitably in the role of host, because the hall 'belongs' to the village. . . . so at the very least space is exchanged for performance" (qtd. in Kershaw, *The Politics of Performance: Radical Theatre as Cultural Intervention* [London: Routledge, 1992], xvii).

53. Rauch, "Connecting Californians," 41.

54. Lynn Jeffries, qtd. in Deb Thiele-Escher, "Cornerstone Theater 'An Imposter in Norcatur,'" *Clarion Ink* (Oberlin, Kansas) (2 November 1987): 9–10.

55. Marvin Carlson, "The Semiotics of Theatre Structure," *Theatre Semiotics: Signs of Life* (Bloomington: Indiana University Press, 1990), 41–55.

56. Turner, *The Ritual Process,* 13–14.

57. Shebar, 30.

58. Sagal, "Playing," 78.

59. Christopher Liam Moore reflects on the phenomenon of audience engagement in community-based productions referring to Cornerstone's first adapted work:

> When we did *Hamlet* in the Badlands it was so terrifying, because we were all suburban kids and we were in ranch country, and I just doubted that anyone would come. And we were packed every single night. Then that first night, Gus came out and couldn't remember his lines as Polonius. It was a moment of incredible—because the audience so knew what was going on,

and were so with him, because they all shopped at his grocery store. I felt that I could do absolutely anything on the stage and it was okay, because this audience is so connected to this piece of theater because this man is on stage and they know him. (Interview with the author, Los Angeles, 29 October 2001)

60. Melanie Aragon, qtd. in *Agai Dicutta Yaduan,* Walker River Paiute Tribe Newsletter (May/June 1988): 1.

61. Brown, letter.

62. Cohen, 55.

63. Durfee 16:61.

64. Hirsch Griffith, letter to Cornerstone, 10 February 1987.

65. Carey, interview, Los Angeles, 3 April 1996.

66. Steven Vineberg, rev. of *The Winter's Tale, Threepenny Review* 13.1 (Spring 1992): 3–4.

4. Rural Routes

1. Carlson, "Theatre Audiences and the Reading of Performance," *Theatre Semiotics,* 18–20.

2. AT&T Foundation had supported Cornerstone's work in its previous season. In contrast to the company's foundation program, AT&T: *OnStage* issued from corporate marketing, thus the more prominent display of sponsorship. Still, the AT&T: *OnStage* cosponsorship headline (the only time in the company's history that a funder received title credit) rubs against texts within the Humanities Flyer that refer to Cornerstone's mission in terms of communities and individuals rather than corporations and foundations. Additionally, while most Cornerstone documents privilege individual contributors, the flyer focused on corporate and foundational support, noting that an individual funding list is "in formation" (12), an unfortunate absence that may be attributed to the scope of the touring enterprise, the increasing quantity of Cornerstone's individual supporters, and the exigencies of a press deadline.

3. Humanities Flyer, 3; *The Winter's Tale* Program Notes; Cornerstone Ensemble and Planning Meeting Notes, 17 December 1990.

4. Jeffries, e-mail to the author, 4 January 2002.

5. Alison Carey, Cornerstone Ensemble and Planning Meeting Notes, 17 December 1990.

6. Bill Rauch, qtd. in Humanities Flyer, 3.

7. Rauch, qtd. in Humanities Flyer, 3.

8. In New York, the one location in which the bus could not be driven, a city cab and driver replaced the bus. Cornerstone Newsletter 5.1 (November 1991): 5.

9. Cornerstone Newsletter Part 2 (Spring 1992): 3.

10. Rauch, qtd. in Humanities Flyer, 3.

11. Rauch, qtd. in Humanities Flyer, 3.

12. Ronald R. Butters, "Whose Language Is It, Anyway? It Belongs to Thee," *Humanities Flyer*, 5.

13. Vineberg, 4.

14. "Cornerstone, Norcatur Shine," *Oberlin Herald* (Oberlin, KS) (4 July 1991): 1.

15. Both crew head Jason Turpin and actor Edret Brinston were under parole restrictions at the time of the production, which prevented them from leaving their respective states. Cobb had to convince their parole officers of the potentially redemptive value of the production. Brinston's officer believed that participating in the production would unfairly "reward" him for social transgressions. Turpin was finally released from parole the day before rehearsals commenced.

16. Susan Esposito, "Cornerstone to Perform Musical in Eastport on August 29 and 30," *Quoddy Tides* (Eastport, ME) (23 August 1991): 1.

17. Rauch, Cornerstone Newsletter 5.1 (November 1991): 3.

18. Humanities Flyer, 2.

19. Rauch, telephone interview with the author, 31 July 1995.

20. Bill Gato, "Troupe Updates Shakespeare," *Miami Herald* (9 August 1991): G1.

21. Mary Feuer, "Cornerstone Theater Company," *Art Dynamo* (Winter 1991): 25.

22. A 1995 article in *Newsweek* exemplifies the reductive nature of reporting on diversity. In an article exploring the multiplicity of "black" identity, the magazine included opinion surveys broken down into responses from "blacks" and "whites" (Tom Morganthau, "What Color Is Black?" *Newsweek* [13 February 1995]: 62).

23. The documentary was of course prey to various dramatic revisions. Mimicking an Aristotelian structure of rising action and conflict, the documentary places Cornerstone's budget cuts in the middle of the film, realigning the events from where they actually occurred far earlier in the process.

24. Cornerstone Planning Meeting Notes, 20 November, 1991.

25. Christopher Liam Moore, Durfee 12:7.

26. Doug Casement, *Cornerstone* Documentary Roll 140. Casement was referring to a young crew member, not to Cornerstone ensemble members.

27. Jim Carrol, qtd. in Feuer, 26.

28. Moore, Durfee 12:7–8.

29. Rosemarie Voorhees, *Cornerstone* Documentary Roll 141.

30. Feuer, 27.

31. Rauch, *Cornerstone* Documentary Roll 155.

32. Rauch, Durfee 12:12.

33. *Cornerstone* Documentary Roll 141.

34. Rod Prichard, *Cornerstone* Documentary Roll 139.

35. Cornerstone Newsletter 5.1 (November 1991): 5.

36. Rauch, Humanities Flyer, 3.

37. Vineberg, 4.

38. Rauch, Durfee 11:63–64. Alison Carey contends that the "schism" was not as great in her mind, and may have resulted from the guest artists' ignorance of Cornerstone process and the fact that many were in particularly difficult financial straits. Telephone interview with the author, 3 April 1996.

39. Cornerstone Newsletter 5.1 (November 1991): 3.

40. David Reiffel Durfee 8:25–26. Bill Rauch acknowledges that Reiffel's critique of Cornerstone's perceived social cowardice had some validity. A lesbian kiss at the end of the show seemed gratuitous, as it was not integrated into the character of Paulina or the action of the play. Rauch also notes, however, that the decision to cast a man rather than a woman as Antigonus, Paulina's spouse, was agreed upon by the company as a whole, including Reiffel. Rauch submits that the moment of the kiss, presented out of the context of the character's imbedded sexuality, may have driven away a former company friend and contact in Dinwiddie, Virginia (13 March 1996). The moment and its consequences suggest the complications of representing sexuality on stage. Expressions that seemed weak and closeted to Reiffel were strong enough to be perceived by others as offensive because of their beliefs about homosexuality.

41. Durfee, 12:6. In contrast to Reiffel's beliefs about homogenization, other ensemble members felt that the art improved through community input. Both Alison Carey and Bill Rauch point out that Reiffel's compositions often neglected the influence of local music.

42. Anne Beresford Clarke, Durfee 12:13.

43. Rauch, Durfee 12:12.

44. Cornerstone Newsletter 5.1 (November 1991): 6.

45. Humanities Flyer, 2.

46. Cornerstone Newsletter 5.1 (November 1991): 6.

47. Cornerstone Planning Day Notes, November 1994.

48. Moore, interview with the author, Los Angeles, 29 October 2001.

5. Urban Revisions

1. Personal journal, 12 September 1994.

2. Stephen Gutwillig, Durfee 14:7.

3. Alison Carey, Durfee 14:6. Some Cornerstone ensemble members do currently supplement their income with work in film and television.

4. Christopher Liam Moore, Durfee 13:36–37.

5. Erik Priestly, qtd. in Hernandez, 39.

6. Bill Rauch, e-mail to the author, 28 November 2001.

7. Shishir Kurup, Durfee 19:19.

8. Fadwa El Guindi, qtd. in Richard Stayton, 73.

9. Pat McDonnell Twair, "*Ghurba* Misses Target of Telling Arab-American Experience in L.A.," *Beirut Times* 9.370 (30 September–7 October 1993): 6.

10. Kari Sprowl, "*Ghurba:* A Different Perspective," *Beirut Times* 9.371 (7–14 October 1993): 6.

11. Cornerstone Newsletter 2.2.1 (November 1993): 2.

12. Kurup, e-mail to the author, 30 November 2001. Additional quotes from this e-mail.

13. Ashby Semple, Durfee 16:14.

14. Cornerstone Ensemble Meeting Notes, 18 November 1995.
15. Cornerstone Planning Day Notes, 13 September 1994, 6.
16. Cornerstone Planning Day Notes, 13 September 1994, 6.
17. Bill Rauch, interview with the Author, Los Angeles, 18 November 1995. Since the time of the interview, Drew has appeared in even more Cornerstone productions, including one ensemble show.
18. Cohen, 12.
19. Qtd. in Hernandez, 39.
20. Rauch, interview with author, Los Angeles, 18 November 1995.
21. Rauch, interview, Los Angeles, 18 November 1995.
22. Benajah Cobb, Durfee 14:2.
23. Ashby Semple, Cornerstone Planning Day Notes, 14 December 1994, 3.
24. Conversation recorded in personal journal, 22 September 1994.
25. Stephen Gutwillig, interview with the author, Los Angeles, 15 December 2001.
26. Carey, e-mail to the author, 6 January 2002.
27. Rauch, Cornerstone Planning Day Notes, 15 September 2000.
28. Molina, interview with the author, Los Angeles, 11 March, 2001. Several Cornerstone members share Molina's opinion. The production, *Los Biombos,* a slow-paced four-hour adaptation of Jean Genet's *Screens,* translated and adapted by Gloria Alvarez, Lynn Jeffries, Peter Galindo, and Peter Sellars, accomplished little in the way of representing or collaborating with either Cornerstone or Boyle Heights, though many members of the community did enjoy working with Sellars. "That has to rank as one of the lowest organizational points in this company," comments Alison Carey in a personal interview (Los Angeles, 30 October 2001).
29. Rauch, interview with the author, Los Angeles, 14 December 2001.
30. Kurup, e-mail to the author, 28 December 2001.
31. Kurup, e-mail, 28 December 2001.
32. Rauch, interview with the author, Los Angeles, 30 June 1995.
33. Jeffries, e-mail to the author, 4 January 2002.
34. Cornerstone Planning Day Notes, 14 December 1994, 2.
35. Cornerstone Planning Day Notes, 14 December 1994, 2.
36. Jeffries elaborates on her design decisions in a 4 January 2002 e-mail:

My choice to do period costumes for *Nightingale* had several factors behind it. First, I wanted to support Ashby in her first directing experience with Cornerstone. Second, the actors present at the read-through expressed very clearly that they understood metaphor, and wanted to do the play as it was written. At the time I was feeling that double outsiderness of "white person not from here," or more specifically, "privileged Harvard-educated white girl from northern California." I thought, "Who am I to tell a group of African Americans in Watts that they can't play ancient Greeks, but they have to play contemporary people in Watts like themselves?" The traditional period costume type of theater is something I had been reacting against, but these particular folks had maybe not had the chance to experience it in the first place.

The other factor, and this was entirely personal and coincidental, was that one of my dearest friends is a classics professor, and a big fan of Cornerstone. She had told me at some point that the ancient Greeks, contrary to the popular image, did not dress all in white, but in brightly colored fabrics with patterned edges. These colors were actually painted on their statues, but they wore off, leaving us with that all-white image. I was interested in this historical tidbit, and thought it would be satisfying to put it into a design.

In the aftermath, when Ashby was criticized so harshly for this decision not to modernize, I was puzzled and hurt. I felt like I was, for once, actually collaborating with community members at the conceptualizing stage of a design, and I was being scolded for it. I thought it was a respectful choice and a worthwhile experiment. Was it fabulously successful? I wouldn't say so particularly, though I thought the costumes were attractive. Is it a direction I think future designs should go in? No. But I don't regret having tried something different.

37. Jeffries responds in a 5 January 2002 e-mail:

Sure, we could have done that. It probably would have been better. We could have made any number of different design choices, I suppose, but it was a chamber show and we didn't have the luxury of a lot of lead time in which to discuss all the options. This was a small show and a quick process, and we just made a simple choice and went with it.

38. For more information about Mexican American and Chicano *Teatro,* see Huerta, *Chicano Theater* or Broyles-González, *El Teatro Campesino.*

39. Cornerstone Newsletter 2.3.2 (Spring 1995): 3.

40. Rauch, interview with the author, Los Angeles, 18 November 1995. All subsequent comments by Rauch are from this interview unless otherwise indicated.

41. Lynn Manning, qtd. in Jan Breslauer, "Parable of Equity Comes to a New 'Circle,'" *Los Angeles Times* (10 November 1995): F26.

42. While Manning's senator visualized his "blackness," another aspect of his playing remained less visible. Manning, a blind man, played Senator Charles as sighted. No audience members that Bill Rauch or I spoke with recognized Manning's blindness in his performance as Senator Charles. Manning's successful choice enacts another aspect of Cornerstone's performance philosophy. Not only does the company work to include and celebrate various ethnic communities but also performances can highlight the constructed nature of identity, offering opportunities for actors to play across gender, ethnic, and, now, physical boundaries. Manning's extraordinary performance reinforced for me the notion that actors shouldn't be confined to playing their limitations. Rauch concurs, noting:

Shishir [Kurup] was one of the people who most strongly supported Lynn's [desire to play the character as sighted] from the very beginning. He said, "Just because I'm Indian I don't always want to play the 7-11 clerk with the accent." He saw Lynn's desire as a direct parallel.

43. *The Central Ave. Chalk Circle* by Lynn Manning and Eric Bentley, adapted from Bertolt Brecht, *The Caucasian Chalk Circle*, 17.

44. In fact, Rauch had earlier misgivings about a totalizing contemporary aesthetic. Many previous Cornerstone shows had incorporated aspects of non-realism including a forty-foot Christmas tree in Norcatur and giant chairs in *Snow Queen* (1986). Rauch has begun to believe more strongly that a nonrealistic or noncontemporary aesthetic could at times illuminate a text more clearly for an audience. He contemplated his growing ambivalence in our November 1995 interview:

> After having done *Romeo & Juliet* (1989), I do remember getting very excited that we should have set it in the late sixties. I had an idea that if it had been a period production, in a time of segregation, it might have been more theatrically charged and also might have invited in the people who needed to pat themselves on the back about how far they'd come in terms of racial segregation. Setting the play in contemporary Mississippi made a lot of people shut down. They felt like they'd come so far and who were we to imply that racial division was still a problem for their community. I remember getting very excited about that possibility and a lot my colleagues in Cornerstone getting really freaked out saying, "Bill, that goes against everything we do in Cornerstone. The whole point is saying these problems still exist today." All of which goes to say that I am surprised that over the years I am increasingly interested in period settings that shed a specific resonance on a play.

45. Lynn Jeffries relates one of her favorite design moments involving the talented community seamstress, Irma Ashe. During *Chalk Circle*, Jeffries approached Ashe with a judge's robe. "I need one of these," she requested, holding up a package of Hefty garbage bags, "made out of these." The Hefty robe fit perfectly (interview with the author, Los Angeles, 14 December 2001).

46. In a 13 March 1996 telephone interview, Rauch noted that the show reflected a great deal of community input and participation. The themes of redevelopment and gentrification upon which the prologue focused arose from community members during a meeting with the playwright. Lynn Jeffries adds a more complex note:

> The set, which was designed by Ed Haynes, was a two-level rough wooden scaffold that wrapped around the audience, and a rotating platform in the middle. It was a very useful design for varied and interesting staging, allowing for lots of movement and dynamic spatial relationships. I thought of it as being a kind of neutral background, like the gray costumes that the actors wore, to which they added more colorful paper accents to define the different characters they were playing. Just as most actors had multiple roles,

the set had to serve as multiple locations, from swank high-rise to mean streets to artist's loft to wine country estate. However, one Watts resident looked at the rough wood with a frown and asked me if it was meant to represent Watts as poor and run-down. I was sad that this is what it said to her. Design is a tricky business. (E-mail to the author, 5 January 2002)

47. LeRoi Jones, qtd. in Gottlieb, 52.

48. In his article on canon formation, John Guillory points out the historical social function of the establishment of canonical texts ("Canon," in *Critical Terms for Literary Study*, ed. Frank Letriccia and Thomas McLaughlin [Chicago: University of Chicago Press, 1990], 233–49.) Initially set aside to teach grammar and literacy in ancient Greek schools, later academic institutions established a canon of "great works" first as a way of teaching Standard English and only recently in order to study the texts themselves. Guillory implies that the texts and their self-evident greatness have never existed outside of the cultural formation specifically institutionalized through schools.

49. Personal journal, 22 November 1995.

50. Bertolt Brecht, qtd. in Willett, 7.

6. Regional Returns: A Tale of Two Collaborations

1. Not only had the company already produced *Good Person* in Long Creek, Oregon (1988) but also ensemble members had ranked the show as their favorite to date in a 1991 meeting discussing artistic standards (Cornerstone Ensemble Meeting Notes, 29 November 1991, audiotape 1, side A). In a 6 January 2002 e-mail, Alison Carey adds that Doug Hughes had, perhaps significantly, seen this production.

2. Christopher Liam Moore, interview with the author, Los Angeles, 29 October 2001.

3. Since 1993, Cornerstone has collaborated with a number of institutions including Arena Stage, the Museum of Contemporary Art in Los Angeles, the Public Theater in New York, Touchstone Theater in Bethlehem, Pennsylvania, Long Wharf Theatre in Connecticut, Great Lakes Theatre in Cleveland, Ohio, and the Mark Taper Forum in Los Angeles. The company defines these collaborations in their current mission statement as sharing their mission and methods.

4. Laurence Maslon, telephone interview with the author, 2 February 1996. All subsequent quotes from this interview unless otherwise indicated.

5. Due to reduced financial resources, the resident acting ensemble, a mainstay of the Arena since its founding, was reduced from twelve members on a four-play contract in the 1993–1994 season to two members on a four-play contract in the 1995–1996 season. At the time, ensemble actors had only a limited voice in choosing season productions and played no part in managing the company.

6. In positioning the organization as an American institution, Arena's Elaboration of Artistic Principles notes, "Even in the very configuration of the Arena space—the most democratic theater space imaginable—we strive to embody our

country's values" (3). This seems a somewhat hyberbolic use of the term *democracy*, which implies direct participation in decision making rather than the ability to view other audience members. Additionally, while arena seating does not display the visually hierarchical audience structures of many seventeenth-century proscenium theaters, the Arena does offer ticket prices that distinguish between good and better seating. In a 5 January 2002 e-mail, Lynn Jeffries adds to the notion that "some seats are more equal than others."

> The expensive seats are on the side of the arena nearest the lobby. This is where the tech tables are set up in rehearsal, and this is where the show is directed and designed from. Bill and I were dismayed when we looked at the set for *Twelfth Night* and saw that it very clearly had a front and a back, with the front, of course, facing this privileged seating area. I tried very hard and very consciously not to favor one side in my design for the Arena Stage. I kept the model in the middle of my hotel room when I was working on it, and I rotated it frequently. I also made sure to move around some during tech week, to check the views from different sides and heights.

7. Doug Wager, telephone interview with the author, 23 January 1996. Additional quotes are from this interview unless otherwise indicated.

8. *The Good Person of New Haven* Program Notes, 11.

9. Long Wharf Theatre Business Circle Pamphlet, 2000.

10. Doug Hughes, interview with the author, New Haven, 7 June 2000. All subsequent quotes from this interview unless otherwise indicated.

11. Bill Rauch, telephone interview with the author, 17 January 1996. All subsequent quotes from this interview unless otherwise indicated.

12. "Collaborations with the Community," unpublished notes, Theater Communications Group (TCG) Panel, 25 June 1994.

13. According to Rauch, the wealthiest member of Arena's board resented any kind of rewriting of classical material. Rauch also alleged that a highly placed staff member grew increasingly skeptical about the project and Cornerstone's mission.

14. Hughes, Letter to John Ostrout, executive director of the Connecticut Commission on the Arts, 17 November 1997, Arts Partnership for Stronger Communities Program 1998 Grant Application.

15. *The Good Person of New Haven,* adapted by Alison Carey from *The Good Woman of Setzuan* by Bertolt Brecht, translated by Ralph Manheim. All textual references refer to the 21 March 2000 script. Subsequent textual references will be included parenthetically in the text.

16. Leslie J. King and Reginald G. Golledge, *Cities, Space, and Behavior: The Elements of Urban Geography* (Englewood Cliffs, NJ: Prentice-Hall, 1978), 4–5.

17. For additional information on urban space, performance, and memory, see Kuftinec, "[Walking Through a] Ghost Town: Cultural Hauntologie in Mostar, Bosnia-Herzegovina."

18. I refer here to Walter Benjamin's meditation on Baudelaire's depiction of the flâneur, or urban stroller, in quest of something new ("On Some Motifs in

Baudelaire," trans. Harry Zohn, in *Illuminations,* ed. Hannah Arendt [New York: Harcourt, Brace and World, 1968]), 155–200.

19. For further explication of social aspects of space, see Edward Soja, *Postmodern Geographies: The Reassertion of Space in Culture and Social Theory* (New York: Verso, 1989); and Henri Lefebvre, *The Production of Space* (Malden, MA: Blackwell, 1991).

20. Hughes had actually initiated conversations with Alison Carey and Bill Rauch prior to learning of the Arts Partnership Grant. The grant did, however, provide incentive and structure for the project's development.

21. Arts Partnerships Grant Proposal Narrative, 1998, 6.

22. Dana Fripp, telephone interview with the author, 7 June 2000. All subsequent quotes from this interview unless otherwise indicated.

23. King and Golledge, 313.

24. "Teen's Goal Is Broadway," *Hamden Journal* (10 May 2000): 1.

25. Horace Little, qtd. in Christopher Arnott, "Streets on Stage," 2.

26. In our telephone interview, Wager noted that the Arena audience base consisted mainly of well-educated white members, one third from Washington, D.C., one third from the Virginia suburbs, and one third from the Maryland suburbs. Wager added that 6 to 7 percent of Arena's audience members were at this time of nonwhite racial and ethnic backgrounds. According to the 1990 census reports, African Americans make up over 60 percent of the population of Washington, D.C., proper.

27. Diana Dale, interview with Laurence Maslon, 15 September 1993. Unpublished notes from Cornerstone Theater's archive.

28. Tamara Sibley, telephone interview with the author, 31 January 1996. All subsequent quotations from this interview unless otherwise indicated.

29. Toni White-Richardson, "Collaborations."

30. White-Richardson, telephone interview with the author, 31 January 1996. All subsequent quotations from this interview unless otherwise indicated.

31. Ella B. Howard-Pearis, qtd. in Joseph Whitaker, "Anacostia's Past," *Washington Post* (14 November 1976): Res. Sec. 1.

32. White-Richardson explains that limits to subway access are compounded by the fact that cabs seldom venture into the Anacostia area. In the Durfee Oral History, Cornerstone members relate an incident that illustrates this difficulty. Participant (and later Cornerstone ensemble member) Damion Teeko Parran was without a ride one day to a performance, and the cab that he called would not venture East of the River:

> They had said that they would come. And he called them back, and it was like oh, no one will go in there. So he had to call another cab company and wait for them to send a cab, so he missed the first half-hour of the show; because he literally couldn't get there. (Durfee 20:13–14)

33. Pamela Tatge, telephone interview with the author, 31 May 2000. All subsequent quotes from this interview.

34. Adelaida Nuñez, qtd. in Collins-Hughes, F2.

35. Nuñez, qtd. in Collins-Hughes, F2.

36. In the Durfee Oral History, Bill Rauch explains:

This is one of many ways the advisory board was really, really useful. We had a whole thing planned that we were gonna basically give them out to individuals like on the streets and in the library and blah-blah-blah. And the advisory board was like, you don't know this community, you don't know what you're talking about. It's gotta be done through groups, 'cause it's all about transportation. People are gonna take your little vouchers on the street and you're never gonna see them 'cause they're gonna have no way to get west of the river. (20:11–12)

37. The casting of the two deaf children proved controversial among some Arena staff members, illustrating to them another example of Cornerstone's over-done political correctness. Rauch felt that *A Community Carol* provided an important opportunity to include hearing-impaired actors on stage. D.C. is home to Galindo University, the largest school for the deaf in the country. Rauch, who has a hearing-impaired brother, felt that given Galindo's presence, it was important to include deaf actors. Arena's access-coordinator was thrilled; the production manager was not. Having an interpreter present at all rehearsals and performances cost Arena a great deal of extra money. When one of the student's parents complained that the sign master (the translator of text to sign) should not be the same person as the interpreter, the production manager grew furious. When the *Washington Times* review appeared disparaging *A Community Carol*'s political correctness (Hap Epstein, "In Tune with the Times," rev. of *A Community Carol, Washington Times* [3 December 1993]: C16), the production manager posted the review on his bulletin board, highlighting a paragraph that detailed the show's "excesses" (Rauch, notes to the author, 20 April 1996).

38. Damion Teeko Parran, interview with the author, Los Angeles, 29 October 2001.

39. Sibley, qtd. in Elizabeth Astor, "Scrooge in Anacostia," *Washington Post* (28 November 1993): G4.

40. Hughes, Letter to John Ostrout.

41. Arts Partnerships Grant Narrative, 1999, 4.

42. Cohen, 25–26.

43. Mark Zaretsky, "'A Little Melting Pot.'" *New Haven Register* (27 June 1999): D1.

44. Zaretsky, D1.

45. Lynn Jeffries, Durfee 20:30.

46. Sabrina Peck, Durfee 20:17.

47. Durfee 20:30.

48. Jeffries, e-mail to the author, 5 January 2002.

49. Maslon, e-mail, 31 December 2001.

50. In a lecture to an American Drama class, Alma Martínez, a former actress with El Teatro Campesino and Ph.D. student at Stanford University, discussed a

complementary experience that Luis Valdez had when producing his play *Zoot Suit* (1978) with the Mark Taper Forum. According to Martínez, Artistic Director Gordon Davidson subjected the production to a similar kind of scrutiny. Davidson insisted on toning down the "rough edges" of the production, including its more overt political references. Martínez referred to the resultant production as the "gringoization" of Chicano theater (23 April 1996).

51. Durfee 20:19.

52. Maslon, e-mail to the author, 31 December 2001.

53. Related by Maslon, e-mail to the author, 31 December 2001.

54. In a 31 December 2001 e-mail, Maslon clarifies that his response referred to early versions of the script. Though over-inclusion remained a problem in the final version, it was "much, much less so when it made its way on-stage with music, staging, etc."

55. Alison Carey, Durfee 20:24.

56. Carey, telephone interview with the author, 17 January 1996. In a later 6 January 2002 e-mail, Carey adds to the story:

> We never actually came to a decision on this one, of course. Someone called the Redskins and found out it would be a cold day in hell before we could use their logo and uniforms. All our non-profit, intramural squabbling was a big waste of time. And, during the production, the audience laughed when we announced "And now, the Washington Potatoskins!" I'm sure all of us would have agreed on the name if we had known that in advance—hey, you don't turn down a laugh line.

57. Damion Teeko Parran relates that this representational conundrum extended into costuming. Cast as Peter Cratchit, Parran at first resisted being clad in a Malcolm X sweatshirt:

> I wasn't sure if I agreed with Malcolm X's philosophy on race and community. I didn't like the assumption that because I'm black, I identify with Malcolm X. But Bill and I talked about it, and I felt like he listened to me. I hadn't understood that there could be a difference between the character and who you are, that there doesn't have to have direct connection to how you feel. By the end I felt comfortable with it. (Telephone interview with the author, 1 June 2000).

58. Rauch, telephone interview with the author, 24 April 1996.

59. Moore, telephone interview with the author, 17 January 1996.

60. Carey, qtd. in Francesco Fiondella, "New Haven: The Play," *New Haven Advocate* (12 November 1998): 8.

61. Arts Partnerships Grant Narrative, 1998, 4.

62. Anonymous audience member, qtd. in Zaretsky, D1.

63. Rauch, interview with the author, New Haven, 29 March 2000.

64. Moore, interview with the author, New Haven, 31 May 2000.

65. Rauch, qtd. in Zaretsky, D1.

66. Rauch, interview with the author, New Haven, 29 March 2000.

67. Long Wharf Theatre Press Release, 4 April 1998.

68. Gracy Brown, qtd. in Frank Rizzo, "Cornerstone of the Community," *Hartford Courant* (7 May 2000): G7.

69. Leididiana Castro, qtd. in Rizzo, G7.

70. Aaron Jafferis, qtd. in Rizzo, G7.

71. William Graustein, qtd. in Rizzo, G6.

72. Aaron Jafferis, qtd. in Zaretsky, D4.

73. *The Good Person of New Haven* Symposium, Long Wharf Theatre, 21 May 2000.

74. See chapter 3, note 17.

75. Jafferis, Qtd. in Rizzo, G7.

76. Brecht, Bertolt, "One or Two Points about Proletarian Actors," trans. John Willett, in *Brecht on Theatre*, ed. and trans. Willett (New York: Hill and Wang, 1964), 148–49.

77. Hans Robert Jauss, qtd. in Marvin Carlson, "Theatre Audiences and the Reading of Performance," *Theatre Semiotics*, 11.

78. Newspaper headlines implied a performance of city as much as play. Examples include Fiondella, "New Haven: The Play"; and "Long Wharf, City Getting Their Act Together," *New Haven Register* (22 October 1998): A1.

79. *The Good Person of New Haven* Program Notes, 9.

80. Hughes, qtd. in Collins-Hughes, F7.

81. Susan Bennett offers a complex analysis of reception to the theatrical event. Discussing the subscriber audience, she notes that while the subscriber may be able to plan ahead for the performance by reading reviews and articles, "the remoteness of the decision to attend from the actual experience of the event might well add an element of unresponsiveness" (*Theatre Audiences: A Theory of Production and Reception* [New York: Routledge, 1997], 124).

82. Carey, telephone interview with the author, 30 May 2000.

83. Deb Clapp, interview with the author, New Haven, 14 June 2000.

84. Rauch, interview with the author, New Haven, 31 May 2000.

85. Moore, interview with the author, New Haven, 31 May 2000.

86. Allison Lee, telephone interview with the author, 3 June 2000. All subsequent quotes from this interview unless otherwise indicated.

87. Jean Routt, interview with the author, New Haven, 14 June 2000.

88. The 1993–94 season included two classics, Shakespeare's *Twelfth Night* and Ibsen's *Hedda Gabler;* two well-known contemporary plays and playwrights, Alan Ayckbourn's *Revengers' Comedies* and Brian Friel's *Dancing at Lugnasha;* and one play originating from Arena's "New Voices for a New America" program, Mustapha Matura's *Small World.* Poster images that feature people prominently suggest a white Hedda, a black character in *A Small World,* the controversial black Santa of *A Community Carol,* a white Irish woman for *Dancing,* and two wrapped faces for *Twelfth Night.* Alison Carey points out that the actors behind the wraps are black and suggests that the wrapping, consciously or unconsciously, potentially conceals this fact (3 April 1996).

89. *A Community Carol* Press Release, 4 November 1993.

90. Rauch, Durfee 20:11

91. Rauch, Durfee 20:11.

92. Jeffries, e-mail to the author, 5 January 2002.

93. Alison Carey adds that several Arena staff members concurred with Cornerstone's perceptions and problems with the poster image (3 April 1996).

94. Durfee 20:12.

95. Susan Clampett, letter to Arena, 3 January 1994.

96. Doug Wager, "Collaborations."

97. Following *A Community Carol,* there was some discussion of a future Cornerstone collaboration:

> In the end it was felt that the project would have drained resources from other artists' projects and thus was not enthusiastically supported. . . . I don't think, really, it was the "community" part Arena objected to; it was the size and unpredictability of a Cornerstone project in a theater with 150 employees and nine other shows to mount. (Maslon e-mail, 27 December 2001)

Doug Wager left Arena Stage in 1998, replaced by Molly Smith, an advocate of community-based performance (she had previously taught Cornerstone members the exercise on cultural mapping referenced in chapter 5). While Arena has not produced another full-length community-based production, Smith has more fully integrated Arena's independent branches of Living Stage, Education, and Audience Enrichment under the umbrella of Community Engagement. Smith has also initiated a major collaboration with Arena's Southwest neighbors, perhaps aided by relations forged during *A Community Carol.* Living Stage, a significant community-based program founded by Robert Alexander in 1966, had always been associated with but distinct from Arena. Performers with the current company have mixed feelings about some of this restructuring, expressing personal concerns to me that the integration might co-opt rather than embrace twenty years of independent community-specific work.

98. Susan Berlin, "Familiar 'Carol' Gets New Harmonies," rev. of *A Community Carol, Gazette* (Washington D.C.) (8 December 1993).

99. Bob Anthony, "It's Showtime," rev. of *A Community Carol,* Jazz 90 WDCU-FM (3 December 1993).

100. Lloyd Rose, "A Scrooge for Our Times at Arena," rev. of *A Community Carol, Washington Post* (3 December 1993): G1, 4.

101. Gary Tischler, "Scrooge, Dickens, and Washington Come to Life in *A Community Carol,*" rev. of *A Community Carol, American Weekly* (13 December 1993).

102. William Henry III, "Putting a Rap on Scrooge," *Time* (20 December 1993): 68.

103. J. Wynn Rousuck, "'A Community Carol': Dickens of a Story, Updated and Unrelentingly PC," rev. of *A Community Carol, Baltimore Sun* (3 December 1993): Live, 20.

Lynn Jeffries adds an intriguing note to this anxiety over political correctness:

I can't resist sharing with you my favorite bit of criticism for the show being too PC. While working on the design, I had been reading a biography
of Dickens, and I came across this reference to *A Christmas Carol,* "The
previous fall [Dickens] had found a topic that embodied his desire to create both a powerful social statement, 'a Sledge hammer' that would respond
to the abysmal treatment of the poor, and something appropriate for the
Christmas season" (Fred Kaplan, *Dickens, a Biography* [New York: Morrow,
1988], 75). I imagined Dickens grinning at Lucia Anderson's review in the
Freelance Star, which was generally very favorable, with the caveat that, "the
message is sometimes delivered with the subtlety of a sledgehammer" (D2).
(E-mail to the author, 5 January 2002)

104. White-Richardson, qtd. in Elizabeth Kastor, "Scrooge in Anacostia," *Washington Post* (28 November 1993): G4.

105. While Maslon stands by his desire for standards, a later e-mail (31 December 2001) clarifies and complicates the nature of professionalism:

Even in a theater like Arena, no one ever agrees on excellence. I think that
there is a difference between work methods that reflect the culture of an
institution (such as lateness, or lack of planning, or lack of diction or commitment on the part of actors, etc.) and the quality of the production, but
the final product is still subjectively assessed. Arena had a large artistic staff
and rarely agreed 100%. I would certainly say . . . that there was clever work
and moving performances and all that, when all was said and done at 10:45,
the piece accomplished what it set out to do. (My dad still thinks it's the
best thing he ever saw at Arena). Community theater can be good too—
when it eventually does what it intended to do. This *Community Carol* did.

106. Maslon, e-mail to the author, 31 December 2001.

107. In a 2 January 2002 e-mail, New Haven Project Coordinator Shana Waterman comments that there were "rumblings of discontent" at various moments
during the initial production process among Long Wharf staff. She attributes Doug
Hughes's leadership in shifting the dynamic towards support of the show. After
initial trepidation, according to both Cornerstone and Long Wharf, the project
proceeded with a great deal of support from the regional theater's staff.

108. Stephen Papa, qtd. in Rizzo, G6.

109. In a 14 June 2000 interview, Jean Routt noted that Long Wharf learned to
ask of local residents and groups, "What do we need to do to help you to come?" If
transportation were an issue, they were able to respond, "We're coming to get you."

110. The Legacy Project focuses on ways of continuing relationships established
among participating partners in the New Haven Project. Focus groups set the
agenda for future initiatives, such as play readings, community festivals, and ongoing orientation and transportation for community members to Long Wharf's
main stage productions.

111. I would like to acknowledge Jan Cohen-Cruz for pointing out this connection.

7. Conclusion: Curtain Calls

1. In *Almost Home: America's Love-Hate Relationship with Community* (Princeton: Princeton University Press, 2000), David L. Kirp outlines an assessment of the dual (and sometimes dueling) nature of conceptions of the individual American as both solitary and communal (5). Kirp locates these tensions historically, in the pull between enlightenment-influenced individual rights and the civic societies and associations Alexis de Tocqueville remarks upon in his early-nineteenth-century observations (7–10).

2. Christopher Liam Moore, Cornerstone Company Meeting, Norcatur, Kansas, 26 November 1991, audiotape.

3. Stephen Gutwillig, Cornerstone Company Meeting, Norcatur, Kansas, 20 November 1991, audiotape.

4. Bill Rauch, Cornerstone Company Meeting, Norcatur Kansas, 26 November 1991, audiotape.

5. Leslie Tamaribuchi, telephone interview with the author, 24 May 2001.

6. Buell, 158.

7. Richard Ford, "The Repressed Community: Locating the New Communitarianism," *Transition* 65: 99.

8. bell hooks, *Yearning,* 29.

9. Ford, 115.

10. Buell, 146.

11. See chapter 1, notes 4 and 15.

12. Mackaye, *Community Drama,* 40.

13. Benajah Cobb, Cornerstone Company Meeting, 20 November 1991, audiotape.

14. Moore, interview with the author, Los Angeles, 29 October 2001

15. Maslon, telephone interview with the author, 2 February 1996.

16. Cornerstone cofounder Alison Carey has expressed critical insight about Cornerstone's success garnering institutional support:

> Frankly, our next big challenge, if you look at per-ticket price—the cost of this organization is obscene and we have to get bigger audience support or Cornerstone will simply choke on its own size. It's just taking all these resources and placing them in a tiny little funnel that is the audience and it's not appropriate. It's too many resources for too few people when there are so many theater companies that are not getting the kind of resources we are. (Interview with the author, Los Angeles, 30 October, 2001)

17. Jill Dolan, "Performance, Utopia, and the Utopian Performative," *Theatre Journal* 53 (2001): 456.

18. Dolan, 455.

19. Moore, interview with the author, 29 October 2001.

20. Michel Foucault, "On the Genealogy of Ethics," in *Ethics: Subjectivity and*

Truth, Vol. 1 of Essential Works of Foucault, 1954–1984, ed. Paul Rabinow, trans. Robert Hurley and others (New York: New Press, 1994), 256. I would like to thank John Fletcher for leading me to this source.

WORKS CITED

Works on Community-Based Theater

Armstrong, Anne Elizabeth. "Paradoxes in Community-Based Pedagogy: Decentering Students Through Oral History Performance." *Theatre Topics* 10.2 (2000): 113–28.

Boal, Augusto. *Rainbow of Desire.* Trans. Adrian Jackson. New York: Routledge, 1995.

———. *Theatre of the Oppressed.* Trans. Charles A. McBride and Maria-Odilia Leal McBride. New York: Theatre Communications Group, 1985.

Brady, Sara. "Welded to the Ladle: Non-Radicality in Community-Based Theater." *The Drama Review* 44.3 (2000): 51–74.

Brophy, Brian. "Perspectives on Urban Community-Based Theater: Peter Sellars in East Los Angeles: The Postcolonial Dilemma of Artistic Occupation." Master's Thesis, California State University Los Angeles, 1999.

Broyles-Gonzalez, Yvonne. *El Teatro Campesino: Theater in the Chicano Movement.* Austin: University of Texas Press, 1994.

Burleigh, Louise. *Community Theatre in Theory and Practice.* Prefatory Letter by Percy Mackaye. Boston: Little, Brown, 1917.

Burnham, Linda Frye. "The Cutting Edge Is Enormous." *High Performance* (Summer 1994): 12–14.

Carey, Alison. Letter to the Editor. *The Drama Review* 45.3 (Fall 2001): 19–22.

Cocke, Dudley, et al., eds. *From the Ground Up: Grassroots Theater in Historical and Contemporary Perspective.* Ithaca: Cornell University Press, 1993.

Coe, Robert. "Verona, Mississippi: Cornerstone Reinvents 'Community Theatre' in America." *American Theater* 6.5 (May 1989): 14–21, 52–57.

Cohen-Cruz, Jan. A conversation on critical writing about community arts, at *National Gathering with an Attitude.* Berkeley, May 2000.

———. "A Hyphenated Field: Community-Based Theater in the USA." *New Theatre Quarterly* 16.4 (2000): 364–78.

———. "When the Gown Goes to Town: The Reciprocal Rewards of Fieldwork for Artists." *Theatre Topics* 11.1 (2001): 55–62.

Community Arts Network Reading Room. www.communityarts.net.

"Connecting Californians." Los Angeles Area Focus Group. Cornerstone Theater, Los Angeles, CA. 18 November 1999. www.communityarts.net/concal/images/lafocus.pdf.

Cornerstone. Documentary produced by Michael Kantor and Steve Ives, 1999.

———. Documentary Rolls.

Croce, Arlene. "Discussing the Undiscussable." *New Yorker* (26 December 1994–2 January 1995): 54–60.

Davol, Ralph. *A Handbook of American Pageantry.* Taunton, MA: Davol, 1914.

Drummond, Alexander. Undated Notes. Department of University Archives and Manuscripts, Cornell University Libraries. In "Alexander Drummond and New York Stories." *Storytelling Theater: Culture, Communication and Community.* The Community-Based Arts Project Final Report. Janet Salmons-Rue, project director. Cornell Center for Theatre Arts and Roadside Theater, 1993.

Dumbold, Charlotte. "Proceedings of the Conference of Cities Held in Connection with the Pageant and Masque of St. Louis, May 29–31, 1914." St. Louis: St. Louis Pageant Drama Association, 1914.

Feuer, Mary. "Cornerstone Theater Company." *Art Dynamo* (Winter 1991): 24–29.

Free Southern Theater by the Free Southern Theater. Ed. Thomas C. Dent, Richard Schechner, and Gilbert Moses. New York: Bobbs-Merrill, 1969.

From the Ground Up: Grassroots Theater in Historical and Contemporary Perspective. Ed. Dudley Cocke, Harry Newman, and Janet Salmons-Rue. Ithaca: Cornell University Press, 1993.

Gard, Robert, and Gertrude S. Burley. *Community Theatre: Idea and Achievement.* New York: Duell, Sloan and Pearce, 1959.

Geer, Richard Owen. "Out of Control in Colquitt: Swamp Gravy Makes Stone Soup." *The Drama Review* 40.2 (1996): 103–30.

Gooch, Steven. *All Together Now: An Alternative View of Theatre and the Community.* London: Methuen, 1984.

Green, Paul. "The American Theatre Today." In *Pioneering a People's Theatre.* Ed. Archibald Henderson. Chapel Hill: University of North Carolina Press, 1945, 62.

Henry, William, III. "Putting a Rap on Scrooge." *Time* 20 (December 1993): 68.

Hill, Jackson. "A Farewell Without Mourning: A Jazz Funeral for Free Southern Theater." *Southern Exposure* 14: 3–4 (1986): 72–76.

Kershaw, Baz. *The Politics of Performance: Radical Theatre as Cultural Intervention.* London: Routledge, 1992.

———. *The Radical in Performance: Between Brecht and Baudrillard.* New York: Routledge, 1999.

Koch, Frederick H. *American Folk Plays.* New York: D. Appleton Company, 1939.

———. *The Carolina Playmakers.* New York: Henry Holt, 1941.

Kuftinec, Sonja. "The Art of Bridge Building in Mostar." Nelhaus and Haedicke, 58–66.

———. "Beyond Brecht: An Interview with Bill Rauch." *Theater InSight* 16 (1996): 35–41.

———. "A Cornerstone for Rethinking Community Theater." *Theater Topics* 6.1 (1996): 91–104.

———. "Cornerstone's Community Chalk Circle." *The Brecht Yearbook* 22 (1997): 239–51.

———. "Fighting Fences: Theatrical Rule-Breaking in the Serbian Republic of Bosnia." *Slavic and Eastern European Performance* 19.2 (1999): 50–57.

————. "Ghost Town: Cultural Hauntologie in Mostar, Bosnia-Herzegovina." *Text and Performance Quarterly* 18.2 (1998): 81–95.

————. "*Odakle Ste? (Where Are You From?)* Active Learning and Community Based Theater in Former Yugoslavia and the US." *Theatre Topics* 7.2 (1997): 171–86.

————. "Playing with the Borders: Dramaturging Ethnicity in Bosnia." *Journal of Dramatic Theory and Criticism* 13.1 (1998): 143–56.

————. Review of *Broken Hearts: A BH Mystery,* by Lisa Loomer. Cornerstone Theater Company, Los Angeles. *Theater Journal* 52.3 (2000): 397–99.

————. "Staging the City with the Good People of New Haven." *Theater Journal* 53.2 (2001): 197–222.

Lacy, Suzanne. "Cultural Pilgrimages and Metaphoric Journeys." *Mapping the Terrain,* 19–47.

————. "Debated Territory: Toward a Critical Language for Public Art." *Mapping the Terrain,* 171–85.

————, ed. *Mapping the Terrain: New Genre Public Art.* Washington: Bay Press, 1996.

Lippard, Lucy. *The Lure of the Local: Senses of Place in a Multicentered Society.* New York: New Press, 1997.

Lordi, Karen. "Santa Claus in the Video Store: An Interview with Bill Rauch." *Yale Theater* (September 1990): 14–19.

Mackay, Constance d'Arcy. *Patriotic Drama in Your Town.* New York: Henry Holt and Company, 1918.

Mackaye, Percy. *The Civic Theatre in Relation to the Redemption of Leisure.* New York: Mitchell Kennerley, 1912.

————. *Community Drama: Its Motive and Method of Neighborliness.* Boston: Houghton Mifflin, 1917.

————. *The New Citizenship: A Civic Ritual Devised for Place of Public Meeting in America.* New York: Macmillan, 1915.

Malpede, John. *Connecting Californians: Finding the Art of Community Change.* Transcript from Los Angeles Focus Group. 18 November 1999. Community Arts Network Reading Room. www.communityarts.net.

McConachie, Bruce. "Approaching the 'Structure of Feeling' in Grassroots Theater." *Theatre Topics* 8.1 (1998): 33–53.

Neal, Larry. "The Black Arts Movement." *The Drama Review* 12.4 (1968): 36–46.

Nelhaus, Tobin, and Susan Haedicke, eds. *Performing Democracy.* Ann Arbor: University of Michigan Press, 2001.

Paterson, Doug. "To For With: Some Observations on Community-Based Theater." In *ReImaging America: The Arts of Social Change.* Ed. Mark O'Brien and Craig Little. Santa Cruz: New Society Publishers, 1990, 237–43.

"Proceedings of the Conference of Cities Held in Connection with the Pageant and Masque of St. Louis, May 29–31, 1914." St. Louis: St. Louis Pageant Drama Association, 1914.

Román, David. "Visa Denied." In *Queer Frontiers: Millennial Geographies, Genders, and Generations.* Ed. Joseph A. Boone. Madison: University of Wisconsin Press, 2000, 350–61.

Russell, Mary. *How to Produce Plays and Pageants.* New York: George H. Doran, 1923.

Schwarzman, Mat. "Drawing the Line at Place: The Environmental Justice Project." *High Performance* 72 (Summer 1996): 1, 8–12.

Shebar, William. "'Three Sisters' in West Virginia." *Theater Week* (18–24 June 1990): 25.

Tsuchiya, Hiroko. "'Let Them Be Amused': The Industrial Drama Movement, 1910–1929." McConachie and Friedman, 97–110.

Vineberg, Steve. Rev. of *The Winter's Tale: An Interstate Adventure. Threepenny Review* (Spring 1992): 3–5.

Ethnography, Community, and Cultural Studies

Aguilar, John. "Insider Research: An Ethnography of a Debate." In *Anthropologists at Home in North America: Methods and Issues in the Study of One's Own Society.* Ed. Donald A. Messerschmidt. New York: Cambridge University Press, 1981, 15–26.

Anderson, Benedict. *Imagined Communities: Reflections on the Origins and Spread of Nationalism.* London: Verso, 1983.

Bell, Colin, and Howard Newby. *Community Studies: An Introduction to the Sociology of the Local Community.* 3rd ed. London: Allen, 1978.

Bhabha, Homi K. *The Location of Culture.* New York: Routledge, 1994.

Buell, Frederick. *National Culture and the New Global System.* Baltimore: Johns Hopkins University Press, 1994.

———. "Theorizing Ethnicity in America." *National Culture and the New Global System.*

Clifford, James. *The Predicament of Culture: Twentieth-Century Ethnography, Literature, and Art.* Cambridge: Harvard University Press, 1988.

Cohen, Anthony. *The Symbolic Construction of Community.* New York: Youngstock, 1985.

Dilthey, William. "The Construction of the Historical World in the Human Sciences." In *W. Dilthey: Selected Writings.* Ed. H. P. Rickman. Cambridge: Cambridge University Press, 1976, 168–245.

Ford, Richard. "The Repressed Community: Locating the New Communitarianism." *Transition* 65 (1995): 96–117.

Geertz, Clifford. "Blurred Genres: The Refiguration of Social Thoughts." Geertz, *Local Knowledge,* 19–35.

———. *Local Knowledge: Further Essays in Interpretive Anthropology.* New York: Basic Books, 1983.

———. "Thick Description: Toward an Interpretive Theory of Culture." *The Interpretation of Cultures.* London: Hutchinson, 1975, 3–30.

Gilroy, Paul. *"There Ain't No Black in the Union Jack": The Cultural Politics of Race and Nation.* London: Hutchinson, 1987.

Kirp, David L. *Almost Home: America's Love-Hate Relationship with Community.* Princeton: Princeton University Press, 2000.

Lawless, Elaine J. "'I was afraid someone like you . . . an outsider . . . would misunderstand' Negotiating Interpretive Differences Between Ethnographers and Subjects." *Journal of American Folklore* 105 (1992): 302–14.

Malinowski, Bronislaw. *A Diary in the Strict Sense of the Term.* New York: Harcourt, Brace, and World, 1967.

Turner, Victor. *From Ritual to Theatre: The Human Seriousness of Play.* New York: Performing Arts Journal, 1982.

————. *The Ritual Process: Structure and Anti-Structure.* Chicago: Aldine, 1969.

Williams, Raymond. *Keywords: A Vocabulary of Culture and Society.* Rev. ed. New York: Oxford University Press, 1985.

Young, Iris Marion. *Justice and the Politics of Difference.* Princeton: Princeton University Press, 1990.

General Works

Alinsky, Saul. *Reveille for Radicals,* 1946. New York: Vintage Books Edition, 1969.

The American Theatre: A Sum of Its Parts: A Collection of the Distinguished Addresses Presented Expressly for the Symposium "The American Theatre—A Cultural Process," at the First American College Theatre Festival, Washington D.C., 1968. New York: Samuel French, 1971.

Anderson, John. *The American Theatre.* Dial Press: New York, 1938.

Baraka, Amiri. *The Autobiography of LeRoi Jones.* New York: Freundlich, 1984.

Benjamin, Walter. "On Some Motifs in Baudelaire." Trans. Harry Zohn. In *Illuminations.* Ed. Hannah Arendt. New York: Harcourt, Brace and World, 1968, 155–200.

Bennett, Susan. *Theatre Audiences: A Theory of Production and Reception.* New York: Routledge, 1997.

Berson, Misha. "Keeping Company." *American Theatre* 7.4 (April 1990): 16–23.

Bourdieu, Pierre. *Distinction: A Social Critique of the Judgment of Taste.* Trans. Richard Nice. Cambridge: Harvard University Press, 1984.

Brecht, Bertolt. "Emphasis on Sport." Willett, 6–9.

————. "One or Two Points about Proletarian Actors." Willett, 148–49.

Brockett, Oscar G. *The History of the Theater.* 8th ed. Boston: Allyn and Bacon, 1999.

————. Introduction to *The American Stage: Social and Economic Issues from the Colonial Period to the Present.* Ed. Ron Engle and Tice L. Miller. Cambridge: Cambridge University Press, 1993, 1–5.

————. "Theater and the New Student." Panel at the annual meeting of the Association of Theater in Higher Education, Chicago, IL, August 2001.

Brook, Peter. *The Empty Space.* New York: Athaneum, 1968.

Burnham, Linda Frye. "Factors for Success." Telling and Listening in Public: Organizers and Artists Building Civic Partnerships. Irvine Foundation. March 2000. Reading Room. www.communityarts.net.

Cambridge Guide to American Theatre. Ed. Don B. Wilmeth with Tice Miller. New York: Cambridge University Press, 1996.

Cambridge History of American Theatre. Vol. 3. Ed. Don B. Wilmeth and Christopher Bigsby. New York: Cambridge University Press, 2000.

Canning, Charlotte. "'The Most American Thing in America': Producing National Identities in Chautauqua, 1904–1932." Mason and Gainor, 91–105.

Carlson, Marvin. "The Semiotics of Theatre Structure." *Theatre Semiotics,* 41–55.

———. "Theatre Audiences and the Reading of Performance." *Theatre Semiotics,* 10–25.

———. *Theatre Semiotics: Signs of Life.* Bloomington: Indiana University Press, 1990.

Chinoy, Helen Krich. "Reunion: A Self-Portrait of the Group Theatre." *Educational Theatre Journal* 28:4 (1976): 490–94.

Concise Oxford Companion to American Theater. Ed. Gerald Bordman. New York: Oxford University Press, 1987.

Dolan, Jill. "Performance, Utopia, and the Utopian Performative." *Theatre Journal* 53 (2001): 455–79.

Eagleton, Terry. *The Ideology of the Aesthetic: From Polis to Postmodernism.* Oxford: Basil Blackwell, 1990.

Eastman, Fred. *The American Saint of Democracy.* In *Plays of Democracy.* Ed. Margaret Mayorga. New York: Dodd, Mead, 1944, 33–54.

Féral, Josette. "'The Artwork Judges Them': the Theatre Critic in a Changing Landscape." *New Theatre Quarterly* 16.4 (2000): 307–14.

Flannery, James. "Southern Theater and the Paradox of Progress." *Southern Exposure* 14:3–4 (1986): 12–17.

Foucault, Michel. "Nietzsche, Genealogy, History." In *The Foucault Reader.* Ed. Paul Rabinow. New York: Pantheon, 1984, 76–100.

———. "On the Genealogy of Ethics." In *Ethics: Subjectivity, and Truth.* Vol. 1 of Essential Works of Foucault, 1954–1984. Ed. Paul Rabinow. Trans. Robert Hurley and others. New York: New Press, 1994, 253–80.

Gottlieb, Saul. "They Think You're an Airplane and You're Really a Bird." Interview with LeRoi Jones. *The Evergreen Review* (December 1967): 50–53, 96–97.

Guillory, John. "Canon." In *Critical Terms for Literary Study.* Ed. Frank Letriccia and Thomas McLaughlin. Chicago: University of Chicago Press, 1990, 233–49.

Hewitt, Bernard. *Theatre USA, 1665–1957.* New York: McGraw-Hill, 1959.

Hirsch, Foster. *A Method to Their Madness: The History of the Actors Studio.* New York: Norton, 1984.

The History of North American Theater from Pre-Columbian Times to the Present. Ed. Felicia Hardison Londré and Daniel J. Watermeier. New York: Continuum, 1998.

hooks, bell. *Yearning.* Boston: South End Press, 1990.

Huerta, Jorge. *Chicano Theater: Themes and Forms.* Ypsilanti, MI: Bilingual Press, 1982.

Hughes, Glen. *A History of the American Theatre, 1700–1950.* New York: Samuel French, 1951.

Jackson, Shannon. "Civic Play-Housekeeping: Gender, Theater, and American Reform." *Theater Journal* 48.3 (1996): 337–61.

Kaplan, Fred. *Dickens: A Biography.* New York: Morrow, 1988.

King, Leslie J., and Reginald G. Golledge. *Cities, Space, and Behavior: The Elements of Urban Geography.* Englewood Cliffs, NJ: Prentice-Hall, 1978.

Kruger, Loren. *The National Stage: Theatre and Cultural Legitimation in England, France, and America.* Chicago: University of Chicago Press, 1992.

Larabee, Anne. "'The Drama of Transformation': Settlement House Idealism and the Neighborhood Playhouse." Mason and Gainor, 123–35.

Lefebvre, Henri. *The Production of Space.* Malden, MA: Blackwell, 1991.

Mason, Jeffrey, and J. Ellen Gainor. *Performing America: Cultural Nationalism in American Theater.* Ann Arbor: University of Michigan Press, 1999.

McConachie, Bruce. "Historicizing the Relations of Theatrical Production." In *Critical Theory and Performance.* Ed. Janelle G. Reinelt and Joseph R. Roach. Ann Arbor: University of Michigan Press, 1992, 168–78.

McConachie, Bruce, and Daniel Friedman, eds. *Theater for Working Class Audiences.* Westport, CT: Greenwood Press, 1985.

McRobbie, Angela. "Strategies of Vigilance: An Interview with Gayatri Chakravorti Spivak." *Block* 10 (1985): 5–9.

Morganthau, Tom. "What Color Is Black?" *Newsweek* (13 February 1995): 62.

Ridgeway, Cecilia. *The Dynamics of Small Groups.* New York: St. Martin's Press, 1983.

Sainer, Arthur. *The Radical Theater Notebook.* New York: Avon, 1975.

Schechner, Richard. *Between Theater and Anthropology.* Philadelphia: University of Pennsylvania Press, 1985.

———. *Performance Theory.* New York: Routledge, 1988.

Shank, Theodore. *American Alternative Theater.* New York: Grove Press, 1982.

Soja, Edward. *Postmodern Geographies: The Reassertion of Space in Culture and Social Theory.* New York: Verso, 1989.

Taylor, Karen Malpede. *People's Theater in Amerika.* New York: Drama Book Specialists, 1972.

Weinberg, Mark. *Challenging the Hierarchy: Collective Theater in the United States.* Westport, CT: Greenwood, 1992.

Willett, John, ed. and trans. *Brecht on Theatre.* New York: Hill and Wang, 1964.

Williams, Jay. *Stage Left.* New York: Scribners, 1974.

Yeatman, Anna. *Postmodern Revisionings of the Political.* New York: Routledge, 1994.

Zeigler, Joseph Wesley. *Regional Theatre: The Revolutionary Stage.* Minneapolis: University of Minnesota Press, 1973.

Newspaper Articles

Agai Dicutta Yaduan, Walker River Paiute Tribe Newsletter (May/June 1988): 1.

Anderson, Lucia. "Contemporary 'Carol' a Treat for the Holidays." Rev. of *A Community Carol. Freelance Star* (Washington, D.C.): D1–2.

Anthony, Bob. "It's Showtime." Rev. of *A Community Carol*. Jazz 90 WDCU-FM (3 December 1993).

Arnott, Christopher. "The People Triumph." *New Haven Advocate* (18 May 2000): 5–6.

———. "Streets on Stage." *New Haven Advocate* (11 May 2000): 2–3.

Berlin, Susan. "Familiar 'Carol' Gets New Harmonies." Rev. of *A Community Carol*. *Gazette* (Washington, D.C.) (8 December 1993).

Breslauer, Jan. "Parable of Equity Comes to a New 'Circle.'" *Los Angeles Times* (10 November 1995): F26.

Chrichlow, Beth. "Ibsen in Eastport." *Down East*. (Eastport, ME) (10 August 1990): 10.

Collins-Hughes, Laura. "Idealism in Action." *New Haven Register* (7 May 2000): F7.

"Cornerstone, Norcatur Shine." *Oberlin Herald* (Oberlin, KS) (4 July 1991): 1.

"Cornerstone Theater Play Set Depicting Dinwiddie 'History.'" *Times-Dispatch/Good Neighbors* (Dinwiddie, VA) (17 May 1987): 4.

Earney, Mary K. "Marfa Residents Catch Stage 'Fever.'" *San Angelo Standard Times* (San Angelo, TX) (30 January 1987): 2.

Erstein, Hap. "In Tune with the Times." Rev. of *A Community Carol*. *Washington Times* (3 December 1993): C16.

Esposito, Susan. "Cornerstone to Perform Musical in Eastport on August 29 and 30." *Quoddy Tides* (Eastport, ME) (23 August 1991): 1.

Fiondella, Francesco. "New Haven: The Play." *New Haven Advocate* (12 November 1998): 8.

Gato, Bill. "Troupe Updates Shakespeare." *Miami Herald* (9 August 1991): G1.

Gillespie, Noel. "An Insignificant Video Store." Rev. of *The Video Store Owner's Significant Other*. *Washington Blade* (9 February 1990): 25.

Hernandez, Sandra. "A Tree Grows in Watts." *LA Weekly* (2–8 September 1994): 39.

Kastor, Elizabeth. "Scrooge in Anacostia." *Washington Post* (28 November 1993): G4.

Keenan, Cheryl. "From the Balcony." *Montgomery Herald* (Montgomery, WV) (November 1989): 1.

Kimmelman, Michael. "In a Square, A Sense of Unity." *New York Times* (19 September 2001): E1, 5.

Lelyved, Nina. "In Cornerstone's Shakespeare, Romeo Raps." Rev. of *Romeo & Juliet* by Cornerstone Theater Company. Adapted from *Romeo and Juliet* by William Shakespeare. *New York Times* (7 May 1989): E6.

"Long Wharf, City Getting Their Act Together." *New Haven Register* (22 October 1998): A1.

McHatton, Wanda. "Roping Nets $1,200 For Theater Group." *Blue Mountain Eagle* (Long Creek, OR) (11 August 1988): 6.

Myers, Leslie R. "Racially Mixed Production Prospers in Port Gibson." *Clarion-Ledger* (Clarion, MS) (19 March 1989): 1.

Rizzo, Frank. "Cornerstone of the Community." *Hartford Courant* (7 May 2000): G6–7.

Rose, Lloyd. "A Scrooge for Our Times at Arena." Rev. of *A Community Carol*. *Washington Post* (3 December 1993): G1, 4.

Rousuck, J. Wynn. "'A Community Carol': Dickens of a Story, Updated and Unrelentingly PC." Rev. of *A Community Carol*. *Baltimore Sun* (3 December 1993): L20.

Sagal, Peter. "Playing America's Backroads." *Los Angeles Times Calendar* (18 August 1991): 7, 78–80.

Sprowl, Kari. "*Ghurba* A Different Perspective." *Beirut Times* 9.371 (October 7–14, 1993): 6.

Stayton, Richard. "Never More Than a Stranger." *Los Angeles Times Calendar* (5 September 1993): 7–9.

"Teen's Goal Is Broadway." *Hamden Journal* (10 May 2000): 1.

Thiele-Escher, Deb. "Cornerstone Theater 'An Imposter in Norcatur.'" *Clarion Ink* (Oberlin, KS) (2 November 1987): 9–10.

Tischler, Gary. "Scrooge, Dickens, and Washington Come to Life in *A Community Carol*." Rev. of *A Community Carol*. *American Weekly* (13 December 1993).

Twair, Pat McDonnell. "Ghurba Misses Target of Telling Arab-American Experience in L.A." *Beirut Times* 9.370 (30 September–7 October 1993): 6.

Whitaker, Joseph. "Anacostia's Past." *Washington Post* (14 November 1976): Res. Sec. 1.

Zaretsky, Mark. "'A Little Melting Pot.'" *New Haven Register* (27 June 1999): D1, D4.

Primary Source Material and Cornerstone Archives

American Festival Project Brochure.

Animating Democracy Initiative Grant Proposal for Cornerstone Theater Company.

Arena Stage Elaboration of Artistic Principles. Arena Stage Archives, Washington, D.C.

Arts Partnership Grant Proposal Narrative, 1998. Long Wharf Theatre Archives, New Haven, CT.

Benjamin, Lucinda. Letter to Cornerstone, June 1988.

Bogart, Ann. Untitled Public Lecture. Minnesota University, Minneapolis, January 1999.

Brady, Sara. E-mail to the author, 15 January 2001.

Brown, Mel. Letter to Cornerstone, June 1990.

Carey, Alison. Telephone interview with the author, 17 January 1996.

———. Interview with the author, Los Angeles, 3 April 1996.

———. Telephone interview with the author, 30 May 2000.

———. Interview with the author, Los Angeles, 30 October 2001.

———. Interview with the author, Los Angeles, 15 November 2001.

———. E-mail to the author, 29 December 2001.

———. E-mail to the author, 6 January 2002.

Clampett, Susan. Letter to Arena Stage, 3 January 1994.

Clapp, Deb. Interview with the author, New Haven, 14 June 2000.

"Collaborations with the Community." Theater Communications Group Panel, 25 June 1994.

A Community Carol Press Release, 4 November 1993.

Cornerstone Ensemble Meeting, Transcriptions from Audiotapes, Norcatur, KS, 25–30 November 1991.

Cornerstone Ensemble Meeting Notes, 1987–2001.

Cornerstone Humanities Flyer, 1991.

Cornerstone Newsletters, 1987–2000.

Cornerstone Planning Day Notes, 1987–2001.

Dale, Diana. Interview with Laurence Maslon, 15 September 1993. Unpublished notes.

Dewey, Ramona. Letter to Cornerstone, June 1988.

Durfee Oral History of Cornerstone, Transcriptions from Audiotapes, Los Angeles, June 1994.

Fripp, Dana. Telephone interview with the author, 7 June 2000.

The Good Person of New Haven Program Notes.

The Good Person of New Haven Symposium, Long Wharf Theatre, New Haven, 21 May 2000.

Griffith, Hirsch. Letter to Cornerstone, 10 February 1987.

Gutwillig, Stephen. Interview with the author, Los Angeles, 15 December 2001.

Hughes, Doug. Letter to John Ostrout, Executive Director of the Connecticut Commission on the Arts, 17 November 1997. Arts Partnership for Stronger Communities Program 1998 Grant Application. Long Wharf Theatre Archives, New Haven, CT.

———. Interview with the author, New Haven, 7 June 2000.

Jeffries, Lynn. Interview with the author, Los Angeles, 14 December 2001.

———. E-mail to the author, 30 December 2001.

———. E-mail to the author, 4 January 2002.

———. E-mail to the author, 5 January 2002.

Kelley, Dorothy. Letter to Cornerstone, June 1987.

———. *Tartoof* Program Notes.

Kuftinec, Sonja. Personal Journal, 1 September 1994–25 December 1995.

Kurup, Shishir. E-mail to the author, 30 November 2001.

———. E-mail to the author, 28 December 2001.

Lee, Allison. Telephone interview with the author, 3 June 2000.

Leonard, Bob. E-mail to the author, 27 July 2001.

Long Wharf Theatre Business Circle Pamphlet, Long Wharf Theatre, 2000.

Long Wharf Theatre Press Release. 4 April 1998.

Martínez, Alma. Untitled Lecture. Stanford University, California, 1996.

Maslon, Laurence. Telephone interview with the author, 2 February 1996.

———. E-mail to the author, 27 December 2001.

———. E-mail to the author, 31 December 2001.

Molina, Armando. Interview with the author, Los Angeles, 11 March 2001.

Moore, Christopher Liam. Telephone interview with the author, 17 January 1996.
———. Interview with the author, New Haven, 31 May 2000.
———. Interview with the author, Los Angeles, 29 October 2001.
Parran, Damion Teeko. Telephone interview with the author, 1 June 2000.
———. Interview with the author, Los Angeles, 29 October 2001.
Payette, Patty. Personal Journal, October 1989.
———. E-mail to the author, 5 March 1995.
Prichard, Rod. Letter to Cornerstone, June 1987.
Rauch, Bill. *The Good Person of Long Creek* Program Notes.
———. Interview with author, Los Angeles, 10 October 1994.
———. Interview with the author, Los Angeles, 30 June 1995.
———. Telephone interview with the author, 31 July 1995.
———. Interview with the author, Los Angeles, 18 November 1995.
———. Telephone interview with the author, 17 January 1996.
———. Telephone interview with the author, 13 March 1996.
———. Notes to the author, 20 April 1996.
———. Telephone interview with the author, 24 April 1996.
———. Interview with the author, New Haven, 29 March 2000.
———. Interview with the author, New Haven, 31 May 2000.
———. E-mail to the author, 5 September 2001.
———. E-mail to the author, 28 November 2001.
———. Interview with the author, Los Angeles, 14 December 2001.
Rice, Otis K. *Three Sisters from West Virginia* Program Notes.
Routt, Jean. Interview with the author, New Haven, 14 June 2000.
Semple, Ashby. Interview with the author, Los Angeles, 15 November 1994.
Sibley, Tamara. Telephone interview with the author, 31 January 1996.
Simile, Dyann. Letter to Cornerstone, 4 December 1989.
Tamaribuchi, Leslie. Telephone interview with the author, 24 May 2001.
Tatge, Pamela. Telephone interview with the author, 31 May 2000.
Three Sisters from West Virginia Program.
Valenzuela, José Luis. Telephone interview with the author, 6 June 2001.
Wager, Doug. Telephone interview with the author, 23 January 1996.
Waterman, Shana. E-mail to the author, 2 January 2002.
White-Richardson, Toni. Telephone interview with the author, 31 January 1996.
The Winter's Tale Program.
———. Evaluation Reports.

Cornerstone Productions (* ensemble production)

* *An Antigone Story.* Adapted and directed by Shishir Kurup from *Antigone* by Sophocles. Subway Terminal Building, Los Angeles, 2000.
A Beautiful Country. Written and directed by Chay Yew. Produced with Chinatown residents. Castelar Elementary School in Chinatown, Los Angeles, 1998.
Los Biombos/The Screens. Adapted by Gloria Alvarez from Jean Genet with the

collaboration of Pete Galindo, Lynn Jeffries, and Peter Sellars. Music by Blues Experiment. Directed by Peter Sellars. Produced with Boyle Heights residents. East Los Angeles Skills Center, Los Angeles, 1998.

Birthday of the Century. Written and composed by Shishir Kurup. Directed by Bill Rauch. Produced with Angelenos born on 30 June. California Plaza, Los Angeles, 1996.

Breaking Plates. Written and directed by Ashby Semple with participants from Watts. Watts Towers Arts Center, Los Angeles, 1994.

Broken Hearts: A BH Mystery. By Lisa Loomer. Music by Michael Abels. Directed by Bill Rauch. Produced in collaboration with participants from four B. H.–initialed neighborhoods including Boyle Heights, Baldwin Hills, Beverly Hills, and Broadway/Hill (Chinatown). Los Angeles Theatre Center, Los Angeles, 1999.

* *California Seagull.* Adapted by Alison Carey from *The Seagull* by Anton Chekhov as translated by Maria Ashot. Directed by Bill Rauch. Premiered at Santa Monica Mall, Santa Monica, CA, 1995.

Candude, or The Optimistic Civil Servant. Adapted from Voltaire by Tracy Young. Music by Joe Romano, Shishir Kurup, Laurence O'Keefe, and Kyle Glass. David Markowitz, music director. Directed by Shishir Kurup. Produced with Los Angeles Police Department, Metropolitan Transportation Authority, Los Angeles Public Library, and U.S. Postal Service employees. Los Angeles Central Library, Los Angeles, 1997.

The Central Ave. Chalk Circle. By Bertolt Brecht, adapted by Eric Bentley and Lynn Manning with Spanish translations by Bernardo Solano. Music by Shishir Kurup. Directed by Bill Rauch. Produced with residents of Watts. Watts Labor Community Action Committee, Los Angeles, 1995.

A Community Carol. Adapted from Dickens by Alison Carey, Edward P. Jones, Laurence Maslon, and Bill Rauch. Music by Michael Keck. Directed by Bill Rauch. Choreography by Sabrina Peck. Produced at Arena Stage with residents of Anacostia. Washington, D.C., 1993.

The Dog Beneath the Skin: An Epidemic Epic. Adapted by the company and members of the Miami AIDS community from W. H. Auden and Christopher Isherwood. Miami Beach, FL, 1987.

* *Everyman at the Mall.* Adapted by Shishir Kurup and Bill Rauch from Anonymous. Directed by Bill Rauch and Shishir Kurup. Premiered at Santa Monica Mall, Santa Monica, CA, 1994.

Los Faustinos. By Bernardo Solano. Music by Robert Ceja. Directed by Juliette Carillo. Produced with residents of Watts. San Miguel Parish Hall, Los Angeles, 1994.

* *Foot/Mouth.* Including Samuel Beckett's *Footfalls* and Alison Carey's adaptation of Luigi Pirandello's *The Man with the Flower in His Mouth.* Directed by Christopher Liam Moore. Premiered in Montclair, CA, 1999.

For Here or To Go. By Alison Carey. Inspired by Francis Beaumont and John Fletcher, *The Knight of the Burning Pestle.* Directed by Bill Rauch. Music by

Michael Abels and Shishir Kurup. Produced with participants from all previous Cornerstone projects in Los Angeles. Mark Taper Forum, Los Angeles, 2000.

Ghurba. Written, composed, and directed by Shishir Kurup. Produced with Los Angeles Arab Americans. Los Angeles, 1993.

The Good Person of Long Creek. Adapted by the company and people of Long Creek from *The Good Woman of Setzuan* by Bertolt Brecht. Long Creek, OR, 1988.

The Good Person of New Haven. Adapted by Alison Carey from *The Good Woman of Setzuan* by Bertolt Brecht as translated by Ralph Manheim. Music by Shishir Kurup. Directed by Bill Rauch. Choreographed by Sabrina Peck. Produced in collaboration with Long Wharf Theatre and New Haven residents. Long Wharf Theatre, New Haven, CT, 2000.

Growing Home. By Bernardo Solano. Directed by Mark Valdez. Produced with residents of Fresno and California State University students. Fresno, CA, 2001.

The House on Walker River. Adapted by the company and people of the Walker River Paiute Tribe and Schurz from *The Oresteia* by Aeschylus. Choreography by Sabrina Peck. Schurz, NV, 1988.

* *I Can't Pay the Rent.* Adapted from familiar melodrama by the company. Premiered 1986.

L.A. Building. Adapted by Alison Carey from Hsia Yen as translated by George Hayden. Music by David Markowitz. Directed by Bill Rauch. Produced with participants from Cornerstone's first three Los Angeles residencies, Angelus Plaza, Pacoima, and Arab Americans citywide. Los Angeles, 1994.

The Love of the Nightingale. By Timberlake Wertenbaker. Music by Jan Mabry. Directed by Ashby Semple. Produced with residents of Watts. Watts Towers Arts Center, Los Angeles, 1994.

Magic Tricks. Adapted by Rickerby Hinds from *Esu and the Vagabond Minstrels* by Femi Osofisan. Music by Shishir Kurup and David Markowitz. Directed by Armando Molina. Produced with residents of Baldwin Hills. Baldwin Hills Crenshaw Plaza, 1998.

* *Mallière.* Adapted by Alison Carey from Molière as translated from the French by Albert Bermel. Directed by Bill Rauch. Santa Monica Place, Santa Monica, CA, 1996.

The Marmarth Hamlet. Adapted by the company and people of Marmarth from *Hamlet* by William Shakespeare. Marmarth, ND, 1986.

* *The Maske Family Musical.* Adapted by the company from Carl Sternheim. Premiered in Front Royal, VA, 1986.

* *A Midsummer Night's Dream.* Adapted by the company from William Shakespeare. Premiered in Radford, VA, 1988.

Our Town. By Thornton Wilder. Produced with residents of Newport News. Newport News, VA, 1986.

Pier Gynt. Adapted by the company, people of Eastport and Perry, Maine, and the Pleasant Point Passamaquoddy Reservation from *Peer Gynt* by Henrik Ibsen. Eastport, ME, 1990.

The Pretty Much True Story of Dinwiddie County. By Douglas Petrie. Produced with residents of Dinwiddie, VA, 1987.

Romeo & Juliet. Adapted by the company and people of Claiborne County, Mississippi, from *Romeo and Juliet* by William Shakespeare. Port Gibson, MS, 1989.

Rushing Waters. By Migdalia Cruz. Music by Danny Vicente, Darren Brady & La Rue Marshall. Directed by Bill Rauch. Produced with residents of Pacoima. Pacoima, CA, 1993.

Sid Arthur. Written and composed by Shishir Kurup. Inspired by Herman Hesse. Directed by Page Leong. Produced with residents of Watts. St. John's United Methodist Church, Watts, 1995.

* *Slides of Our Trip.* A revue of Cornerstone songs by David Reiffel. Codirected by Sabrina Peck and Bill Rauch. Premiered in San Francisco, CA, 1988.

The Snow Queen. Adapted by the company from *The Snow Queen* by Hans Christian Anderson. Produced with students from Prince George County, VA, 1986.

Steelbound. Adapted by Alison Carey. Inspired by *Prometheus Bound* by Aeschylus. Music by Ysaye M. Barnwell. Directed by Bill Rauch. Movement Director Jennie Gilrain. Produced with Touchstone Theater Company and residents of Bethlehem. Bethlehem Steel Plant, Bethlehem, PA, 1999.

Tartoof (Or, An Imposter in Norcatur—and at Christmas!). Adapted by the company and people of Norcatur from *Tartuffe* by Molière. Norcatur, KS, 1987.

That Marfa Fever. Adapted by the company and people of Marfa from *Hay Fever* by Noel Coward. Marfa, TX, 1987.

Three Sisters from West Virginia. Adapted by the company and people of the Kanawha Valley from *Three Sisters* by Anton Chekhov. Montgomery, WV, 1989.

The Too Noble Brothers. Adapted by Alison Carey and hundreds of members of the Seward Park High School community from *Two Noble Kinsmen* by William Shakespeare and John Fletcher. Directed by Bill Rauch. Choreographed by Sabrina Peck. Produced in association with the New York Shakespeare Festival/ Public Theater at Seward Park High School. New York, 1997.

The Toy Truck. Adapted by the company and Peter Sagal from *The Clay Cart* by King Sudraka as translated by J. A. B. Van Buitenen. Music by Nathan Wang. Directed by Bill Rauch. Produced with residents of the Angelus Plaza Senior Center. Los Angeles, 1992.

* *The Video Store Owner's Significant Other.* Adapted by the company from *The Shoemaker's Prodigious Wife* by Frederico Garcia Lorca. Premiered at the American Place Theater, Washington, D.C., 1990.

The Winter's Tale: An Interstate Adventure. Adapted by the company from *The Winter's Tale* by William Shakespeare. Choreography by Sabrina Peck. Produced with participants from prior Cornerstone residencies. 1991.

* *Zones.* By Peter Howard. Directed by Bill Rauch. Los Angeles, 2001.

INDEX

Sonja Kuftinec is an assistant professor at the University of Minnesota, where she teaches courses in theater historiography and performance and social change. She has published several articles on Cornerstone Theater and on her own community-based work in the Balkans. Kuftinec also works as a director and dramaturg in the former Yugoslavia and as a facilitator with Seeds of Peace, an organization advocating coexistence between youth from the Middle East and Balkan regions.

THEATER IN THE AMERICAS

The goal of the series is to publish a wide range of scholarship on theater and performance, defining theater in its broadest terms and including subjects that encompass all of the Americas.

The series focuses on the performance and production of theater and theater artists and practitioners but welcomes studies of dramatic literature as well. Meant to be inclusive, the series invites studies of traditional, experimental, and ethnic forms of theater; celebrations, festivals, and rituals that perform culture; and acts of civil disobedience that are performative in nature. We publish studies of theater and performance activities of all cultural groups within the Americas, including biographies of individuals, histories of theater companies, studies of cultural traditions, and collections of plays.

R

WITHDRAWN